MEMORY FOR ACTION

COUNTERPOINTS: *Cognition, Memory, and Language*
SERIES EDITOR: Marc Marschark
Rochester Institute of Technology
National Technical Institute for the Deaf

STRETCHING THE IMAGINATION
Representation and Transformation in Mental Imagery
C. Cornoldi, R. Logie, M. Brandimonte, G. Kaufmann, D. Reisberg

MODELS OF VISUOSPATIAL COGNITION
M. de Vega, M. J. Intons-Peterson, P. N. Johnson-Laird, M. Denis, M. Marschark

WORKING MEMORY AND HUMAN COGNITION
J.T.E. Richardson, R. W. Engle, L. Hasher, R. H. Logie, E. R. Stoltzfus, R. T. Zacks

RELATIONS OF LANGUAGE AND THOUGHT
The View from Sign Language and Deaf Children
M. Marschark, P. Siple, D. Lillo-Martin, R. Campbell, V. Everhart

GENDER DIFFERENCES IN HUMAN COGNITION
P. J. Caplan, M. Crawford, J. S. Hyde, J.T.E. Richardson

FIGURATIVE LANGUAGE AND THOUGHT
A. Katz, C. Cacciari, R. W. Gibbs, M. Turner

COGNITION AND EMOTION
E. Eich, J. F. Kihlstrom, G. H. Bower, J. P. Forgas, P. M. Niedenthal

BECOMING A WORD LEARNER
A Debate on Lexical Acquisition
R. M. Golinkoff, K. Hirsh-Pasek, L. Bloom, L. B. Smith, A. L. Woodward, N. Akhtar,
M. Tomasello, and G. J. Hollich

MEMORY FOR ACTION
A Distinct Form of Episodic Memory?
H. D. Zimmer, R. Cohen, M. J. Guynn, J. Engelkamp, R. Kormi-Nouri, M. A. Foley

MEMORY FOR ACTION
A Distinct Form
of Episodic Memory?

HUBERT D. ZIMMER
RONALD L. COHEN
MELISSA J. GUYNN
JOHANNES ENGELKAMP
REZA KORMI–NOURI
MARY ANN FOLEY

OXFORD
UNIVERSITY PRESS

2001

OXFORD
UNIVERSITY PRESS

Oxford   New York
Athens   Auckland   Bangkok   Bogotá   Buenos Aires   Calcutta
Cape Town   Chennai   Dar es Salaam   Delhi   Florence   Hong Kong   Istanbul
Karachi   Kuala Lumpur   Madrid   Melbourne   Mexico City   Mumbai
Nairobi   Paris   São Paulo   Shanghai   Singapore   Taipei   Tokyo   Toronto   Warsaw

and associated companies in
Berlin   Ibadan

Copyright © 2001 by Oxford University Press

Published by Oxford University Press, Inc.
198 Madison Avenue, New York, New York 10016

Oxford is a registered trademark of Oxford University Press, Inc.

Library of Congress Cataloging-in-Publication Data
Memory for action : a distinct form of episodic memory? / Hubert D. Zimmer . . . [et al.].
p.   cm. — (Counterpoints)
Includes bibliographical references and index.
ISBN 0-19-511553-8 (cloth) — ISBN 0-19-511554-6 (paper)
1. Memory.   2. Recollection (Psychology)   I. Zimmer, H. D. (Hubert D.), 1953–   II.
Counterpoints (Oxford University Press)
BF371.M4485   2001
153.1'3—dc21   00-025019

1 3 5 7 9 8 6 4 2

Printed in the United States of America
on acid-free paper

Preface

Let me provide a context for this *Counterpoints* volume.

Take a minute or two and imagine that you are being interviewed by the police. They think you might have some information they need to solve a crime, and they want to know, rather precisely, the details of your morning.

Now, before going any farther, think about what came to mind. You may have reported that you got out of bed, had a shower, and then ate breakfast. You might admit that you became a bit angry when one of your children spilled orange juice all over the kitchen table. You had to clean it up, and you already were running late. You wiped the table with a dishcloth and put the dishes into the sink and the milk into the refrigerator. Perhaps you gathered up your work from the evening before, still spread out on the dining room table, and stuffed it into your briefcase. You ran down to the corner to catch the bus, but you missed it and had to come back to the house to get your car.

Whatever the content details of your morning, the general format probably ran something like the description in the previous paragraph. What I would like you to notice is that most of your everyday memories are about *actions*. And that is what this book is all about. Much of the discussion in the following chapters concerns retrospective memory of the sort that you have just experienced—something that you do frequently everyday in a variety of contexts. In the laboratory, memory for action is investigated through what is called *subject-performed tasks* or SPTs. This label highlights what it is that makes this task special: participants perform the named actions themselves during the study. They thus are intimately involved in the generation of what is to the remembered.

This type of encoding task is not commonly used in research on human memory and was introduced only 20 years ago, independently, by Ronald Cohen and Johannes Engelkamp. Since that time, action memory and SPT research has yielded a number of interesting findings. Perhaps most important, memory for subject-performed tasks, like other mental imagery tasks, is extraordinarily high.

But it also produces a number of unexpected effects that deviate from traditional verbal memory tasks and help to further define the nature of memory.

After several discussions beginning in 1996, investigators working in this area thought that research on action memory, and what it tells us about human cognition, should be shared with a broader audience. The hope was that we could both inform others about the importance of these findings and encourage further research in the area. I was fortunate to be able to convince Ronald Cohen to work with me on a book on this topic in order to achieve these goals. Our primary focus was on presenting an overview of the main results from research on memory for actions while giving readers a feel for the impact of this research on current models of memory. At present, the psychology of memory is relatively input-oriented, and we thought it important to demonstrate the limitations of existing models in dealing with output-oriented information like SPTs.

As we planned the book, we were able to recruit several contributors who were among the major players in this field. Consistent with the *Counterpoints* model, each agreed to write a chapter in which they present their specific views on action memory and also confront the differences among them. Chapter 1 provides a brief overview of these individual contributions.

Oxford University Press agreed to publish the book, and we all were optimistic that we could complete the project in a reasonable amount of time. Soon after we began, however, Ronald Cohen became seriously ill. Although he could not contribute to the book in the way he had planned, Ronald wanted to remain involved in the project, and we worked within and around his limitations. The preparation of this book thus took quite a bit longer than we had expected, but, as you can see, we finally succeeded. Unfortunately, this does not bring us to an entirely happy ending. Ronald Cohen died in September 1999 and was unable to see the publication of this work.

Despite the obstacles and delays, this volume is very much what Ronald and I had in mind at the beginning. I owe much to the collaboration of the contributors, and I thank them all for their patience and for their willingness to update their chapters in order to include the recent findings in the area. I hope that the volume will achieve its aim and make action memory a more prominent theme in the psychology of memory. I also hope that the reader will enjoy the book, consider the challenges that it raises, and perhaps become more interested in SPT research.

I would like to thank Marc Marschark, the *Counterpoints* series editor, and all of the others who have contributed to making this book a reality. On behalf of all of the participants in this project, we dedicate it to the memory of our friend and colleague Ronald Cohen.

August 2000   H. Z.
Saarbrücken, Germany

Contents

Contributors

Ronald L. Cohen, Glendon College, York University, Canada

Gilles O. Einstein, Furman University

Johannes Engelkamp, Saarbrücken, Germany

Mary Ann Foley, Skidmore College

Melissa J. Guynn, New Mexico State University

Reza Kormi-Nouri, Stockholm University, Sweden

Mark A. McDaniel, University of New Mexico, Albuquerque

Lars-Göran Nilsson, Stockholm University, Sweden

Hilary Horn Ratner, Wayne State University

Hubert D. Zimmer, Saarland University, Germany

MEMORY FOR ACTION

CHAPTER 1

Remembering Actions

A Specific Type of Memory?

Hubert D. Zimmer and Ronald L. Cohen

INTRODUCTION

Actions: A Specific Memory Content

Imagine that you came home from the office or from a day trip and someone asked you what had happened during the day. What would you tell him or her? You would probably describe the events that had happened and you would talk about the *things you had done*. Similarly, if you described your working day, it is very likely that you listed a series of *activities* that you had performed over the course of the day.

Is there anything peculiar in these memory tasks that makes them of specific interest for memory psychologists and that justifies the specific attention paid to them? Can we learn something by studying these tasks, which cannot be discovered using standard verbal learning experiments? At first glance, this doesn't seem to be the case. The only apparent difference seems to be that people remember another content than is usually studied in the laboratory, for instance, lists of words, but in principle, remembering is expected to be comparable to the standard memory conditions.

However, a closer look reveals that the mentioned situations have a number of unique features that are specific to them and distinguish these everyday tasks from traditional (laboratory) research on memory. In the mentioned situations, the persons asked had to remember things that they had actively established. Therefore, the things that had to be remembered were usually *actions*, and, additionally, these actions were *self-performed*. This aspect is an important fea-

3

ture, as we will demonstrate in this book. We want to decide whether traditional memory psychology, which is mainly concerned with the memory of information that was taken in, can successfully explain the remembrance of self-performed actions, an output behavior, and whether such output components also contribute to this memory performance.

Interestingly, these ordinary memory situations, in which actions are to be remembered, differ in several aspects from the traditional memory experiments conducted in the laboratory. In the laboratory experiments, participants are usually assigned the role of observers who only have to record and memorize what the experimenter has exposed them to. Koriat and Goldsmith (1996) described this traditional approach as the storehouse metaphor, in which memory is a depository of input elements. In contrast, in everyday life, at least outside of educational contexts, people often remember output elements. They perform actions in order to change their environment and to reach their action goals, and the memory of these actions is a by-product of performing them. A large amount of the everyday memory situations can therefore be characterized by at least three aspects that are peculiar for these tasks and somewhat different from laboratory memory research:

1. Everyday memory is usually memory for situations in which people were *active*. They were seldom only passive observers in a situation where they had to record an input presented to them.
2. The generation of these memory traces was most often *unintentional*. Everyday memory is usually *involuntary memory*. A person would rarely make a conscious effort to memorize the actions she or he performed. Memory of these activities appears to be rather "automatic."
3. Additionally, activity memory is a record of *input and output* elements. It is not only a record of the information picked up, but also a record of the overt (and covert) (re)actions that were performed as a response to the environmental stimulus.

Especially the latter aspect, that output processes are part of information processing and that this information may also contribute to memory, is a frequently ignored fact in psychology. Already Rosenbaum (1991) complained about the relative neglect of motor output in psychology. He wrote, "Most of the work . . . about the information processing system has been concerned with information *intake* rather than information *output*. Research into the structure of the information processing system has largely ignored motor function" (p. 101), and one can add that researchers on memory behaved in the same way. There are a few exceptions, but they do not disprove that research on episodic memory was mainly research about verbal memory, and rarely research about actions.

With the present book, we want to change this and bring action memory more into focus.

Looking more systematically at the remembrance of actions, we are able to find further peculiarities at the *retrieval stage*. From introspection, a strong *retrieval intention* does not seem to be necessary to retrieve self-performed events. Self-performed actions often spontaneously pop into conscious memory. Sometimes an environmental cue or random reflection elicits this memory. Retrieving action is therefore experienced as relatively effortless. In addition, actions often have to be remembered outside of memory tasks, that is, during the *monitoring* of the execution of one's own behavior. During performance, it is always necessary to remember one's own actions in order to keep track of things that one has done and that one has yet to do. To give some examples: Did I switch off the coffee machine this morning and did I lock the door before I left the house? Did I pay the plumber's bill? Have I taken my heart medication? The management of one's life would become very difficult if one was unable to remember these actions.

Similarly, while performing, one has to remember which part processes were already done in order to successfully perform the present action. One has to know whether one has already tightened the screw so that one can continue with the assembly process. Even in action planning, one often makes use of the memory of previously performed actions. For instance, one tries to remember what steps were executed, the last time one formatted the text with this specific text processing system, in order to guide the present action. In all these cases, people make use of the memory of actions that they have performed previously, although they do not consciously experience these situations as real memory tasks.

Finally, in the case of self-performed actions, a further type of memory task becomes relevant. If one intends to perform a specific action in the future, one has to retrieve the action, at the right moment, which has been planned, and then the action is initiated. This is *prospective memory*, and prospective memory is memory of actions. Admittedly, it is not the memory of actions that had already been performed, but it is memory of actions that the actor encoded in order to remember and perform them at some time in the future. This task has to be considered as a kind of action memory as well, and it is no less important than the retrospective memory of actions.

Obviously, remembering self-performed actions or remembering to-be-self-performed actions are both common, everyday memory tasks. As the examples have shown, this type of memory is highly important for humans to function successfully. Remembering what should be done, what was done, and whether something has already been done or not are preconditions of a successful interaction with the environment. Action memory is therefore of great ecological importance, and it should not be surprising if the *human memory is specifically prepared to remember actions*. It might be that actions are the typical content of memory for which the episodic memory system was "designed," and it was even speculated that memory evolved from the necessity to keep action-relevant information (Glenberg, 1997).

The Aim and the Structure of the Book

Taking into consideration the importance of action memory for managing everyday life, a sharp contrast becomes obvious if we look at the amount of research that has been dedicated to this memory performance. In the laboratories, memory was commonly investigated by way of word lists. Partially nonverbal stimuli, such as pictures, sounds, or watched movies, were investigated, but the active output, that is, performing an action, as an encoding manipulation, was rarely considered as relevant. Only a few exceptions are to be mentioned.

In the field of working memory, which is a more recent view of short-term memory, motor processes are explicitly acknowledged as relevant. It is discussed that spatial working memory is used to remember visuo-spatial information as well as the movement trajectories that guide spatially aimed movements (e.g., Smyth, Pearson, & Pendleton, 1988; Smyth & Pendleton, 1990). However, this is also a very recent development, and it has not yet aroused broad interest. In the context of long-term memory research, one might think about experiments on schema memory and scripts, for instance, Abelson (1981) or Lichtenstein & Brewer (1980). However, these experiments had a different focus than the influence of performance on memory. The focus was not the execution of the action that causes the schemata, but it was on the relationship between general and specific (episodic) memory and on the effect of top-down processes on the perception and reconstruction of memory. The only real exception was a suggestion of Bruner (1968), who postulated that enactive memory may be a specific form of remembering alongside verbal and pictorial memory. However, in our opinion, this suggestion had minimal consequences for memory research. In our view, one therefore can conclude that, compared to the long tradition of memory research, it was only recently that action memory became more relevant to memory researchers. However, even today, compared to all those people who do memory research, only a few research groups are active in the field of memory for performed actions.

This discrepancy was the reason for this book. A central aim of this book is to demonstrate the extraordinary memory of actions, to bring into consciousness the specific memory effects that are observed if self-performed actions are to be remembered, and to present the readers a state-of-the-art overview of action memory and its explanations, as well as to inform about the controversies between divergent explanations. In addition, we hope that this book is able to arouse interest in this topic and, with this, make action memory a more favorable topic in memory research in general. In this book, people from the most active research groups in the field of action memory present their actual results and their specific views on this type of memory task. We anticipate that there are several results that are worth looking at more closely, and the following chapters will demonstrate this.

All presented papers were written with two requirements. On the one hand, the collection of papers should give an overview about the actual topics in research on action memory, executed by the different research groups. On the other hand, the controversial topics should become visible. Therefore, the authors were requested to stress the differences instead of searching for the commonalties among the competing approaches. The authors focus on their own interpretations of the results and stress aspects in which their own interpretations deviate from that of other research groups. This latter effort was especially devised to fulfill the spirit of the *Counterpoints series*. We wanted to make explicit which topics are controversial in the field of action memory and to present unique positions on important aspects of action memory. These requirements culminated in two results. On the one hand, the papers familiarize the reader with the effects observed by the investigation of memory for self-performed actions, and, on the other hand, the presented selections provide different explanations for these effects.

Historically, in about 1980, in three different laboratories, a new paradigm of memory research was introduced nearly at the same time and independently of each other. In these experiments, subjects were required to remember a series of items. These items were mini-tasks, for example, close a book, comb your hair, light a cigarette, etc. The unique aspect of these studies was that subjects were not only instructed to remember these items but were, additionally, required to do so by actually performing the denoted actions during encoding. This change was the important aspect that was new for laboratory memory experiments.

These mini-tasks were less extended than everyday actions or activities, for instance, to go shopping or to prepare a salad, but nevertheless the mini-tasks shared with everyday actions the important feature that *they were overtly executed by the subjects during study*. One can therefore say that by applying these experiments, memory of actions was simulated in the laboratory, and a new line of memory research was set up that put less importance on verbal material than the traditional memory research did. Of course, subjects usually had to verbally recall what they did, but the focus of memory was now the action and not the verbal command. In other words, this paradigm brought action memory into the laboratory, and much of the research that will be reported in this book is based on this paradigm.

In the remainder of the introductory chapter, we want to give, as an advanced organizer, an overview of the main developments and results within the field of action memory. This overview should make the readers familiar with the main results to prepare them for the more specific topics of the following chapters. Afterward, the keynote articles will follow, in which four distinct positions on action memory are developed. Melissa Guynn, Mark McDaniel, and Gilles Einstein will present their view on the prospective memory of actions. In the chapter that follows, Johannes Engelkamp will present a system-oriented approach to explain action memory. He will stress that the motor aspects of the performed actions contribute considerably to the memory of actions. Next, Reza Kormi-Nouri and Lars-Göran Nilsson will present their arguments against a "motor view" of action memory. Then action memory will be put in the broader context of activity memory by Mary Ann Foley and Hilary Ratner. From their perspective, the performed actions should be seen in the context of larger plans and action sequences. Self-performed actions are, in this view, specific, not only because they were performed but also because they were functional—whether they were successful or not—for reaching a given goal, and because they were usually performed in a social context. Finally, two comments will follow, one from Lars-Göran Nilsson and Reza Kormi-Nouri and one from Johannes Engelkamp, in which these authors offer comments in response to each other's chapters. That only these two comments are presented was motivated by the fact that these two positions are in strong opposition to each other, whereas the other positions differ only in the relative importance that is given to different aspects of action memory. In the concluding chapter, Hubert Zimmer will discuss the presented positions in relation to each other. For this purpose, he will outline a common framework that is suitable to analyze the different positions and that might also suggest possible topics for future research.

MEMORY EFFECTS OF PERFORMING ACTIONS: A BRIEF REVIEW

Executing Actions: The Optimal Encoding for Episodic Memory?

Laboratory research on action memory began in 1980. Engelkamp and Krumnacker (1980) at Saarland University, Germany, instructed subjects to perform a series of mini-tasks, of the previously mentioned type, on verbal commands. The list comprised 48 actions. After presentation, the subjects were required to recall the actions and to write up the names of the actions they had previously performed. The main result was that memory of actions, measured by phrase recall, was much better after performing the actions (.62) than after listening to the phrases (.45), and it was even better than imagining the actions (.53). Due to the observation of this increased memory performance after subjects had enacted the denoted actions, Engelkamp and Krumnacker called the effect *enactment effect* to underline that the effect was caused by performing the actions.

A similar procedure was chosen by Cohen (1981), at that time, at the University of Umeå, Sweden, and later at Glendon College, Toronto, Canada. He required his subjects to study four lists of 15 phrases either under standard learning instructions or by self-performing the actions. Memory was also tested by free recall. Consistent with Engelkamp and Krumnacker, Cohen observed that memory was much better after self-performance than after standard learning. He called the encoding condition, in which subjects performed the actions themselves, subject-performed task, and he therefore spoke of the *SPT-effect*.

Since this term is neutral with regard to a possible explanation of the effect, we will use *subject-performed task* (SPT) in the following to refer to those conditions in which subjects encoded the to-be-remembered actions by performing the actions themselves and *verbal task* (VT) for those conditions in which subjects studied phrases under standard learning instructions.

Saltz and Donnenwerth-Nolan (1981), at Wayne State University in Detroit, Michigan, independently of each other, compared memory after motor-encoding, that is, performing, with memory for imagined actions, (imagining the actor performing the actions). The actions were presented as subject-predicate-object sentences, for example, "The bride STIRRED the COFFEE" or "The dentist NAILED the SIGN on the wall." In addition, they administered two different secondary tasks; either they presented pictures or the subjects were required to perform actions. Leaving aside the latter factor, the authors also observed an increased memory performance if the actions were performed during study.

Finally, Kausler and Lichty (e.g., Kausler & Lichty, 1986, Lichty, Kausler, & Martinez, 1986) started to investigate memory for self-performed activities. They did their research from a lifelong developmental perspective. They were interested in memory and aging, and their aim was to have a memory task with which the elderly participants were more familiar. These researchers also demonstrated a clear memory advantage of performing the actions.

Around the same time other researchers started to conduct SPT memory experiments. We want to mention only a few other active groups: Tore Helstrup, from Bergen University, today at Oslo University, Norway (e.g., Helstrup, 1984, 1986), did research mainly on serial position effects and strategic encoding with SPT. Lars-Göran Nilsson, at that time at the University of Umeå and today at the University of Stockholm, Sweden, together with Lars Bäckman, at the Stockholm Gerontology Research Center, were also initially foremost interested in the effects of performance on the memory of elderly people (e.g., Bäckman & Nilsson, 1984; Bäckman, 1985). Later, they became interested in memory for subject-performed tasks in general. In Germany at that time Monika Knopf, at the Max-Planck Institute for Psychological Research, Munich, and today at the University of Frankfurt, started her research on action performance and the development of memory (e.g., Knopf, 1989, 1991). Later, SPT also aroused the interest of other research groups, as the following contributions will demonstrate.

The common feature of these beginnings was that in all studies excellent memory performances were observed in the SPT condition that were clearly higher than those of other types of encoding, especially standard verbal encoding. This is the *SPT advantage*, and since that time it has been confirmed in a large number of experiments. The effect was demonstrated with different types of material (verbs, phrases, actions with real objects and without real objects, common and bizarre actions, etc.), with different samples of subjects (students, elderly people, children, mentally retarded subjects, memory impaired subjects, Alzheimer patients, etc.), and in different tests (free recall, cued recall, recognition). Reviews of this research can be found in Cohen (1985, 1989), in Engelkamp (1997), in Engelkamp & Zimmer (1985, 1989, 1994), and in Nilsson (in press).

Memory performances, in the SPT condition, were sometimes highly impressive. To give an example from a recent experiment, we presented our subjects with 200 action phrases during study, 100 of which were performed, while the others were encoded by other means. Afterward, a recognition test followed, in which subjects saw 300 action phrases, all of the old ones plus 100 new phrases. Subjects had to decide whether the denoted action was on the study list or not. In this recognition test we observed, for the performed items, hit rates between .94 and .97 and a false alarm rate for new items of less than .04. Under comparable conditions, for standard verbal encoding, we obtained hit rates lower than .70 and false alarm rates of about .23 (Zimmer, 1996a). These high recognition performances, after action performance, were observed even if the study condition was incidental, in which case we informed our subjects that we were interested in the times necessary to plan the actions for overt performance. It seemed to be that performing the actions was sufficient for good memory, whereas the intention to memorize the material was not critical (cf. also Kausler, Lichty, Hakami, & Freund, 1986).

The observation that performance supports memory without any additional encoding operations made researchers believe that performance is sufficient to lay down an efficient memory trace. For this reason, the subject-performed task was called a non-strategic way of encoding (e.g., Cohen, 1981, 1983) or an effortless encoding (Kausler, 1989), and it was even speculated that in SPT "additional implicit memory components might be involved" (Nilsson & Bäckman, 1989, p. 181). Kausler (1989) summarized his results with the statement: "Memory for the content of our own activities seems to me to be an everyday example of rehearsal independent memory" (p. 63). A long series of results is cited in favor of this assumption. A part of these observations comes from experiments in which one looked at the influence of individual differences in memory, and another part is from experiments in which encoding variations were investigated.

The experiments on individual differences revealed no or reduced influences of the subject variable on memory. Mentally retarded subjects showed impaired performances with verbal encoding, whereas their memory was comparable in size to a control group if the actions were performed during study (Cohen & Bean, 1983). Similarly, if the items were performed during study neither elderly subjects (e.g., Bäckman & Nilsson, 1984, 1985) nor children (Cohen & Stewart, 1982) showed a memory deficit compared to middle-aged subjects. However, it has to be considered that contradictory results regarding the aging effects have also been reported. For example, Cohen, Sandler, and Schroeder (1987) as well as Brooks and Gardiner (1994) observed that, after SPT encoding, elderly people recalled as much as younger adults of the short lists but not of the long lists, and Knopf (1995) reported even additive effects of age and type of encoding. Kausler (1989) observed a reduced aging effect in recall, and no aging effects in recognition if performed actions were to be remembered. Obviously, the size of the compensating effect of performance on memory is modulated by the retrieval demands of the task. More details of this aspect will be discussed in the chapter from Foley and Ratner.

However, critical words were also put forward against the position that action memory is a non-strategic, already optimal encoding (e.g., Helstrup, 1987). Helstrup argued that the rather passive encoding of subjects in SPT is a strategy in itself and that subjects can also actively encode actions if they are specifically instructed to do so, which he was able to show. We agree with the latter argument, but we want to note that this conclusion is only in opposition to the extreme interpretation of the passive encoding position, but it is not incompatible with the more liberal interpretation (cf. Zimmer & Engelkamp, 1989a). The extreme position would state that performing actions during study excludes any other kind of active processing. This is, of course, not correct, and to our knowledge nobody has taken this position. Proponents of the non-strategic SPT memory view claim that subjects do not need intentional encoding processes or active rehearsal in order to remember actions. The results seem to support this. However, it must also be admitted that this conclusion does not yet explain why memory in SPT is so good, although the subjects were rather passive during encoding. One should expect that subjects' memories are bad if they made little effort during study to memorize the items, whereas in fact the opposite was shown.

Similarly, several encoding variations were proven to be less important for SPT learning than for VT learning. A number of variables that influence the encoding of individual items and that usually influence memory performances were not efficient in the context of performing. During study, emphasizing some

items as more important for recall than others enhanced memory for these emphasized items in VT, but recall was independent of this variation if the actions
were performed (Cohen, 1983). Cohen (1981) reported that no levels-of-
processing effects were obtained with SPT, and Nilsson & Craik (1990) reported
only small and nearly insignificant effects when the actions were performed.
Contrary to these results, however, we were recently able to show that under
appropriate conditions SPT memory was also consistently impaired if the subjects were oriented to the verbal surface during encoding, but the levels of
processing effects were clearly reduced with SPT (Zimmer & Engelkamp, 1999).
Furthermore, verbal encoding, but not SPT, showed a generation effect. In VT,
subjects recalled more actions if they themselves generated the to-be-recalled
actions, which were to be performed on an object, than if the items were pre-
specified by the experimenter. In SPT, this variation did not matter (Nilsson &
Cohen, 1988). Varying the study time also had much larger effects on VT than
on SPT (Cohen, 1985). The amount of elaboration of an item was unimportant
for memory if the denoted action was performed (Helstrup, 1987; Zimmer,
1984). Finally, bizarre items were recognized better than common items in VT
but not in SPT (Engelkamp, Zimmer, & Biegelmann, 1993; Knopf, 1991). All
these results are compatible with the assumption that *pure performance is an
optimal type of encoding for actions*.

What Is Not Enhanced by Enactment

However, the previously mentioned results should not be overgeneralized. Performing the to-be-memorized actions during study does not enhance all types
of memories. There are specific tasks that are solved with other types of encoding as well as or even better than with performance. With all of these tasks, it
is not sufficient to know that an item was there, but rather beyond simply remembering the occurrence, it is necessary to know something about the relations
between different previously unrelated items or the relation between the item
and the actual context. Engelkamp (1997) called this *"episodic-relational" information*.

Engelkamp (1986) observed that pair-associated learning was even worse
after enactment than after standard verbal encoding. Subjects studied unrelated
pairs of verbs, either under standard conditions or by performing the denoted
actions. If subjects were allowed to recall the items freely, they reported more
items with SPT than with VT, but if they were requested to give the correct
target word to one of the pair elements as a cue, they were unable to do so.
Helstrup (1991) demonstrated that this disadvantage did not occur if subjects
were explicitly instructed on how to integrate the pair-elements. However, we
could later show that this integration was based on a surplus of processes that
was done in addition to performing the actions (Engelkamp, Mohr, & Zimmer,

1991). Performance itself, therefore, does not seem to support the integration of unrelated actions.

It was also shown that *serial recall* was not enhanced by enactment. If subjects studied a list of items and were later instructed to recall the items in the correct order or to rearrange the items in their correct order, SPT was not better than VT (Olofsson, 1996; Zimmer, Helstrup, & Engelkamp, 1993). In addition, the serial recall task changed the serial position effects, that is, the recall probabilities of items as a function of input positions, in comparison with free recall tasks. Usually, in free recall, SPT showed strong recency but no primacy effects, whereas VT showed primacy as well as recency effects (Cohen, 1981; Helstrup, 1986). In serial recall, however, both conditions had identical primacy and recency effects (Helstrup, 1987; Olofsson, 1996; Zimmer, Helstrup, and Engelkamp, 1993). One might speculate that this change of the serial position curve is a consequence of output interference (subjects reconstructed the sequence from the list's beginning), and it therefore does not tell us anything about SPT memory. However, this is not the case. In these studies, subjects were not obliged to start with the first item—they only had to rearrange the represented items in the correct order. It is more likely that the position effects indicate the availability of positional cues in SPT and VT. The shapes and performances of the memory functions, with these two types of encoding, are comparable for VT and SPT, and this demonstrates that the positional cues are not enhanced by enactment.

It was furthermore disclosed that SPT does not strengthen the *association between the item and the context*. This was demonstrated for locations as well as for situations. The loci method, which usually strongly enhanced recall, was inefficient in the SPT condition (Helstrup, 1989), and this was even the case if the loci were prominent geographical places (Cornoldi, Corti, & Helstrup, 1994). In the same way, enactment did not assist in the recall of the positions of objects in the environmental space compared to a visual encoding condition (Zimmer, 1994, 1996b)—in this case enactment means actively placing an object in a specific location during encoding. Furthermore, although subjects remembered more items in the SPT than in the VT condition (occurrence memory), their source memory was worse after performing. In the latter case, subjects had to discriminate in which of two contexts the item was studied (Koriat, Ben-Zur, & Druch, 1991).

Finally, performance did not enhance remembrance in *short-term memory* tasks. In Sternberg's memory task, subjects gained no advantage from performing the actions. The search rate was the same for both encoding conditions. Subjects' decision times increased, as in VT, if the memory set was made longer, and this was even the case if the subjects had performed only one item of a memory set, and this item was the target (Zimmer & Saathoff, 1996). However, in the latter case, a main effect in favor of the performed item was observed.

The SPT item was accepted somewhat faster than a non-performed item from the remaining part of the list. In other words, it was not the speed of access to an item that was enhanced if the denoted action was performed, but more likely the acceptance of an already accessed item, an "old" item, was accelerated.

Controversial Topics on Action Memory

The picture of action memory, which we have developed so far, seems to be pretty clear. Apparently, except for a few details, no contradictory results and positions seem to exist. However, this impression is deceptive. A part of the empirical results and especially the explanation of the SPT effect are controversial. The differences in the explanations of the SPT effects will become clear in the following chapters, we will therefore only mention some of the contradictory empirical results.

The first controversy concerns *the role of objects* in SPT memory. The laboratories differ in the importance they gave to objects. The Swedish group (Nilsson and Bäckman) emphasized the importance of object features for SPT memory. They usually ran SPT experiments with real objects—at least in the beginning—and an important role in SPT memory was given to the objects' features, including their color, weight, smell, taste, texture, etc. (e.g., Bäckman, Nilsson, & Chalom, 1986; Nilsson & Bäckman, 1989). The Saarbrücken group also used actions that had to be performed with objects, but these objects were usually not present. If the command was "to fill a glass," no real glass and no liquid was present. Subjects had to pretend to fill a glass. In this group, it was shown that the presence of physical objects also contributes to memory but that this influence is independent of the effect of performance. Both factors, real objects and enactment, enhanced memory (Engelkamp & Zimmer, 1983, 1996). These authors therefore spoke of the enactment instead of the SPT effect to refer to the influence of enactment on memory, and they properly distinguished this enactment effect from the additional effect of the real objects used in the action (cf. Chapter 3 of this book). Due to the fact that presenting objects as well as enacting the denoted action enhance memory, real objects were usually not presented during study in SPT experiments ran in Saarbrücken, in order to investigate the pure SPT effect. In other laboratories, this was different. In these research groups, SPT with objects was compared against VT without objects (e.g., Kormi-Nouri & Nilsson, 1999, and Chapter 4 of this book). This difference has been often overlooked (cf. Engelkamp & Zimmer, 1996).

Another controversy deals with the relationship between *experimenter-performed task (EPT) and SPT*. In EPT, subjects do not perform the actions themselves, but instead they watch the experimenter perform the actions. The EPT-SPT distinction was already made in the beginning of SPT research (Cohen, 1981). Cohen reported that these two encoding conditions led to comparable memory performances. In contrast, in other experiments, it was found that SPT memory was better than EPT memory (Engelkamp & Zimmer, 1983). Later, a distinction was proven to be important for the occurrence of this effect, which varies across the different laboratories. In the Saarbrücken group, subjects usually only studied one long list of items—between 24 and 48 items—followed by the memory test. Cohen and the Swedish group often used several short lists of 12 items each, followed by a memory test. With such short lists, no difference between SPT and EPT was found if the encoding conditions were blocked, that is, all items of the list were encoded under one condition. In contrast, if encoding conditions were mixed within the list or if lists were long, memory in the SPT condition was usually higher than in the EPT condition (Engelkamp & Zimmer, 1997). However, the details of the differences between these two tasks are still up for discussion.

A third controversial fact is the influence of enactment on *relational information*. Relational information is the information that relates items within a list or to a specific context. Traditional examples for relational information are the organization into categories, schemata, scripts, etc. (e.g., Mandler, 1984). The question is whether performing actions enhances this relational processing or not. Bäckman, Nilsson, & Chalom (1986) concluded, on the basis of their results, that performance enhanced relational processing. Zimmer & Engelkamp (1989b, 2000) came to the opposite conclusion. Performance, per se, does not necessarily enhance the available relational information, which was recently confirmed by further experiments (Engelkamp & Zimmer, 1996). Nevertheless, other results have been interpreted in support of the position that enactment also enhances relational information (see the contribution of Kormi-Nouri & Nilsson, Chapter 4 in this book, and 1999).

Finally, the discussion about *automatic and effortful processing* of performed actions should be mentioned if one is listing controversies in SPT research. It was already said that SPT encoding was qualified as non-strategic and effortless. Later, it was shown that SPT also suffers from divided attention during encoding (see Table 2 of the contribution from Kormi-Nouri & Nilsson, Chapter 4, or Bäckman, Nilsson, & Chalom, 1986; Engelkamp, Zimmer, & Biegelmann, 1993). This result was taken as evidence that encoding by performing actions needs resources and is not effortless (automatic). A further result that was given as an argument for the importance of strategic processes in SPT was the developmental effect that was observed with SPT (cf. Chapter 5). Both results indicate that the effectiveness of encoding may also vary under enactment, and that at least a part of these encoding processes needs attention.

However, the question still remains as to what is the limited resource and what is the "substance" that is consumed by these effortful encoding processes. Neumann and others (e.g., Neumann, 1992) argued against the "fuel metaphor" of limited resources. He offered the alternative view that it is not a question of limitation in the true sense of the word; instead, the observed limitations are a consequence of the necessity to inhibit concurrent activities during performance. In order to finish the ongoing action efficiently, concurrent activities, that do not contribute to goal achievement have to be suppressed. Performing, as an action, must therefore compete with other concurrent activities and vice versa, independent of a limitation of any capacity. In the concluding chapter, we want to come back to this aspect of performing actions, and we will discuss its consequence on memory.

Similarly, automatic processes were discussed for memory testing. It was suggested that an *"automatic" retrieval* process contributes to free recall in SPT, and that in addition to an enhanced conscious recollection recognition performances are also enhanced by a *familiarity-based* decision that can be categorized as automatic. In free recall of SPTs an automatic retrieval component is assumed, which we had called the *pop-out mechanism*. This mechanism is enhanced if items were performed during study, and we were able to show that this process strongly contributes to memory in SPT free recall (Zimmer 1991, Zimmer, Helstrup, & Engelkamp, 2000). Due to this mechanism, a number of items should pop into mind without subjects intentionally having had to search for them. Items that are highly accessible because they are still active to some degree, or because their features are easily reintegrated, are prone to this process. Since this process is a function of the recency of encoding, the recency effect in SPT is strongly enhanced in its absolute size as well as in its length; furthermore, it is independent of the depth of encoding, and it is not influenced when a secondary task is executed during retrieval (Zimmer, Helstrup, & Engelkamp, 2000).

In addition, it was suggested that *automatic and intentional retrieval contribute to recognition* performances (e.g., Mandler, 1980; Yonelinas & Jacoby, 1994). The automatic retrieval makes use of the familiarity of an item, whereas intentional retrieval results in a recollection of an item. Engelkamp and Dehn (1997) conducted three experiments in which they investigated recognition memory in SPT in order to separate controlled from automatic processes. They used the remember-know technique (Gardiner, 1988) and the process dissociation method (Jacoby, 1991). Based on their results, Engelkamp and Dehn concluded that SPT enhanced especially controlled processes. However, this latter conclusion causes methodological problems. The methods that are used to estimate automatic and controlled memory retrieval in recognition make use of information that is not necessarily related to the automaticity of retrieval. The observed effects may only reflect source memory (cf. Buchner, Erdfelder, Steffens, & Martensen, 1997; Dehn & Engelkamp, 1997). Since performance can influence source memory it is difficult to determine the contribution of automatic and controlled processes to recognition of performed actions.

In the process dissociation method, subjects study two lists, and later they have to recognize the items under two different conditions: an inclusion and an exclusion condition. In the exclusion condition subjects have to discriminate between the two studied lists; they have to decide whether the presented item belonged to list one or to list two. This is different in the inclusion condition in which they have to accept items from both encoding conditions. The extent to which subjects are able to discriminate, in addition to only recognizing the item, is taken as an estimation of the subjects' ability to recollect the episodic information. Mathematically, it is the difference between the proportion of old decisions in the inclusion condition and in the exclusion condition. In other words, it is assumed that recollection is enhanced if subjects can successfully discriminate a higher proportion of the recognized items. Engelkamp and Dehn (1997) observed exactly this result. The proportion of discriminated items was clearly higher in the SPT than in the VT condition. Hence they concluded that recollection is higher in SPT than in VT and that therefore conscious processing is enhanced by performing.

However, it is questionable whether this conclusion can be drawn in this way. In the SPT condition, one of the lists was encoded using performance, and the other one using verbal means. Because subjects know which items they had performed and which they had not, they are relatively good at discriminating between these two lists. Therefore, subjects have better conditions to discriminate the two lists in SPT than in VT, where both lists were encoded under two different verbal tasks. The extent to which performing enhances controlled memory processes (conscious recollection) may therefore be overestimated by this method. It is possible that the better discrimination, in the SPT condition, does not have much to do with automatic and controlled processes. In contrast, it is likely that the better performances in the exclusion condition reflect the availability of information that allows to discriminate between lists. The same argument can be put forward for the second technique: the remember-know method. Due to these difficulties, it has not yet been decided to what extent performing enhances conscious processes in recognition.

MEMORY OF ACTIONS: ACTIVITIES, SELF-PERFORMED ACTIONS, MOVEMENTS, AND TO-BE-PERFORMED ACTIONS

So far, we have discussed some central topics regarding the subject-performed tasks and also given a brief summary of the main results. Now we want to provide information about the topics and contents of the following chapters and to the relation of SPT research to action memory in general.

In the introduction, we stated that SPT brought actions into the laboratory. However, SPTs are only mini-tasks. Examples are: open a purse, tear up a letter, wipe the table, knock, wave your hands, shake your head, etc. These actions are "smaller" than everyday actions, and the used items are not homogeneous. Some of them are body-related, while others involve objects. In addition, sometimes they are performed with real objects, and thus they might produce observable outcomes; other times subjects only pretend to perform the actions. Can all these different tasks be taken as equivalent realizations of common actions?

Foley & Ratner (Chapter 5) will discuss in more detail what *components constitute everyday actions*. They point to the fact that actions, in their full range, include numerous aspects beside the action itself, for instance, the goal, a motivation, an emotion, social aspects, success or failure, etc. Contrary to that, subject-performed tasks, in the laboratory, comprise only a part of these components. Intention is necessary only in the sense of being willing to perform the verbal commands with which subjects are presented. An outcome, beyond the overt movement, is only available if real objects are used. Only performance and, in part, planning are shared by both types of actions. These differences, put forward by Foley and Ratner, make our position doubtful that SPT memory can be taken as a laboratory example for memory of everyday actions. However, for the moment, we still want to take this position, and we want to assay SPT memory as a model for action memory in general. The two core processes, planning and performance, are common to SPT in the laboratory and to everyday actions. In the final chapter, further arguments supporting this position will be presented.

The fact that full actions include a broad range of different components draws our attention to the different features that, in principle, can cause the SPT effect. Each of these features, alone or in combination, can be responsible for the SPT memory advantage. One should therefore not be surprised that the different research groups addressed different topics, and they preferred different explanations of the effects. For example, in some studies the focus relied on the commands and their meaning, while in other studies the focus was either on planning or on enactment, and still in others, it was the perception of the situation and of the outcomes of actions, may it be the movement or the effects on the objects.

The Swedish group, for example, focused initially on the perceptual effects. They looked especially at the perception of the used objects and of the perception of one's own movement. Although the encoded effects were produced by generating the output (performance), the memory record was seen primarily as a consequence of *input* processes (perception), and *not output* processes (enactment). In addition, these authors looked at SPT memory mainly as a kind of verbal memory. The central task in action memory is, in their view, a verbal memory task that was supported by performance. *From this perspective, SPT memory is not unique.* The instruction to perform the denoted action is one encoding instruction among several others that enhances the encoding operations. This point is elaborated by Kormi-Nouri & Nilsson in Chapter 4.

The Saarbrücken group took another perspective. They focused mainly on the overt performance and therefore categorized the effect as output effect. Initially, they made the physical enactment solely responsible for the effects (e.g., Engelkamp & Zimmer, 1985). The fact that so much importance was given to the *overt motor output* clarified why the term "motor memory" was used by these researchers. Sometimes this terminology was misunderstood because SPT research was subsumed under motor learning or motor skills, whose relationship was never intended. The subjects' task in SPT experiments was an episodic one: remember "what was done," and they were rarely asked how they did it. Later, the Saarbrücken group also discussed the contribution of other part processes besides the overt movement (e.g., Engelkamp & Zimmer, 1994; Zimmer & Engelkamp, 1989b, 1992, 1996), but the contribution of the output processes, the physical enactment, was still emphasized. It was postulated that performing actions made motor information available, and that this information became part of the memory trace. This point is further elaborated by Engelkamp in Chapter 3.

A third position was held by Cohen. He used not only object-related and body-related motor actions, but also activities, for example, spell C-O-L-D, name four colors, add 2 + 3 (Cohen, 1981). The fact that he was dealing with these three types of items as equivalent makes clear that he focused neither on the overt (motor) enactment nor the perception of objects. His focus was the *activity or the action component.* He claimed that memory of actions is different from verbal memory, and he speculated that action memory might follow specific laws (Cohen, 1985). To remember what one has and has not done has a high ecological relevance, and thus action memory might differ from other memories, for instance, verbal memory. The organism might be specifically prepared to encode activities (Cohen, 1983). This perspective is not only related to the position of Foley and Ratner, but also to the already mentioned necessity to remember future actions, which is dealt with in Chapter 2.

SPT tasks are related to prospective memory because a high proportion of actions cannot be performed immediately, but instead have to be remembered to be performed in the future. The memory task of the subjects is to remember the to-be-performed action (the content of the intended action), and at the right moment (if the critical condition is realized) they have to retrieve "what to do," and if they are aware of the to-be-performed action, then the specific action is executed. This specific type of memory performance is dealt with in the chapter from Guynn, McDaniel, & Einstein (Chapter 2). These authors are specifically interested in the processes that enable a given cue to trigger off the retrieval of the intended action. They restrict their thinking to these *event-based types of prospective memory tasks*. They do not discuss other types of prospective memory in which subjects have to perform actions, for example, in a time-based manner without external cues (cf. the relevant chapters in Brandimonte, Einstein, & McDaniel, 1996).

In closing, a few words should be said about issues that are *not discussed* in the book. Although the book is on action memory, we do not deal with personal experiences as they are discussed under the heading of "auto-biographical memory" (e.g., Cohen, 1996, Chapter. 6) or with memory of real actions experienced in everyday life. We restrict ourselves to results from experimental research. This restriction is necessary due to the intention to isolate the relevant components that influence memory of actions. The focus of autobiographical memory is more on the selection of episodes that are remembered, on the correctness of this memory, and on the reconstructive process of remembering (Rubin, 1995; Thompson, Skowronski, Larsen, & Betz, 1996; Wright & Gaskell, 1998). We also do not handle general knowledge such as action schemata (e.g., Vallacher & Wegner, 1987) and scripts (e.g., Abelson, 1981) because we only want to discuss episodic memory for actions and not general knowledge about actions. Finally, for the same reason, we will not discuss skills and the physical substrates of movements (e.g., Rosenbaum, 1991). Although we think that these aspects, which include motor planning and motor control, are relevant to the effects of performance on action memory, these processes themselves are not included in this book. However, in the final chapter of this book, the topic of motor programs and their neurological substrates will be picked up, and it is briefly discussed which brain modules will be additionally activated in action memory compared to verbal memory.

REFERENCES

Abelson, R. (1981). Psychological status of the script. *American Psychologist, 36*, 715–729.

Bäckman, L. (1985). Further evidence for the lack of adult age differences on free recall of subject-performed tasks: The importance of motor action. *Human Learning, 4*, 79–87.

Bäckman, L., & Nilsson, L. G. (1984). Aging effects in free recall: An exception to the rule. *Human Learning, 3*, 53–69.

Bäckman, L., & Nilsson, L. G. (1985). Prerequisites for the lack of age differences in memory performance. *Experimental Aging Research, 11*, 67–73.

Bäckman, L., Nilsson, L. G., & Chalom, D. (1986). New evidence on the nature of the encoding of action events. *Memory & Cognition, 14*, 339–346.

Brandimonte, M., Einstein, G. O., & McDaniel, M. A. (Eds.). (1996). *Prospective memory*. Mahwah, N.J.: Erlbaum.

Brooks, B. M., & Gardiner, J. M. (1994). Age differences in memory for prospective compared with retrospective subject-performed tasks. *Memory & Cognition, 22*, 27–33.

Bruner, J. (1968). *Processes of cognitive growth: Infancy.* Worcester: Clark University Press.

Buchner, A., Erdfelder, E., Steffens, M. C., & Martensen, H. (1997). The nature of memory processes underlying recognition judgments in the process dissociation procedure. *Memory & Cognition, 25*, 508–518.

Cohen, G. (1996). *Memory in the real world.* Hillsdale: Erlbaum.

Cohen, R. L. (1981). On the generality of some memory laws. *Scandinavian Journal of Psychology, 22*, 267–281.

Cohen, R. L. (1983). The effect of encoding variables on the free recall of words and action events. *Memory & Cognition, 11*, 575–582.

Cohen, R. L. (1985). On the generality of the laws of memory. In L. G. Nilsson & T. Archer (Eds.), *Animal learning and human memory* (pp. 247–277). Hillsdale: Erlbaum.

Cohen, R. L. (1989). Memory for action events: The power of enactment. *Educational Psychological Review, 1*, 57–80.

Cohen, R. L., & Bean, G. (1983). Memory in educable mentally retarded adults: Deficit in subject or experimenter? *Intelligence, 7*, 287–298.

Cohen, R. L., Sandler, S. P., & Schroeder, K. (1987). Aging and memory for words and action events: Effects of item repetition and list length. *Psychology and Aging, 2*, 280–285.

Cohen, R. L., & Stewart, M. (1982). How to avoid developmental effects in free recall. *Scandinavian Journal of Psychology, 23*, 9–16.

Cornoldi, C., Corti, M. T., & Helstrup, T. (1994). Do you remember what you imagined you would do in that place? The motor encoding cue-failure effect in sighted and blind people. *Quarterly Journal of Experimental Psychology, 47A*, 311–329.

Dehn, D., & Engelkamp, J. (1997). Process dissociation procedure: Double dissociation following devided attention and speeded responding. *Quarterly Journal of Experimental Psychology A, 50A*, 318–336.

Engelkamp, J. (1986). Nouns and verbs in paired-associate learning: Instructional effects. *Psychological Research, 48*, 153–159.

Engelkamp, J. (1997). *Memory for actions.* Hove: Psychology Press.

Engelkamp, J., & Dehn, D. M. (1997). Strategy and consciousness in remembering subject-performed actions. *Sprache & Kognition, 16*, 94–109.

Engelkamp, J., & Krumnacker, H. (1980). Imaginale und motorische Prozesse beim Behalten verbalen Materials [Imagery and motor processes in memory of verbal material]. *Zeitschrift für experimentelle und angewandte Psychologie, 27*, 511–533.

Engelkamp, J., Mohr, G., & Zimmer, H. D. (1991). Pair-relational encoding of performed nouns and verbs. *Psychological Research, 53*, 232–239.

Engelkamp, J., & Zimmer, H. D. (1983). Zum Einfluß von Wahrnehmen und Tun auf das Behalten von Verb-Objekt-Phrasen [The influence of perception and action on memory for verb-object phrases]. *Sprache & Kognition, 2*, 117–127.

Engelkamp, J., & Zimmer, H. D. (1985). Motor programs and their relation to semantic memory. *German Journal of Psychology, 9*, 239–254.

Engelkamp, J., & Zimmer, H. D. (1989). Memory for action events: A new field of research. *Psychological Research, 51*, 153–157.

Engelkamp, J., & Zimmer, H. D. (1994). *The human memory: A multimodal approach.* Seattle: Hogrefe & Huber.

Engelkamp, J., & Zimmer, H. D. (1996). Organisation and recall in verbal tasks and subject-performed tasks. *European Journal of Cognitive Psychology, 8*, 257–273.

Engelkamp, J., & Zimmer, H. D. (1997). Sensory factors in memory for subject-performed tasks. *Acta Psychologica, 96*, 43–60.

Engelkamp, J., Zimmer, H. D., & Biegelmann, U. E. (1993). Bizarreness effects in verbal tasks and subject-performed tasks. *European Journal of Cognitive Psychology, 5*, 393–415.

Gardiner, J. M. (1988). Recognition failures and free-recall failures: Implications for the relation between recall and recognition. *Memory & Cognition, 16*, 446–451.

Glenberg, A. M. (1997). What memory is for. *Behavioral and Brain Sciences, 20*, 1–55.

Helstrup, T. (1984). Serial position phenomena: Memory for acts, contents and spatial position patterns. *Scandinavian Journal of Psychology, 25*, 131–146.

Helstrup, T. (1986). Separate memory laws for recall of performed acts? *Scandinavian Journal of Psychology, 27*, 1–29.

Helstrup, T. (1987). One, two, or three memories? A problem-solving approach to memory for performed acts. *Acta Psychologica, 66*, 37–68.

Helstrup, T. (1989). Loci for act recall: Contextual influence on processing of action events. *Psychological Research, 51*, 168–175.

Helstrup, T. (1991). Integration versus nonintegration of noun pairs and verb pairs under enactment and nonenactment conditions. *Psychological Research, 53*, 240–245.

Jacoby, L. L. (1991). A process dissociation framework: Separating automatic from intentional uses of memory. *Journal of Memory and Language, 30*, 513–541.

Kausler, D. H. (1989). Impairment in normal memory aging: Implications of laboratory evidence. In G. C. Gilmore, P. J. Whitehouse, & M. L. Wykle (Eds.), *Memory aging & dementia* (pp. 41–73). New York: Springer.

Kausler, D. H., & Lichty, W. (1986). Activity duration and adult age differences in memory for activity performance. *Journal of Psychology, 1*, 80–81.

Kausler, D. H., Lichty, W., Hakami, M. K., & Freund, J. S. (1986). Activity duration and adult age differences in memory for activity performance. *Journal of the Psychology of Aging, 1*, 80–81.

Knopf, M. (1989). Die Entwicklung des Gedächtnisses für Handlungen bei 4- und 6jährigen Kindern [The development of memory for actions with 4 to 6 year old children]. *Vortrag auf 9. Tagung Entwicklungspsychologie München, 18–21. September*. München: Max-Planck-Institut.

Knopf, M. (1991). Having shaved a kiwi fruit: Memory of unfamiliar subject-performed actions. *Psychological Research, 53*, 203–211.

Knopf, M. (1995). Neues zum Gedächtnis im Alter. In K. Pawlik (Ed.), *Bericht über den 39. Kongreß der Deutschen Gesellschaft für Psychologie in Hamburg 1994* (pp. 335–340). Göttingen: Hogrefe.

Koriat, A., Ben-Zur, H., & Druch, A. (1991). The contextualisation of input and output events in memory. *Psychological Research, 53*, 260–270.

Koriat, A., & Goldsmith, M. (1996). Memory metaphors and the real-life/laboratory controversy: Correspondence versus storehouse conceptions of memory. *Behavioral and Brain Sciences, 19*, 167–188.

Kormi-Nouri, R., & Nilsson, L. G. (1999). Negative cueing effects with weak and strong intralist cues. *European Journal of Cognitive Psychology, 11*, 199–218.

Lichtenstein, E. H., & Brewer, W. F. (1980). Memory for goal-directed events. *Cognitive Psychology, 12*, 412–445.

Lichty, W., Kausler, D. H., & Martinez, D. R. (1986). Adult age differences in memory for motor versus cognitive activities. *Experimental Aging Research, 12*, 227–330.

Mandler, G. (1980). Recognizing: The judgment of previous occurrence. *Psychological Review, 87*, 252–271.

Mandler, J. M. (1984). *Stories, scripts, and scenes: Aspects of schema theory.* Hillsdale: Erlbaum.

Neumann, O. (1992). Theorien der Aufmerksamkeit: Von Metaphern zu Mechanismen. *Psychologische Rundschau, 43*, 83–101.

Nilsson, L. G. (2000). Remembering actions and words. In F. I. M. Craik & E. Tulving (Eds.), *Oxford handbook of memory* (pp. 137–148). Oxford: Oxford University Press.

Nilsson, L. G., & Bäckman, L. (1989). Implicit memory and the enactment of verbal instructions. In S. Lewandowsky, J. C. Dunn, & K. Kirsner (Eds.), *Implicit memory: Theoretical issues* (pp. 173–183). Hillsdale: Erlbaum.

Nilsson, L. G., & Cohen, R. L. (1988). Enrichment and generation in the recall of enacted and non-enacted instructions. In M. M. Gruneberg, P. E. Morris, & R. N. Sykes (Eds.), *Practical aspects of memory: Current research and issues* (pp. 427–432). Chichester: John Wiley.

Nilsson, L. G., & Craik, F. I. M. (1990). Additive and interactive effects in memory for subject-performed tasks. *European Journal of Cognitive Psychology, 2*, 305–324.

Olofsson, U. (1996). The effect of motor enactment on memory for order. *Psychological Research, 59*, 75–79.

Rosenbaum, D. A. (1991). *Human motor control.* San Diego: Academic Press.

Rubin, D. C. (Ed.). (1995). *Remembering our past.* Cambridge: Cambridge University Press.

Saltz, E., & Donnenwerth-Nolan, S. (1981). Does motoric imagery facilitate memory for sentences? A selective interference test. *Journal of Verbal Learning and Verbal Behavior, 20*, 322–332.

Smyth, M. M., Pearson, N. A., & Pendleton, L. R. (1988). Movement and working memory: Patterns and positions in space. *Quarterly Journal of Experimental Psychology, 40A*, 497–514.

Smyth, M. M., & Pendleton, L. R. (1990). Space and movement in working memory. *Quarterly Journal of Experimental Psychology, 42A*, 291–304.

Thompson, C. P., Skowronski, J. J., Larsen, S. F., & Betz, A. L. (1996). *Autobiographical memory: Remembering what and remembering when.* Mahwah: Erlbaum.

Vallacher, R. R., & Wegner, D. M. (1987). What do people think they're doing? Action identification and human behavior. *Psychological Review, 94*, 3–15.

Wright, D. B., & Gaskell, G. D. (Eds.). (1998). *Surveying memory processes*. Hove: Psychology Press.

Yonelinas, A., & Jacoby, L. L. (1994). Dissociations of processes in recognition memory: Effects of interference and of response speed. *Canadian Journal of Experimental Psychology, 48,* 516–534.

Zimmer, H. D. (1984). *Enkodierung, Rekodierung, Retrieval und die Aktivation motorischer Programme* [Encoding, re-coding, retrieval and the activation of motor programs]. (Arbeiten der Fachrichtung Psychologie, Vol. 91). Saarbrücken: Universität des Saarlandes.

Zimmer, H. D. (1991). Memory after motoric encoding in a generation-recognition model. *Psychological Research, 53,* 226–231.

Zimmer, H. D. (1994). Representation and processing of the spatial layout of objects with verbal and nonverbal input. In W. Schnotz & R. W. Kulhavy (Eds.), *Comprehension of graphics* (pp. 97–112). Amsterdam: Elsevier, North Holland.

Zimmer, H. D. (1996a). Subject-performed tasks enhance item-specific information but not context integration. Paper presented at the XXVI World Congress of Psychology, Montreal, Canada.

Zimmer, H. D. (1996b). Memory for spatial location and enactment. *Psychologische Beiträge, 38,* 404–418.

Zimmer, H. D., & Engelkamp, J. (1989a). One, two or three memories: Some comments and new findings. *Acta Psychologica, 70,* 293–304.

Zimmer, H. D., & Engelkamp, J. (1989b). Does motor encoding enhance relational information? *Psychological Research, 51,* 158–167.

Zimmer, H. D., & Engelkamp, J. (1992). *Gedächtnispsychologische Aspekte der Planung, Wahrnehmung und Ausführung von Handlungen* [Aspects of planning, perceiving, and performing actions seen from memory psychology]. (Arbeiten der Fachrichtung Psychologie, Vol. 171). Saarbrücken: Universität des Saarlandes.

Zimmer, H. D., & Engelkamp, J. (1996). Routes to actions and their efficacy for remembering. *Memory, 4,* 59–78.

Zimmer, H. D., & Engelkamp, J. (1999). Levels-of-process effects in subject-performed tasks. *Memory & Cognition, 27,* 907–914.

Zimmer, H. D., & Engelkamp, J. (2000). What type of information is enhanced in subject-performed tasks. Submitted.

Zimmer, H. D., Helstrup, T., & Engelkamp, J. (1993). Memory of subject-performed task and serial position effects. Unpublished manuscript.

Zimmer, H. D., Helstrup, T., & Engelkamp, J. (2000). Pop-out into memory: A retrieval mechanism that is enhanced with the recall of subject-performed tasks. *Journal of Experimental Psychology: Human Learning, Memory and Cognition, 26,* 658–670.

Zimmer, H. D., & Saathoff, J. (1996). The influence of enactment on short-term recognition. *Acta Psychologica, 95,* 85–95.

CHAPTER 2

Remembering to Perform Actions

A Different Type of Memory?

Melissa J. Guynn, Mark A. McDaniel, and Gilles O. Einstein

People remember and forget numerous things every day. If I asked you to tell me the last thing you forgot, perhaps you would say that you forgot to do some task that you had intended to do, like take a vitamin, run an errand, or give someone a message. In keeping with earlier terminology (e.g., Harris, 1984), we will call this type of memory (remembering to perform actions) prospective memory. Prospective memory can be contrasted with remembering actions previously performed or, more generally, previously encountered episodes, called retrospective memory. Compared to the vast theoretical and empirical literature on various retrospective memory phenomena, there is a much smaller literature in the relatively newer field of prospective memory. Perhaps it is at least somewhat due to this discrepancy that one important question in the area of prospective memory has been, "To what extent is prospective memory similar to, and to what extent is it different from, retrospective memory?"

One readily apparent difference between retrospective memory (as it is typically studied in the laboratory) and prospective memory is that there is usually an agent prompting remembering in retrospective memory tasks. The prompt may be quite specific (Did this word appear in the list you studied?) or more general (Recall the list of words you studied). In contrast, an intriguing feature of prospective memory tasks is that there is not an external agent prompting remembering. A friend does not ask you, "What message were you supposed to give me?" but instead you must remember on your own to give the friend the message. And an experimenter in a prospective memory experiment does not tell you, when a target word appears, "Remember to press the key you were supposed to press." It is in this way that prospective memory tasks require something of an individual that retrospective memory tasks do not: Not only must the individual remember the information that he or she learned, but he or she must also act on that information at the appropriate point, without a prompt or a reminder to do so.

Put another way, in typical retrospective memory tasks studied in the laboratory, experimenters put subjects in a retrieval mode (Tulving, 1983), which initiates remembering and sensitizes subjects to the meaning of retrieved memories. By contrast, in prospective memory tasks, internal or external events must trigger remembering that it is time to perform an intended action, in the absence of being in a retrieval mode. In this sense, prospective memory is more similar to the involuntary remembering (Ebbinghaus, 1964; Richardson-Klavehn, Gardiner, & Java, 1994) that occurs when thoughts spontaneously come to mind—a phenomenon that occurs frequently in everyday life. This difference between retrospective and prospective memory tasks raises an interesting question: How is a memory process initiated when there is no external agent to prompt remembering? We offer an answer to that question in the remainder of this chapter.

As a departure point, we initially propose that prospective memory involves the same processes assumed by some theorists to mediate one type of retrospective memory, namely recognition memory. We then proceed to answer the question of how a memory process might be initiated when there is no external agent to prompt remembering. Although retrospective and prospective memory tasks differ in that subjects are in a retrieval mode in the former but not in the latter, one theoretical view of prospective memory, called the *familiarity plus search view*, assumes that processes mediating recognition memory can fully account for prospective memory (Einstein & McDaniel, 1996; McDaniel, 1995). We develop the theoretical implications of the familiarity plus search view, and we review some of our existing work and report a new experiment that addresses the plausibility of this view. We then outline a new theoretical view, and its implications, that was stimulated by the empirical work that we review. In the context of this new view, called the *automatic associative activation view*, we highlight both the overlap in prospective and retrospective memory processes, as well as how they are unique. We contrast the automatic associative activation view with a formulation that emphasizes the involvement of a supervisory system in prospective memory (Ellis, 1996; Shallice & Burgess, 1991), a system that presumably requires attentional resources for implementing the processes the system recruits to achieve prospective remembering. We then describe some of our existing work and report some preliminary data that are consistent with the automatic associative activation view. Finally, we account for some apparently discrepant data in the context of this new theoretical view.

Before proceeding, we briefly describe the type of prospective memory task to which our theoretical discussion and empirical work apply. Real-world prospective memory tasks often demand that individuals interrupt an activity in order to perform another intended action. We simulate this feature of real-world prospective memory in our experiments by having subjects do a "cover" activity. The prospective memory task is embedded in this cover activity, as the goal is to have subjects busily involved in the cover activity and not maintaining the prospective memory task in mind. Following a delay (to introduce some forgetting) after the instructions for the cover activity and the prospective memory task, we measure whether subjects perform the prospective memory task (e.g., press a key on the computer keyboard) at the appropriate instance (e.g., when a particular target word appears in the context of the cover activity).

FAMILIARITY PLUS SEARCH

We first adopt the strong position that, despite the fact that retrospective memory tasks often involve a prompt to remember, and prospective memory tasks do not, prospective memory is mediated by the same processes that mediate recognition memory. According to Atkinson and Juola's (1974) model of recognition memory (see also Mandler, 1980, for a similar view), when a word is presented on a recognition test, a subject directly accesses the word's familiarity (hereafter referred to as the familiarity index), which is a function of the amount of time since the word was last encountered, relative to the number of times the word was encountered in the past. Presenting a familiar or frequently-occurring word produces a smaller increase in its familiarity index, and presenting an unfamiliar or infrequently-occurring word produces a larger increase in its familiarity index. Sometimes the familiarity index of the word can be a reliable indicator as to whether or not the word was recently encountered. If the word has a high familiarity index, an individual can quickly decide that the word was recently encountered, and if the word has a low familiarity index, an individual can quickly decide that the word was not recently encountered. If the word has an intermediate familiarity index, however, the individual cannot make a quick decision based on familiarity, and instead must initiate a memory search to decide whether the word was recently encountered.

We propose that these dual processes assumed to mediate recognition memory might also be recruited to support prospective memory (see also Einstein & McDaniel, 1996; McDaniel, 1995). Specifically, the idea is that when a subject encounters a prospective memory target event (e.g., a target word) in a cover task in a prospective memory experiment, the subject's response to the target event is determined in part by the familiarity of the target event. Familiarity processes are presumed to be relatively automatic and nondirected (Jacoby, 1991), like in the case of context-free recognition. For example, one may experience a sense of familiarity upon seeing a person on a bus, but not identify the person without further reflection. In much the same way, we suggest that the familiarity of a prospective memory target event may stimulate a memory search to determine the significance of the prospective memory target event. The idea is that if the familiarity index of a target event exceeds a criterion, then a subject is stimulated to search memory to identify the source of the familiarity. If a subject were in a retrieval mode (e.g., for a recognition test), then the subject might use the high familiarity to decide quickly that an item is old. In contrast, when a subject is not in a retrieval mode (e.g., as in the case of prospective memory), then the high familiarity is likely to lead to a search for the source of the familiarity. In the course of searching memory, the subject may identify the word as a prospective memory target event (in which case he or she performs the prospective memory task) or the subject may attribute the familiarity to some other source (in which case he or she does not perform the prospective memory task). If the familiarity index does not exceed a criterion, then the subject does not identify the word as a target event and does not perform the prospective memory task. Further, we propose, like others (e.g., Mandler, 1980), that rather than the absolute familiarity of the word, the increment in the familiarity of the word (e.g., as a result of presentation of the word in the experiment) determines the feeling of familiarity that stimulates the memory search.

If the application of dual-process models of recognition memory to prospective memory is valid, then recognition memory phenomena should extend to prospective memory. For example, prospective memory should be more accurate when prospective memory target events are less familiar or lower frequency words than when prospective memory target events are more familiar or higher frequency words (as is the case for recognition memory). Recent experience (exposure to the target events during encoding of the prospective memory task) should produce a greater increment to the familiarity of lower frequency target events than to the familiarity of higher frequency target events, such that the familiarity of the lower frequency target events is more likely to exceed criterion. Consequently, a memory search is more likely to be attempted with lower frequency target events, and intended actions are more likely to be performed.

Support for this prediction comes from an experiment by Einstein and McDaniel (1990, Experiment 2; McDaniel & Einstein, 1993, reported similar results). Subjects were given the prospective memory task of pressing a key on a computer keyboard if they ever saw a particular target word in the context of a cover task. The cover task required subjects to study short strings of unrelated words for an immediate serial recall task, and a prospective memory target word occurred three times during the 42 short-term memory trials. Half of the subjects were given a familiar target word (e.g., rake or method) and half of the subjects were given an unfamiliar target word (e.g., sone or monad). The results appear in Table 2.1 and show that prospective memory was more accurate when the target events were unfamiliar words than when the target events were familiar

TABLE 2.1. Unfamiliar Target Events Produced Better Prospective Memory than Familiar Target Events for Both Younger and Older Subjects

	Familiar Target Events	Unfamiliar Target Events
Younger Subjects	.28	.83
Older Subjects	.36	.94

Einstein and McDaniel (1990, Experiment 2)

words. This was true for both the young and the old subjects (who did not differ in prospective memory), indicating the robustness of the effect.

To test the familiarity plus search view of prospective memory more directly, we conducted several experiments in which we manipulated the familiarity of the target words in a different way: We varied the number of encounters with the target words within the experiment (Guynn, McDaniel, & Einstein, 1998, Experiments 1a and 1b). Subjects performed an implicit memory cover task (word fragment completion in one experiment and anagram solution in the other). Subjects tried to complete (or to solve) 100 different word fragments (or anagrams). The prospective memory task was embedded within this cover task, in that 3 of the 100 word fragments (or anagrams) could be completed (or solved) with prospective memory target events. Subjects were instructed that if they ever saw one of three prospective memory target words (anatomy, office, and shadow for half of the subjects, and anybody, freckle, and bravado for half of the subjects) as a completion (or a solution), to circle the word on their cover task answer sheet.

We manipulated the familiarity of the target words by reminding some subjects of the target words three times during the cover task. The reminder was the instruction to "Remember the three words that you studied at the beginning of the experiment." Other subjects were not reminded of the target words. We expected that because the prospective memory target events were familiar words, they would receive a fairly small increment in familiarity by our presenting them once during the prospective memory instructions. We expected that they would receive a relatively larger increment in familiarity by our reminding subjects of them three times during the experiment.

The results appear in Table 2.2 and show that subjects were no more likely to circle the target words when they were reminded of them three times than when they were not reminded of them. To the extent that reminding subjects of the target words increased the familiarity of the target words, the results indicate that increasing the familiarity of the target words does not improve prospective memory.

TABLE 2.2. Target-Only Reminders Did Not Improve
Prospective Memory over That in a No-Reminder
Control Condition

	No-Reminder Control	Target-Only Reminder
Experiment 1a	.59	.60
Experiment 1b	.66	.57

Guynn, McDaniel, and Einstein (1998, Experiments 1a and 1b)

One possibility is that we did not manipulate familiarity appropriately. Evidence that this was the case comes from finding that recognition memory (which is presumed to be sensitive to differences in familiarity) for the target words was not better in the reminder condition than in the no-reminder control condition. Reminding subjects may not have increased the familiarity of the target words because the target words were not actually ever visually re-presented to the subjects (the subjects were asked to remember the target words). If perceptual fluency affects the familiarity of a word (Jacoby, 1991; Mandler, 1980), then perhaps the words must actually be visually re-presented to increase their familiarity (because perceptual fluency depends on reinstating perceptual processes).

A New Experiment

We conducted a new experiment, not previously reported, to address this concern. In this experiment, subjects performed a prospective memory task in the context of a word search cover task. We manipulated the number of exposures of the prospective memory target events by varying whether or not subjects were given prospective memory reminders during the experiment (0 reminders versus 12 reminders). To ensure that this manipulation would affect the perceptual fluency and thus the familiarity of the target events, the target words were actually visually re-presented to the subjects during the reminders.

The subjects were 64 male U.S. Air Force recruits who participated as part of a basic training requirement. Subjects were tested in two groups of 32 subjects. In each group, half of the subjects were given 12 prospective memory reminders and half of the subjects were not given reminders.

The 976 words for the experiment were selected from Clusters 4–8 of the Toglia and Battig (1978) norms. Four words (power, curb, mild, sweat) were the prospective memory target events. Twenty-eight words were target words for the word search cover task (two words for each of the two practice trials and the 12 test trials). The remaining 944 words were distracters for the word search cover task. The word search cover task involved searching for certain retrospective memory target words in successive four-word displays. Examples of the four types of displays appear in Table 2.3.[1]

Subjects were first given the instructions and a practice trial on the word search cover task. They were told that we were interested in how quickly they could search a display of words for certain target words, and a trial on this task consisted of the following components: (1) the instruction to "Remember These Target Words" and two target words on the computer screen for 2 s, (2) the instruction to "Prepare for Display" for 2 s, and (3) 20 four-word displays, presented one at a time for 1 s each. A display was simply four words presented in a square on the computer screen, and subjects were instructed always to attend to just two words in the display (the valid words). For half of the subjects, the valid words were in the upper left and the lower right of the display, and for half of the subjects, the valid words were in the upper right and the lower left of the display. Subjects were told that the valid words were important and to ignore the invalid words.

Subjects were instructed that, if either of the two target words matched either of the two valid words, press a designated key (for yes) on the computer keyboard. If neither of the two target words matched either of the two valid words, press another key (for no) on the computer keyboard. Subjects were then given a practice trial on the task.

Next, subjects received the prospective memory task instructions, which first involved learning four words (i.e., the prospective memory target events; power, curb, mild, sweat). The words were presented one at a time, for 2 s each. Subjects were instructed to press a designated key for the prospective memory task if they ever saw any of the four words later in the experiment. Because the

TABLE 2.3. Examples of the Four Types of Displays Used in the Word Search Cover Task

Prospective Memory Target Events: Power, Curb, Mild, Sweat
Memory Set Items: Second, Podium
Valid Diagonal: Upper Left and Lower Right Words

Display Type 1	bare	pull
	home	mild
Display Type 2	clumsy	power
	power	grow
Display Type 3	podium	starch
	curfew	sink
Display Type 4	foot	empty
	guilt	gold

entire set of instructions was complex, we repeated and summarized the instructions.

Subjects were then given another practice trial, followed by 12 test trials. Each test trial consisted of presentation of two new target words, followed by 20 new four-word displays (presented one at a time). Before each test trial, subjects receiving reminders were given the instruction to "Remember the four words that you studied at the beginning of the experiment," and the four prospective memory target events were presented. Each reminder appeared on the computer screen for 5 s. A different prospective memory target event occurred once on the valid diagonal on the 3rd, 5th, 8th, and 12th test trials.

At the end of the word search cover task, subjects were asked to recall and to recognize the four prospective memory target events. The distracters for the recognition test were the 28 target words from the 14 cover task trials (12 test trials and two practice trials), and 68 distracters from the 12th cover task test trial, for a total of 100 words on the recognition test.

The results appear in Table 2.4 and show no effect of reminding subjects of the target events on prospective memory. Subjects were no more likely to perform the prospective memory task when they received 12 reminders, including visual re-presentation of the target events, than when they did not receive reminders. Similarly, using a latency measure of responding, there was no effect of reminding subjects on prospective memory.

In contrast, the retrospective memory measures were affected by the manipulation of familiarity. Recall and recognition of the prospective memory target events were better for subjects who received 12 reminders than for subjects who did not receive reminders.

We expected that visual re-presentation of the target words during the reminders would increase the perceptual fluency and thereby the familiarity of the target words. Evidence that familiarity was increased by the reminders comes from finding that subjects receiving reminders recognized the target words better than subjects not receiving reminders. Apparently, however, increased familiarity

TABLE 2.4. Target-Only Reminders Improved Recall and Recognition but Not Prospective Memory

	No-Reminder Control	Target-Only Reminder
Prospective Memory	.35	.41
Recall	.58	.88
Recognition	.66	.96

Guynn, McDaniel, and Einstein (unpublished)

(at least increased familiarity produced by the present procedure) does not mediate prospective memory as it does recognition memory, because prospective memory did not differ for subjects receiving reminders and subjects not receiving reminders.

The results of the three experiments just discussed, in which there was no effect of reminding subjects of the target events on prospective memory, do not support the familiarity plus search view of prospective memory. Note that the familiarity plus search view places a premium on the target events per se, and our results suggest that the view may be incorrect in this regard.[2] Rather, it may be that the associative link between the target events and the intended action plays a central role in prospective memory. If so, then reminders that focus on the associative link between the target events and the intended action may improve prospective memory. We have conducted two experiments to test this idea (Guynn, McDaniel, & Einstein, 1998).

In both experiments (Guynn McDaniel, & Einstein, 1998, Experiments 2 and 3), subjects performed a word fragment completion implicit memory cover task similar to the one described earlier (Guynn McDaniel, & Einstein, 1998, Experiment 1a). As before, one group of subjects was not reminded about the prospective memory target events, and another group of subjects was reminded three times about the prospective memory target events. A final group of subjects was reminded three times about both the target events and the intended action. The reminders to this third group of subjects consisted of the instruction to "Remember the three words that you studied at the beginning of the experiment," plus the instruction to "Remember what you have to do if you ever see any of those three words" (Experiment 2), or the instruction to "Remember the key that you have to press later in the experiment if you ever see one of the three words" (Experiment 3).[3]

The results appear in Table 2.5. As in the prior experiments, subjects were no more likely to perform the prospective memory task when they were reminded of the target words three times than when they were not reminded of the target words. The results differed for the target plus action reminders, however, in that subjects were more likely to perform the prospective memory task

TABLE 2.5. Target-Plus-Action Reminders (but Not Target-Only Reminders) Improved Prospective Memory

	No-Reminder Control	Target-Only Reminder	Target + Action Reminder
Expt. 2	.42	.28	.95
Expt. 3	.31	.36	.82

Guynn, McDaniel, and Einstein (1998, Experiments 2 and 3)

when they were reminded of the target words and the intended action three times than when they were not reminded of them.

These results have stimulated a framework that we develop next, proposing that event-based prospective memory depends on the target event automatically evoking retrieval of the intended action (cf. McDaniel, Robinson-Riegler, & Einstein, 1998). We link this process to an automatic associative episodic memory module, a module posited by Moscovitch (1994) as being partly responsible for mediating performance on explicit episodic memory tasks. In the next section, we briefly outline the assumptions of Moscovitch's model, develop the ideas with regard to prospective memory, and report new experimental work to demonstrate the utility of the model in understanding prospective memory.

AUTOMATIC ASSOCIATIVE ACTIVATION

According to Moscovitch's (1994) model, explicit episodic (retrospective) memory is mediated by several subsystems corresponding to unique neuropsychological components. One primary subsystem is the medial-temporal/hippocampal module, which mediates the encoding, storage, and retrieval of associative information. A central feature of this subsystem is that it processes information specifically for the purposes of associative retrieval, with retrieval proceeding in an automatic, nonstrategic fashion. In particular, this module accepts consciously-attended information (cues for memory retrieval) and automatically produces interactions between the cues and memory traces previously associated with the cues. If the cue is sufficient (i.e., if the attended information produces enough interaction [ecphory] with a memory trace), then the module delivers that memory trace to consciousness rapidly, obligatorily, and with few cognitive resources. Further, the module operates reflexively, such that if the attended information (a cue) does not interact sufficiently with a particular memory trace, then that memory trace is not retrieved (unless another subsystem strategically generates additional cues for input to the hippocampal module [following Moscovitch we use the term "hippocampal" to refer to this module, but we remain neutral on precisely what neuropsychological structures might support this automatic associative module]). Moscovitch assumed that such strategic processes are mediated by a prefrontal subsystem and that both the automatic, hippocampal module and the strategic, prefrontal subsystem are involved in explicit episodic retrospective memory.

Our working assumption is that prospective memory retrieval is supported by the automatic associative memory module (McDaniel, Robinson-Riegler, & Einstein, 1998). This assumption provides an account of how prospective remembering occurs despite the fact that there is no external agent to prompt memory retrieval. The idea is that when a prospective memory target event is encountered, if the target event is consciously processed, then it is input to the associative memory module. If there is sufficient interaction (ecphory) between the cue (the target event) and the memory trace that specifies the intended action, then that intended action is automatically delivered to consciousness (i.e., the idea to perform the intended action is retrieved). If there is not sufficient ecphory, then the intended action is not delivered to consciousness and prospective remembering does not occur.

Before considering the relevant empirical work, it is worth noting that one prevailing view assumes that a Supervisory Attentional System, subserved by prefrontal systems, is involved in prospective memory, in terms of creating markers for nonhabitual or nonroutine intended actions, monitoring for the markers, and using the markers to trigger retrieval of the intended actions (Bisiacchi, 1996; Burgess, 1996; Burgess & Shallice, 1997; Ellis, 1996; Shallice & Burgess, 1991). Although this view does not explicitly address the degree to which self-initiated and/or strategic processes are involved in monitoring for markers and in using the markers to trigger retrieval of intended actions, the rationale for assuming the involvement of a Supervisory Attentional System is that it is required for nonhabitual or nonroutine intended actions because "well-learned triggering procedures are not sufficient to ensure an intended outcome" (Ellis, 1996, p. 12). Thus, one reasonable assumption is that the monitoring and triggering procedures that are thought to be associated with prospective memory are somewhat strategic and resource demanding. This version of the Supervisory Attentional System account of prospective memory, along with the familiarity plus search view, provides a direct contrast to our new view as detailed in the remainder of this chapter.

The attractiveness of our framework is that it can account for a diverse array of existing empirical work, which we briefly review. For instance, the absence of age differences on simple (e.g., one target event) event-based prospective memory tasks is consistent with our framework (Einstein, Holland, McDaniel, & Guynn, 1992; Einstein & McDaniel, 1990). According to our framework, when a cue (i.e., a target event) is presented, and the cue interacts with the memory trace of an intended action, the hippocampal module automatically delivers the intended action to consciousness. Age differences are not expected when memory retrieval occurs automatically.

Additionally, the absence of an effect of target-only reminders on prospective memory can be understood by noting that target-only reminders would not be expected to affect the interaction between the target events and the memory traces of the intended actions. However, target plus action reminders would be expected to increase the associative interaction between the target events and the memory traces of the intended actions, thereby increasing the likelihood that the associative module would automatically output the intended action when the target event is presented. It is not obvious how a view of prospective memory based on a strategic monitoring system (e.g., a Supervisory Attentional System) would account for the differential effectiveness of reminders reported by Guynn, McDaniel, and Einstein (1998) and reviewed earlier.

Further, Moscovitch (1994) suggested that semantic or distinctive encodings facilitate the subsequent automatic interaction of a cue with a memory trace. If so, then prospective memory should be better when the target event and intended action are encoded under semantic orienting tasks than under nonsemantic orienting tasks. McDaniel, Robinson-Riegler, and Einstein (1998) reported just such a finding. They also reported that prospective memory is better when the target event is presented as a picture at encoding than when the target event is presented as a word at encoding. On the assumption that pictures provide a more distinctive encoding than words (cf. Weldon & Coyote, 1996), this finding is consistent with the presumed operation of an automatic associative module.

On a more informal note, in much of our previous work, we have recorded the latencies of prospective memory responding. We typically do not report these data, because if subjects respond, they do so immediately upon presentation of the target event (Einstein & McDaniel, 1990). This pattern of responding is consistent with the assumption that the automatic associative module rapidly delivers the retrieved information to consciousness. Finally, in our previous work, we have queried subjects about their strategies for prospective memory retrieval. Subjects typically report that they did not do anything strategic—the memory just "popped into mind" (Einstein & McDaniel, 1990). This phenomenological report suggests that prospective memories might be analogous to spontaneous retrospective memories that pop into mind, for which the hippocampal module is thought to be responsible.

Direct Tests of the Automatic Associative Activation Framework

To provide more direct tests of the idea that an automatic associative system supports prospective memory retrieval, we have conducted two lines of work. In one pilot experiment, we manipulated the pre-experimental association of the target events and the intended actions. A prospective memory task was embedded in the word fragment completion cover task described previously. The prospective memory task was to write down a particular response word if a word fragment was ever completed with a prospective memory target word. In one condition, the target words and the response words were associatively related to each other. (For half of the subjects, the word pairs were eraser-pencil, steeple-church, and wallet-money. For the other half of the subjects, the word pairs were library-books, spaghetti-sauce, and thread-needle.) In another condition, the target words were re-paired with the response words from the other stimulus set, such that there was no obvious associative relationship between the words in a pair. (For half of the subjects, the word pairs were eraser-needle, steeple-books, and wallet-sauce. For the other half of the subjects, the word pairs were library-money, spaghetti-church, and thread-pencil.)

The familiarity plus search view anticipates equivalent performance in the associatively related and unrelated conditions because the target events (and hence the familiarities of the target events) were identical in the two conditions. Only the response words, and more important the nature of the pre-experimental association between the target events and the response words, differed between the two conditions. According to the familiarity plus search view, it is the familiarity of the target event that affects whether or not the target event stimulates a feeling of familiarity and whether or not a memory search is attempted to determine the reason for the feeling of familiarity. Given that the target events were identical in the two conditions, the familiarity plus search view predicts equivalent performance in the two conditions.

Similarly, a view based on strategic monitoring for cues anticipates equivalent performance in the two conditions, because it is the detection of a cue as a target event that determines the likelihood that the prospective memory task will be performed. Given that the target events were identical in the two conditions, a view based on strategic monitoring for cues predicts equivalent performance in the two conditions.

In contrast to these two views, the automatic associative activation view predicts better prospective memory in the condition in which the target events and the response words were associatively related than in the condition in which the target events and the response words were not related. According to the automatic associative activation view, it is necessary that the target event (the cue) has sufficient interaction or ecphory with the memory trace of the intended action in order for the automatic associative module to deliver the memory trace of the intended action into consciousness. Factors that increase that potential for interaction are expected to increase the likelihood of the module delivering the memory trace into consciousness, and thus of improving prospective memory. Associative relatedness between the target event and the intended action would seem to be one factor that would affect the potential for interaction.

The preliminary results of the pilot experiment are consistent with the predictions of the automatic associative activation framework. With 14 subjects tested (six in the associatively related condition and eight in the unrelated condition), prospective memory was better in the condition in which the target words and response words were associatively related ($M = .89$) than in the condition in which the target words and response words were not related ($M = .63$).

The results of some other recent work are also consistent with the automatic associative activation view. Einstein, Smith, McDaniel, and Shaw (1997, Experiment 2) reported an experiment examining the effects of dividing attention (with a digit-monitoring task) during either the encoding phase or the retrieval phase of a prospective memory task. The familiarity plus search view predicts that dividing attention at retrieval would reduce the likelihood of conducting a successful search in response to the familiarity of the target event, and thereby reduce prospective memory (compared to that in a full attention condition). (Note that dividing attention at retrieval would not be expected to affect the likelihood of noticing the familiarity of the target event, which is assumed to be an automatic process that is not affected by dividing attention.) Alternatively, a view based on strategic monitoring for cues predicts that dividing attention at retrieval would reduce the likelihood of detecting a prospective memory target event as a cue to perform the intended action.

The automatic associative activation view, however, predicts no detrimental effect of dividing attention at retrieval. According to this view, if there is sufficient interaction or ecphory between the target event (the cue) and the memory trace of the intended action, then the hippocampal module will automatically deliver the memory trace into consciousness. Because it is thought to be an automatic process, it is not expected to be affected by dividing attention (cf. Moscovitch, 1994).

The data appear in Table 2.6 and show that the effect of dividing attention was consistent with the automatic associative activation view of prospective memory. Specifically, dividing attention at retrieval had no effect on prospective memory. Otani et al. (1997) have also provided evidence that dividing attention at retrieval does not impair event-based prospective memory. The absence of a divided attention effect in Einstein et al.'s (1997) experiment cannot readily be explained by suggesting that the divided attention manipulation was ineffective, because dividing attention at encoding reduced prospective memory. Dividing attention at encoding presumably reduced the quality of the encoding of the association between the target event and the intended action.

TABLE 2.6. Dividing Attention at Encoding, but Not at Retrieval, Reduced Prospective Memory for Younger Subjects

Retrieval Condition	Encoding Condition	
	Full Attention	Divided Attention
Full Attention	.66	.47
Divided Attention	.64	.55

Einstein, Smith, McDaniel, and Shaw (1997, Experiment 2, younger subjects)

Extensions of the Framework

The two experiments just described provide support for the idea that an automatic associative (hippocampal) module mediates performance on at least some kinds of prospective memory tasks. We now report some additional results that at first appear to challenge this approach to prospective memory. We then present another component of this approach that can be invoked to account for these apparently discrepant results as well. We previously reported the results for the younger subjects of Einstein et al.'s (1997) experiment as being consistent with the automatic associative activation framework. Einstein et al. (1997) also tested older subjects (their results appear in Table 2.7), and at first it appears that their results are not consistent with the framework. Specifically, older subjects' prospective memory was impaired by dividing attention at encoding (as was the case for younger subjects) and by dividing attention at retrieval (in contrast to younger subjects). The automatic associative activation framework as presented thus far is less able to account for this latter result, because an automatic process should be spared in older subjects, even when attention is divided.

On our view, this impaired prospective memory for older subjects when attention is divided at retrieval may reflect the role of the frontal system in prospective memory. Recently, McDaniel, Glisky, Rubin, Guynn, and Routhieaux (1999) reported evidence that the frontal system is involved in prospective memory. They found that older adults with lower than average scores on neuropsychological tests associated with frontal functioning performed less well on a laboratory prospective memory task than did older adults with higher than average scores. On many accounts, the frontal system is intimately involved with working memory (Frith & Dolan, 1996; Kimberg, D'Esposito, & Farah, 1998; Kimberg & Farah, 1993; Shimamura, 1994; or analogous types of executive function, Shallice & Burgess, 1991). Working memory would presumably be instrumental in holding the intended action in mind once it was retrieved, scheduling an appropriate sequence of responses (i.e., performing the divided attention task, performing the cover task, and performing the prospective memory task), and monitoring the execution of those responses. (See Cherry & LeCompte,

TABLE 2.7. Dividing Attention at Encoding or at Retrieval Reduced Prospective Memory for Older Subjects

Retrieval Condition	Encoding Condition	
	Full Attention	Divided Attention
Full Attention	.58	.54
Divided Attention	.38	.17

Einstein, Smith, McDaniel, and Shaw (1997, Experiment 2, older subjects)

1999, and Einstein, McDaniel, Manzi, Cochran, & Baker, in press, for evidence that working memory is correlated with prospective memory.) Further, older adults are thought to have limited resources associated with working memory functioning (Salthouse & Babcock, 1991), and perhaps not coincidentally, aging appears to produce disproportionate neurological decline in frontal areas (Shimamura, 1994). Thus, if age-related frontal decline or, in psychological terms, "declining working memory resources" are further compromised by the demands of a concurrent divided attention task, then performance of the prospective memory task would be expected to suffer. The idea is that limited working memory resources (declining frontal functioning) would impair the ability of older adults to hold the intended action in mind (after it was retrieved) concurrently with several other ongoing tasks, interrupt those tasks, and monitor the status of the execution of the prospective memory task.

One straightforward prediction of this view is that requiring subjects to maintain the intended action in mind over a short delay after it is retrieved should produce disproportionate declines in prospective memory for older as compared to younger adults. To test this prediction, Einstein et al. (in press) examined the effects of allowing subjects to execute the intended action immediately after it was retrieved versus requiring subjects to maintain the retrieved intended action in mind over a short delay before executing the intended action. The cover task involved reading short, three-sentence paragraphs, each followed by trivia questions. The prospective memory task was to press the F1 key if a prospective memory target event appeared as a word in a paragraph. In the immediate (no-delay) condition, the instruction was to press F1 as soon as a target word appeared, and in the delayed condition the instruction was to wait and press F1 when the trivia questions began (delays of 10–40 s). Einstein et al. (in press) used salient target events (the target words were presented in all uppercase letters) to help ensure that they were investigating maintenance of a retrieved intended action (rather than actual retrieval of the intended action). Prior work (McDaniel, Guynn, & Einstein, 1997) had indicated that these salient target events resulted in automatic (i.e., obligatory) retrieval of the intended action.

Our new automatic associative activation view predicts that aging should impair the ability to maintain the intended action in mind over the short delay after it is retrieved (by reducing the working memory resources that are required for the task). The older subjects' impaired ability to maintain the intended action in mind over the short delay should therefore increase any age differences in prospective memory (compared to that in a no-delay condition).

The data appear in Table 2.8 and show that the results were consistent with our new view. When subjects were allowed to execute the intended action as soon as a target word appeared, aging did not significantly affect prospective memory. In contrast, when subjects were required to wait until the trivia questions began to execute the intended action, aging significantly reduced prospec-

TABLE 2.8. Maintaining the Retrieved Intended Action in Mind over a Short Delay Disproportionately Affected Older Subjects and Produced Age Differences in Prospective Memory

	No Delay	10-s Delay	30-s Delay
Younger Subjects	.98	.75	.79
Older Subjects	.95	.44	.56

Einstein, McDaniel, Manzi, Cochran, and Baker (in press)

tive memory (even at delays as short as 10 s). This effect presumably occurred because the reduced working memory resources associated with aging particularly impaired the older subjects' ability to maintain the intended action in mind over the delay (compared to the younger subjects).

Further evidence for a role for working memory in maintaining an intended action in mind over a short delay comes from finding a positive correlation between working memory and prospective memory in the delayed condition (but not in the immediate, no-delay condition).

A related and more specified explanation of how concurrent interference, or maintaining an intended action in mind over a short delay, might disrupt prospective memory for older adults in particular can be sketched via an extension of Kimberg and Farah's (1993; Kimberg, D'Esposito, & Farah, 1998) formal model of frontal functioning and working memory. In this model, performance of complex tasks is mediated by production systems (condition-action plans) that are activated when appropriate information is encountered. Importantly, associations between elements in working memory are responsible in part for resolving conflict between competing productions (responses) that match subsets of the contents of working memory. Some of these contents involve relations between current goals and other information in working memory, thereby allowing behavior to be adaptive and goal-directed. If the associative strengths between these contents of working memory are attenuated (e.g., by frontal damage or deterioration), then the productions that are most consistent with some goals of the task may not be activated; instead, other mechanisms will capture relatively more control over production activation, such as priming of competing productions due to their recent execution. In terms of the present situation, the associative strengths between: (1) the intended prospective memory activity (present in working memory as a result of the hippocampally-mediated retrieval stimulated by the target event) and the stimulus at hand (the particular stimulus in working memory as determined by the presentation trial); (2) the cover task and the stimulus; and (3) the divided attention task and the stimulus, become degraded. Thus, the particular production that is activated will depend somewhat less on the current goals and somewhat more on other factors, like the most recent use of a production. Because productions that support cover task and divided attention task performance have been recently and frequently initiated, activation of productions for the cover task and the divided attention task is heightened, and such competition might then interfere with activating the prospective memory production. Note that without the concurrent divided attention task, there is less competition with the prospective memory production, and so its likelihood of being activated is not necessarily impaired (see Kimberg, D'Esposito, & Farah, 1998; Kimberg & Farah, 1993, for details). Also, without the requirement to maintain the retrieved intended action in mind over a short delay, there is less likelihood that the attenuated associative strengths will be further degraded by the passage of time.

Accordingly, by our model, the intended action may come to mind for older subjects as readily as for younger subjects (at least in a simple event-based task) through a relatively automatic (hippocampal) process. However, if other concurrent tasks place too much demand on working memory, as in our divided attention retrieval condition, or when the retrieved intended action must be maintained in mind over a short delay, then older subjects do not have the cognitive resources or perhaps the frontal functioning to successfully carry out the required tasks. More generally, this formulation suggests that age differences on simple event-based prospective memory tasks may be modulated by the demands to working memory of the activities concurrent with the prospective memory task.

In particular, this formulation predicts that older subjects should be impaired to a greater extent than younger subjects by any manipulation (e.g., divided attention, maintaining an intended action in mind over a short delay) that places additional demands on resources that are already somewhat limited in older adults. This would be the case if any of the various tasks that subjects are asked to do are resource-demanding such that older subjects' working memory resources are occupied such that they can not simultaneously perform the cover task, the prospective memory task, and the divided attention task. For example, if the cover task is one that is particularly demanding for older adults (e.g., retrieving names; see Maylor, 1990), then age differences would be expected even on a simple event-based prospective memory task. Consistent with this prediction, Maylor (1993; 1996) has shown that older subjects are impaired on simple event-based prospective memory, compared to younger subjects, when the cover task involves naming famous faces.

Returning to our prior discussion of the effects of dividing attention, Einstein et al.'s (1997) results for both younger and older subjects are especially interesting given the effects of dividing attention in younger and older subjects in a retrospective memory task. In Einstein et al.'s (1997) experiment, there was an interaction of age group with dividing attention at retrieval (the older were more impaired than the younger by dividing attention) but no interaction of age group with dividing attention at encoding (the older and the younger were equally impaired by dividing attention). In contrast to these results for prospective memory, Park, Smith, Dudley, and Lafronza (1989) have reported quite different results for retrospective memory. In Park et al.'s (1989) experiments, there was an interaction of age group with dividing attention at encoding (the older were more impaired than the younger) but no interaction of age group with dividing attention at retrieval. One would expect similar patterns for prospective memory and retrospective memory if performance on the two types of tasks is mediated by the same processes. That the interactions were in opposite directions for prospective memory and retrospective memory gives further support to the idea that these different types of remembering involve differences in the functional interplay of underlying memory systems. We further develop this idea in the next section.

Continuing with the prospective memory framework that we introduced earlier, younger subjects' prospective memory could also be expected to be impaired by dividing attention. This would be the case if younger subjects' working memory resources were occupied such that they could not simultaneously perform the cover task, the prospective memory task, and the divided attention task. Consistent with this possibility, McDaniel, Robinson-Riegler, and Einstein (1998) have shown that dividing attention at retrieval can impair event-based prospective memory in younger subjects.

Marsh and Hicks (1998) have also shown that dividing attention at retrieval can impair event-based prospective memory in younger subjects. Their results are consistent with the idea that younger subjects' working memory resources can be occupied to the extent that they cannot simultaneously perform the cover task, the prospective memory task, and the divided attention task. Further evidence for this interpretation comes from finding that prospective memory was impaired by dividing attention when the divided attention task demanded central executive working memory resources, but not when the divided attention task demanded non-executive working memory resources.

CONCLUSION

Our current theoretical perspective on prospective memory is that it involves some of the same memory systems as cued retrospective memory—an automatic, hippocampal module and a strategic, frontal system. These are the components of Moscovitch's (1994) multiple memory systems model that are presumed to mediate performance on explicit episodic retrospective memory tasks (see Craik, Govoni, Naveh-Benjamin, & Anderson, 1996, for evidence on the role of these two memory systems components in encoding and retrieval in explicit episodic retrospective memory tasks). On our view, these components, or the functions they subserve, are presumed to mediate performance on prospective memory tasks as well. A schematic diagram of performance on these two types of tasks appears in Figure 2.1. What differs between prospective memory and retrospective memory are the dynamics of utilizing the memory systems components, and the particular frontal subsystems involved. On both types of tests, the automatic associative activation (hippocampal) component is presumed to be responsible for the spontaneous retrieval of a memory trace when a cue interacts with that memory trace. We suggest that the role and even the particular subsystem of the strategic (frontal) component differs depending on the type of memory test. On retrospective memory tests, the role of the strategic frontal subsystem is to query memory or to initiate a search of memory for the desired contents (if they are not retrieved automatically via the hippocampal module). Using PET technology, Petrides (1995) has reported that the ventral lateral frontal region is highly active during deliberate attempts to remember information on explicit retrospective memory tests.

In contrast, for prospective memory tests, if the desired contents are not retrieved automatically via the hippocampal module, then there is no search of memory for the desired contents. For prospective memory tests, the role of the strategic frontal subsystem is not to query memory or to initiate a search of memory, but to coordinate and to schedule the various activities or tasks involved—for example, holding the concurrent tasks in mind, holding the intended action in mind once it has been retrieved, and interrupting the ongoing cover task in order to execute the intended action. This strategic subsystem may be considered to be a different frontal region (the mid dorsal lateral frontal region) from that involved in deliberate attempts to remember past information. Petrides (1995) has reported that this mid dorsal lateral region is highly active during tasks requiring planning, organizing information, and keeping track of the products of memory.

Thus we have moved away from the view that prospective memory can be completely explained by existing models of retrospective (recognition) memory. We have moved to a view, based on a neuropsychological systems approach to memory, of prospective memory and retrospective memory as representing different dynamic interactions of these memory systems, as well as involvement of somewhat different subsystems. Although existing data provide some support for this view of prospective memory retrieval, other views can probably account for most of the data as well. We offer this view in the spirit of stimulating more direct tests of these different views of prospective memory, as well as new perspectives and a more complete understanding of prospective memory.

CUED RETROSPECTIVE MEMORY

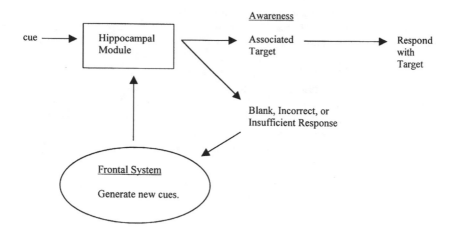

PROSPECTIVE MEMORY

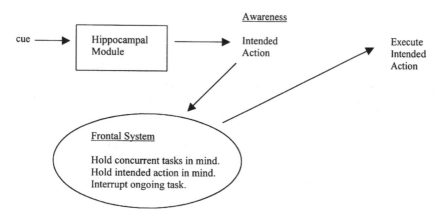

FIGURE 2.1. A representation of how the automatic, hippocampal module and the strategic, frontal subsystem mediate performance in cued retrospective memory and in prospective memory.

NOTES

Preparation of this chapter was supported in part by NIA grant AG08436. Data collection for the unpublished experiment reported herein (Guynn, McDaniel, & Einstein, unpublished) was supported in part by a National Science Foundation Graduate Research Fellowship to Melissa J. Guynn and by Grant AF 49620–92–J–0437 from the Air Force Office of Scientific Research to Henry L. Roediger, III.

1. There were four possible types of displays: (1) a prospective memory target event on the valid diagonal and distracters in the other three locations, (2) a prospective memory target event in both locations of the invalid diagonal and distracters in the other two locations, (3) a memory set item on the valid diagonal and distracters in the other three locations, and (4) distracters in all four locations in the display.

2. We note that Burkes (1994) has some unpublished data that could be interpreted as being consistent with the familiarity plus search model of prospective memory.

3. The prospective memory task was changed to pressing the F10 key on the computer keyboard for Experiment 3.

REFERENCES

Atkinson, R. C., & Juola, J. F. (1974). Search and decision processes in recognition memory. In D. H. Krantz, R. C. Atkinson, R. D. Luce, & P. Suppes (Eds.), *Contemporary developments in mathematical psychology: Learning, memory, and thinking* (Vol. 1). San Francisco: Freeman.

Bisiacchi, P. S. (1996). The neuropsychological approach in the study of prospective memory. In M. Brandimonte, G. O. Einstein, & M. A. McDaniel (Eds.), *Prospective memory: Theory and applications* (pp. 297–318). Mahwah, NJ: Erlbaum.

Burgess, P. (July 1996). *Prospective memory following frontal lobe damage.* Paper presented at the International Conference on Memory, Abano Terme, Italy.

Burgess, P. W., & Shallice, T. (1997). The relationship between prospective and retrospective memory: Neuropsychological evidence. In M. A. Conway (Ed.), *Cognitive models of memory* (pp. 247–272). Cambridge: MIT Press.

Burkes, M. (July 1994). *The effect of local context on prospective memory performance in a semantic processing task.* Paper presented at the Practical Aspects of Memory Conference, College Park, MD.

Cherry, K. E., & LeCompte, D. C. (1999). Age and individual differences influence prospective memory. *Psychology and Aging, 14,* 60–76.

Craik, F. I. M., Govoni, R., Naveh-Benjamin, M., & Anderson, N. D. (1996). The effects of divided attention on encoding and retrieval processes in human memory. *Journal of Experimental Psychology: General, 125,* 159–180.

Ebbinghaus, H. (1964). *Memory: A contribution to experimental psychology* (H. A. Ruger & C. E. Bussenius, Trans.). New York: Dover. (Original work published 1885; translated 1913).

Einstein, G. O., Holland, L. J., McDaniel, M. A., & Guynn, M. J. (1992). Age-related deficits in prospective memory: The influence of task complexity. *Psychology and Aging, 7,* 471–478.

Einstein, G. O., & McDaniel, M. A. (1990). Normal aging and prospective memory. *Journal of Experimental Psychology: Learning, Memory, and Cognition, 16*, 717–726.

Einstein, G. O., & McDaniel, M. A. (1996). Retrieval processes in prospective memory: Theoretical approaches and some new empirical findings. In M. Brandimonte, G. O. Einstein, & M. A. McDaniel (Eds.), *Prospective memory: Theory and applications* (pp. 115–142). Mahwah, NJ: Erlbaum.

Einstein, G. O., McDaniel, M. A., Manzi, M., Cochran, B., & Baker, M. (in press). Prospective memory and aging: Forgetting intentions over short delays. *Psychology and Aging*.

Einstein, G. O., Smith, R. E., McDaniel, M. A., & Shaw, P. (1997). Aging and prospective memory: The influence of increased task demands at encoding and retrieval. *Psychology and Aging, 12*, 479–488.

Ellis, J. (1996). Prospective memory or the realization of delayed intentions: A conceptual framework for research. In M. Brandimonte, G. O. Einstein, & M. A. McDaniel (Eds.), *Prospective memory: Theory and applications* (pp. 1–22). Mahwah, NJ: Erlbaum.

Frith, C., & Dolan, R. (1996). The role of the prefrontal cortex in higher cognitive functions. *Cognitive Brain Research, 5*, 175–181.

Guynn, M. J., McDaniel, M. A., & Einstein, G. O. (1998). Prospective memory: When reminders fail. *Memory & Cognition, 26*, 287–298.

Harris, J. E. (1984). Remembering to do things: A forgotten topic. In J. E. Harris & P. E. Morris (Eds.), *Everyday memory, actions, and absentmindedness* (pp. 71–92). New York: Academic.

Jacoby, L. L. (1991). A process dissociation framework: Separating automatic from intentional uses of memory. *Journal of Memory and Language, 30*, 513–541.

Kimberg, D. Y., D'Esposito, M., & Farah, M. J. (1998). Cognitive functions in the prefrontal cortex—Working memory and executive control. *Current Directions in Psychological Science, 6*, 185–192.

Kimberg, D. Y., & Farah, M. J. (1993). A unified account of cognitive impairments following frontal lobe damage: The role of working memory in complex, organized behavior. *Journal of Experimental Psychology: General, 122*, 411–428.

Mandler, G. (1980). Recognizing: The judgment of previous occurrence. *Psychological Review, 87*, 252–271.

Marsh, R. L., & Hicks, J. L. (1998). Event-based prospective memory and executive control of working memory. *Journal of Experimental Psychology: Learning, Memory, and Cognition, 24*, 336–349.

Maylor, E. A. (1990). Recognizing and naming faces: Aging, memory retrieval, and the tip of the tongue state. *Journal of Gerontology: Psychological Sciences, 45*, P 215–P 226.

Maylor, E. A. (1993). Aging and forgetting in prospective and retrospective memory tasks. *Psychology and Aging, 8*, 420–428.

Maylor, E. A. (1996). Age-related impairment in an event-based prospective-memory task. *Psychology and Aging, 11*, 74–78.

McDaniel, M. A. (1995). Prospective memory: Progress and processes. In D. L. Medin (Ed.), *The psychology of learning and motivation* (Vol. 33, pp. 191–221). San Diego: Academic.

McDaniel, M. A., & Einstein, G. O. (1993). The importance of cue familiarity and cue distinctiveness in prospective memory. *Memory, 1*, 23–41.

McDaniel, M. A., Glisky, E. L., Rubin, S. R., Guynn, M. J., & Routhieaux, B. C. (1999). Prospective memory: A neuropsychological study. *Neuropsychology, 13*, 103–110.

McDaniel, M., Guynn, M., & Einstein, G. (November 1997). *Prospective memory: Two views and some new data.* Paper presented at the 38th Annual Meeting of the Psychonomic Society, Philadelphia, PA.

McDaniel, M. A., Robinson-Riegler, B., & Einstein, G. O. (1998). Prospective remembering: Perceptually-driven or conceptually-driven processes? *Memory & Cognition, 26*, 121–134.

Moscovitch, M. (1994). Memory and working with memory: Evaluation of a component process model and comparisons with other models. In D. L. Schacter & E. Tulving (Eds.), *Memory systems* (pp. 269–310). Cambridge: MIT Press.

Otani, H., Landau, J. D., Libkuman, T. M., St. Louis, J. P., Kazen, J. K., & Throne, G. W. (1997). Prospective memory and divided attention. *Memory, 5*, 343–360.

Park, D. C., Smith, A. D., Dudley, W. N., & Lafronza, V. N. (1989). Effects of age and a divided attention task presented during encoding and retrieval on memory. *Journal of Experimental Psychology: Learning, Memory, and Cognition, 15*, 1185–1191.

Petrides, M. (1995). Functional organization of the human frontal cortex for mnemonic processing: Evidence from neuroimaging studies. *Annals of the New York Academy of Sciences; 769*, 85–96.

Richardson-Klavehn, A., Gardiner, J. M., & Java, R. I. (1994). Involuntary conscious memory and the method of opposition. *Memory, 2*, 1–29.

Salthouse, T. A., & Babcock, R. L. (1991). Decomposing adult age differences in working memory. *Developmental Psychology, 27*, 763–776.

Shallice, T., & Burgess, P. W. (1991). Deficits in strategy application following frontal lobe damage in man. *Brain, 114*, 727–741.

Shimamura, A. P. (1994). Neuropsychological perspectives on memory and cognitive decline in normal aging. *Seminars in the Neurosciences, 6*, 387–394.

Toglia, M. P., & Battig, W. F. (1978). *Handbook of semantic word norms.* Hillsdale: Erlbaum.

Tulving, E. (1983). *Elements of episodic memory.* Oxford: Clarendon Press.

Weldon, M. S., & Coyote, K. C. (1996). Failure to find the picture superiority effect in implicit conceptual memory tests. *Journal of Experimental Psychology: Learning, Memory, and Cognition, 22*, 670–686.

CHAPTER 3

Action Memory

A System-Oriented Approach

Johannes Engelkamp

This chapter explains why action phrases such as "brush your teeth" are better retained when we perform them than when we only listen to them or watch and imagine them, respectively. This memory advantage of performing actions is called subject-performed task effect (SPT effect). Although there are some boundary conditions for this SPT effect (e.g., Engelkamp & Zimmer, 1997; Zimmer & Engelkamp, 1999), this effect is very robust and has been demonstrated in numerous experiments (see Engelkamp, 1998, for a comprehensive review). In trying to explain this effect, it is proposed that more than one memory system is involved. Demonstrating that one needs several systems to explain the SPT effect is the topic of this chapter.

WHAT IS A SYSTEM-ORIENTED APPROACH?

There are different ways in which memory is subdivided in subsystems. What I do not mean when I speak of a system-oriented approach is a multi-store approach as proposed by Atkinson and Shiffrin (1968) in the classical multi-store model.

What I do not focus on either is the system distinction between episodic and semantic memory proposed by Tulving (1972 and later) that he later (1985a, 1985b) extended to include a procedural system. According to Tulving (1985a, 1985b), these systems are closely connected to different states of awareness, and they are hierarchically ordered in the sense that they developed succesively during evolution. Basically, I will refer only to the episodic memory system of Tulving. Nevertheless, in order to make the difference clear between Tulving's classification system and the system approach I pursue, I will briefly describe the memory systems of Tulving.

The procedural system is the phylogenetically oldest system. It allows acquisition of stimulus-response connections. Information on this level is prescriptive for behavior. The organism has no awareness of this kind of information. Information of the semantic and episodic systems is on the contrary descriptive, and persons may be aware of information from these systems, although in different forms. In both systems, external information (among others) is represented internally. In the semantic system, this information is not context-specific, whereas in the episodic system, there is additional information represented about the circumstances under which external information was acquired in space and time. Both forms of information may become conscious. In the former case, we become aware of external facts, in the latter case of autobiographical external facts. Tulving speaks of noetic and autonoetic consciousness, respectively. Consciousness is in both of the cases not dependent on the actual presence of the external facts.

I am particularly interested in autonoetic consciousness, which "allows an individual to become aware of his or her own identity and existence in subjective time." It provides the familiar phenomenal flavor of recollective experience characterized by "pastness" and subjective "veridicality" (Tulving, 1985a, p. 388). Hence, the retrieval of information from the episodic memory system is accompanied by the experience of remembering some autobiographical fact, and the method to measure performance of memory from the episodic system is to request subjects to recollect autobiographical facts or episodes.

The system-oriented approach that I am pursuing assumes that recollection may be based on information stemming from different systems in still another meaning of the term. What I mean by system refers also to type of information, albeit in a different sense than Tulving. I do not debate whether episodic information becomes conscious, but whether different aspects of autobiographical information are processed by different memory systems. An experienced fact may be verbal or nonverbal, visual or acoustic, sensory or motor, or conceptual. Thus, the systems that I propose here differ with respect to the kind of information that they handle. To make clearer what I mean, I will review the code debate in history. To make my position with regard to Tulving's (1985a, 1985b) explicit, I share the distinction between semantic and episodic information insofar as episodic information refers to a single episode (in time and space), and semantic information is context-free. I do not assume, however, that episodic information is necessarily dependent on an autonoetic conciousness if it is remembered. Episodic information can also be reflected in an implicit memory test. I agree, however, that performance in an explicit memory test refers to episodic information. Because I consider episodic information as the information of an event in time and space, it is legitimate to distinguish different aspects by which the episode can be described (e.g., with regard to the occurence of an object where it occurred, what color it has, how it was oriented, etc.). The critical question of such an informational systems approach is whether the different kinds of informational aspects are handled by different memory systems. In this sense, Schacter's (1990, 1994) perceptual representation system (PRS) is an informational system.

One of the first who proposed that episodic memory performance may be based on different code systems was Paivio (1969, 1971): In his dual code theory, he claimed essentially that there is a verbal and nonverbal (essentially he focused on the nonverbal visual) code and that memory performance may be based on either or both of these codes. When verbal material is presented, subjects mainly rely on the verbal system, and when nonverbal pictorial material is presented, they rather rely on the nonverbal system. The nonverbal system was assumed to be more efficient than the verbal system. The picture superiority effect was partly explained by this difference. One critical feature of Paivio's dual code theory (e.g., 1986) was that both code systems were also semantic systems. Thus, the verbal system was a verbal-semantic and the nonverbal system a nonverbal-semantic or a visual-semantic system. The relationship between both systems was associative, that is, there were learned connections. The relations were not logically founded. They were not an inherent part of the whole system. This associationistic feature raises a central problem. It does not assume any "qualitative" differences between (associative) connections. Concretely spoken, that means the association between say the internal verbal representation of the word "shoe" to the internal nonverbal representation of the visually perceived object "shoe" or the picture of it is not basically different from the association between the representation of the word "shoe" and the representation of the object "socks" or "shoe polish" or "foot." That is, there is no inherent relation between an object and its label in Paivio's theory.

All other code theories assume—as far as I see—such an inherent relation between the representation of objects and their verbal labels. What the related representations have in common is called meaning or more often concept. That is, in other code theories a verbal code system (for word forms), a semantic code system (for concepts), and as a natural consequence, a nonverbal code system (for picture forms) analogue to the verbal code system are postulated (e.g., Glass, Holyoak, & Santa, 1979; Nelson, 1979; Schacter, 1994; Seymour, 1979; Snodgrass, 1984; Warren & Morton, 1982). Interestingly, there was much more resistance to accept the assumption of a nonverbal (nonsemantic) visual code system than to accept the assumption of a nonsemantic verbal code system (or lexicon) (e.g., Schreuder, 1987; Hoffmann; 1986). This situation has changed only recently due to studying explicit and implicit episodic memory in comparison (Schacter, 1990, 1994; Biederman & Cooper, 1992; Zimmer, 1995) and due to the increasing interest in cognitive neuropsychology (Ellis & Young, 1989; McCarthy & Warrington, 1990; Riddoch et al., 1988). Nowadays, researchers speak also of entry systems to the semantic system. They claim these entry systems (mainly the verbal and nonverbal visual) as interfaces between the early presemantic and the semantic information processes (e.g., Bruce & Young, 1986). The entry systems are considered to be modality-specific. The semantic system serves on the one hand to represent the relations between representations of different modality-specific systems (e.g., word form of the word "shoe," picture form of the object "shoe") in a corresponding concept (concept of SHOE), and it serves on the other hand to represent connections among concepts in so-called propositions. In episodic memory, typical connections are predicates to objects such as "the shoe is dirty."

There was a great debate in the 1970s about whether we need any modality-specific (presemantic) visual representations in addition to concepts and propositions in order to explain behavioral phenomena (e.g., Kosslyn, 1981; Pylyshyn, 1973, 1981). Although this debate had led to no result (e.g., Anderson, 1978), the number of researchers who assume a system approach has increased steadily (see Engelkamp, 1994, for some reasons why the debate led to no decision).

While the claim of different entry systems followed quite naturally from the variations of stimulus modalities (such as words vs. pictures), output systems were ignored until recently. In the field of explicit memory, this situation is due to the fact that in typical memory tasks, stimuli were either words or pictures, and as far as encoding instructions are concerned they aimed at varying internal processes (e.g., degree of semantic elaboration) and not overt reactions. Thus, the output system was not varied, and correspondingly, its relevance for memory performances was overlooked. That one needs also representations at the output side independent of concepts became mainly obvious in the field of neuropsychology. The observations that some patients were unable to understand words but were able to name objects; that there were other patients who demonstrated in word-picture matching tasks that they understood the meaning of words but that they could not speak them aloud; that there were again other patients who could speak words aloud but who could not write them, etc. (Ellis & Young, 1989), led neuropsychologists to claim besides an input lexicon an output lexicon (e.g., Riddoch et al., 1988) or even two output lexicons, one for speaking and one for writing (Ellis & Young, 1989).

In the field of psycholinguistics (e.g., Garnham, 1985; Harley, 1995) and in the field of cognitive neuropsychology, one distinguishes moreover three routes to word production (a route from letter to sound or sound to sound, a route from word form representation in the input lexicon to word production and a route from a word form via a concept to word production). At least, the latter two distinctions also imply the assumption of an output lexicon besides an input lexicon.

Having reached this point, it is only a small step to claim also a nonverbal output system for actions. Such a claim was formulated by Engelkamp and Krumnacker (1980) and Engelkamp and Zimmer (1983). This claim was motivated by the observation that remembering action phrases is increased when subjects performed the denoted actions during learning. This SPT effect was of course by itself insufficient to argue that memory after enactment benefitted from an action output system just as the picture superiority effect was insufficient to argue that memory for pictures benefits from a visual entry system. It is therefore my main goal to present further evidence for the assumption that there is an action output system and that information from this system can support memory for enacted actions.

Before I do so, I will try to summarize the system construct used here and discuss what kind of evidence can be used to support such a system-oriented approach.

What characterizes the so-called code approach is that it claims the existence of systems that are specialized with regard to the kind of information that they can handle and that the kind of information depends on the physical appearance of stimuli and on the pattern of movement produced.

The systems based on the physical appearance of stimuli differ essentially according to the sense modality in which stimuli are perceived. Stimuli that we see provide us with other information than those that we hear or those that we touch or those that we smell. The critical assumption of a system-oriented approach in memory psychology is that these kinds of information are stored in memory and remembered in episodic recollection. Our episodic experiences do not only differ subjectively, for instance, when we recognize a rose upon seeing it or smelling it or touching it, they also differ in terms of the memory traces that they create, and these trace differences are due to the component traces laid down in the different entry systems.

The distinction between a verbal and a nonverbal entry system is more abstract insofar as it is not defined by specific sense systems but by the goal for which the stimuli are used. Verbal stimuli usually refer to objects and facts that are arbitrarily connected to them. In everyday life, verbal stimuli are used to refer to these external facts. Nonverbal stimuli usually constitute facts. They are simply there and are not usually used by other people to communicate about them. These few remarks on differences between verbal and nonverbal stimuli may suffice to give the idea that they serve deeply different functions (see Engelkamp, 1990, for a more extended discussion). It is plausible to assume that specialized systems have evolved to process verbal and nonverbal stimuli.

Finally, although it is still widely ignored in memory research, our motor actions are also part of episodic experiences. We may name an object "rose," or we may pick it. These motor activities also create different sensory experiences, and it is as plausible (as it is for other sense-dependent aspects of experiences) that they are stored and that they can be recollected. Again, labeling objects or events usually serves other functions than using objects or doing things nonverbally.

What is claimed by a system-oriented approach is therefore that information processing is complex when we experience episodes, that specialized part-systems are involved—specialized for processing specific kinds of information (such as color or form with objects) and specialized for processing specific movement patterns depending on specific purposes—and that correspondingly part traces are laid down in memory that can be used in recollecting episodes. A specific assumption that I make is: I assume that recollecting episodes necessarily involves conceptual information, and that non-conceptual information, which I will globally refer to as modality-specific information, may accompany the conceptual information to a varying degree, depending on the specific memory task. This assumption is further specified below.

A last remark that I would like to add here is that if I speak of representations and memory traces, I do not assume that these representations are locally circumscript. They may well be distributed within a system, but they are restricted to a specific system. Furthermore, usually several systems are involved in processing and recollecting episodes. Some are automatically used given a specific stimulus in a memory task, while others depend on the specific goals pursued. Their use is flexible.

These last considerations lead us to the question: What kind of phenomena do we expect with such a system-oriented approach?

WHAT KIND OF EVIDENCE SUPPORTS A SYSTEM-ORIENTED APPROACH?

It is not without reason that in the imagery debate it was Kosslyn (e.g., 1981) who had to defend the assumption of a visual system and not Pylyshyn (e.g., 1981), whose pure propositional position was rather taken for granted and did not need to be defended. It seems self-evident that we have access to meaning and that we remember meaning. Therefore it does not come as a surprise that conceptual information was considered to be the only basis for explicit episodic memory performance until into the 1980s (Anderson, 1985; Klatzky, 1980; Roediger & Weldon, 1987). In my opinion (see also Engelkamp, 1990, 1991; Engelkamp & Zimmer, 1994a), explicit memory performance can be also dependent on modality-specific information. The position that explicit episodic memory performance is only based on conceptual information overlooked that memory tasks are often constructed in a way that subjects can rely (completely) on conceptual information. In assessing whether explicit episodic memory performance is based on conceptual information only, the specific manner in which memory is tested has to be taken into account. Typically, the instruction to recollect an episode requires that the subject recollect concepts, that is, the meaning of episodes (for instance, the meaning of pictures they saw). This means there are good reasons to assume that explicit memory performance is (also) based on conceptual information. However, the fact that conceptual information is involved in, and is even essential for, performance does not mean that modality-specific information is not stored in episodic memory and that it cannot be used in appropriate explicit memory tasks. This fact becomes particularly obvious, when conceptual information is not sufficient to make the memory judgment, for instance, when a subject has to assess whether he or she saw a photograph that shows the identical objects but black-white instead of colored (e.g., Homa & Viera, 1988; or Snodgrass, Hirshman, & Fan, 1996). Hence, to explore whether we need a system approach to explain memory performance we have to design the memory tasks appropriately.

What tasks are considered appropriate depends on the theoretical assumptions, particularly on what is considered conceptual and on what is considered modality-specific information. I make three assumptions concerning this difference.

The first relates to a definition based on the stimuli presented in an experiment. I consider conceptual the meaning of a stimulus, that is, its categorical status (e.g., that an apple is a fruit, a tulip a flower, a collie a dog, a bus a means of transportation, and so on). In this sense, content words (such as apple, tulip, collie, bus, etc.) have a conceptual meaning, and the conceptual meaning of objects such as an apple, a tulip, etc. is reflected in a naming response (e.g., Bruce & Young, 1986; Humphreys & Bruce, 1989, for such an assumption). Analogously, actions such as "open the door" have meanings representing the corresponding action concepts, and again these conceptual meanings are reflected in naming the corresponding action phrases.

From the meaning of a stimulus object, I distinguish its physical properties, such as its color, its size, its orientation, its distance from the person perceiving, and so on. Similarly, a word might be written by hand or in print, in capitals or small letters, in blue or in black, etc. without changing its meaning. Further, actions also have physical properties that are different from their meaning. The same action (e.g., to wave) may be performed slow or fast, with one or with two hands, etc. All these physical features are considered modality-specific.

The important implication of this distinction is that conceptual and modality-specific aspects of stimuli can be manipulated independently of each other, and as a consequence their influence on memory performance can be studied. Thus, two stimulus words may be conceptually similar and "physically" dissimilar, such as "mouse" and "rat," or they may be conceptually dissimilar and "physically" similar, such as "mouse" and "house." Correspondingly, two motor actions may be conceptually similar and "physically" dissimilar, such as "opening a door" when it is a "normal" door, or a "sliding" door, or they may be conceptually dissimilar and "physically" similar such as "stir the paint" and "stir the soup." The term "physical" is here synonymously used to the term modality-specific.

There are two special cases of modality manipulations that deserve special mention. One is specific for words. Words may be presented in two modalities: acoustically and visually. The specific aspect here is that the identical meaning can be presented in two physically completely different forms. The other case is that a specific meaning can be presented as a written word and as a picture (such as the word "apple" and a picture of an apple). In this case, both stimuli are presented in the visual modality, but at the same time one is presented in a verbal and one in a nonverbal modality. The latter distinction (as mentioned above) refers to modality in a more abstract sense.

In summary, the essential point made here is that the distinction between conceptual and modality-specific aspects of stimuli allows manipulation of both types of information independently, and as a consequence the effects of both kinds of manipulation on memory performance can be studied separately.

The second assumption relating to the distinction between conceptual and modality-specific information concerns the question of how we encode a stimulus. On the one side, it is assumed that every stimulus activates its specific entry system. That is, to come from a word to its meaning, one has to pass the verbal entry system. Or to come from a picture of an object to its meaning, one has to pass the pictorial entry system. On the other side, a word does not automatically activate information in the pictorial system, and a picture does not automatically activate information in the verbal system. Similarly, an action phrase does not automatically induce the performance of the action, and the action does the other way around not automatically activate its label in the verbal system. However, optionally the systems can become activated. We may strategically activate the labels of objects, we may actively generate mental pictures of referents of word meaning, and we may actively perform the action denoted by an action phrase. In brief, there are systems that are obligatorily activated dependent on the stimulus modality, and there are systems that are not automatically activated given a specific stimulus, but that can be strategically activated, for instance, when a specific task is given. Particularly, the output systems are strategically used. We do not automatically label a picture whenever we see one, and we do not automatically perform an action when we are presented with its description (as when hearing "to knock at the door").

In summary, we must distinguish between modality-specific information that is activated automatically given a specific stimulus, and modality-specific information that is activated strategically dependent on a self-instruction or an experimenter-given instruction. Varying the encoding instructions with given stimuli therefore also allows to manipulate the use of specific types of information and as a consequence to study the effects of these manipulations on memory performance.

The third assumption that we have to consider in this context is the type of memory task used to test the effects of conceptual and modality-specific information. The central aspect of studying explicit memory performances is that subjects are requested to recollect meanings. That is, when they have studied a list of words such as "apple, store, church, ball, hammer," etc. they try to remember these words in terms of their meanings; and when they have studied a list of action phrases such as "bend the wire," "open the purse," "lift the arm," etc. they try to remember these phrases in terms of their meanings. Nevertheless, it has to be analyzed carefully how the memory of meanings is tested and whether modality-specific information is given the opportunity to influence the memory performance. I will first consider free recall, then recognition under this perspective.

Free recall is considered the prototypical test requiring recollection of meanings. Although it seems relatively irrelevant how subjects recall meanings, that is, whether they give, for instance, an oral or a written recall, it is not irrelevant how the meaning is presented at study. This becomes obvious in the so-called picture-superiority effect. Subjects recall more items when they learn them as pictures than as their labels (e.g., Madigan, 1983; Roediger & Weldon, 1987). The presentation of verbal and nonverbal stimuli at study is however a rather large variation, and its effects are therefore difficult to interpret. It is not surprising that researchers, being prone to accept a pure conceptual basis of explicit memory performance, attribute the picture-superiority effect simply to better conceptual encoding of pictures than of words (e.g., Roediger & Weldon, 1987). It is therefore more convincing for a multiple system position if effects of the physical appearance of pictures and words, respectively, are varied. For pictures, their physical richness could, for instance, be manipulated. Such manipulations have been applied to pictures, and it turned out that physical richness of pictures enhances their recall (e.g., Gollin & Sharps, 1988; Madigan & Lawrence, 1980; Ritchey, 1982). But even if a more detailed picture—say of an apple—was better recalled than a less detailed picture, one could still postulate, although perhaps less convincingly so, that physically richer stimuli lead to a richer semantic encoding than physically less rich stimuli. However, such an explanation does not seem straightforward and rather post hoc. From a conceptual position, it is difficult to specify in advance what changes of surface structure should have what effect on recall.

Still more straightforward is therefore the technique of selective interference. By the multiple system approach, it is assumed that the processes between different systems take place rather independently of each other. If two different systems are, for instance, used simultaneously or in close temporal contiguity, then their processes should little interfere. If, however, information is processed simultaneously or in close temporal contiguity by the same system, the processes should impair each other by mutually overwriting their traces. If therefore a list of pictures is encoded, their recall should be more impaired when other pictures are simultaneously processed than when words are simultaneously processed. And, correspondingly, if a list of words is encoded, their recall should be worse when words are simultaneously processed than when pictures are simultaneously processed. Such findings have been reported (e.g., Pellegrino, Siegel, & Dhawan, 1975; Warren, 1977). A pure conceptual theory of retention has difficulties explaining such an outcome, were it observed. The important point remains that, from a multiple system point of view, modality-specific and conceptual information can be varied independently.

The situation becomes more complex when a more specific aspect of meaning has to be encoded and will be tested. When a subject is requested, for instance, to encode and recollect a physical aspect of a stimulus such as its color or its orientation, in this case, by definition color or orientation are conceptually encoded and its recollection is conceptual recollection. The concept to be recollected is the color of an object (say of a tulip) or even the concept of color itself (as when dots of different color have to be retained). Particularly in the latter situation, memory performance is usually poor. This is so because these (atypical) concepts are not well interconnected in memory. It is as if one learns a nonsense syllable. There is no richness of meaning. If now the stimuli vary on a physical dimension (e.g., color), this dimension defines at the same time the conceptual similarity (which by definition is also color). In this case we cannot distinguish whether the memory performance is determined by conceptual or modality-specific information because both are correlated.

To summarize, in the particular case when a physical aspect of a stimulus is focused on at study and test, that is, when it is processed as conceptual information at study and test, there are two consequences: (a) There is no rich meaning of the stimulus; it is more or less meaningless, and (b) aspects of meaning and modality (or physical appearance) are correlated in this situation, and their effects can not be disentangled.

Recognition memory is also considered a concept-based test, although according to the two process theories of recognition (e.g., Mandler, 1980; Jacoby & Dallas, 1981), a less pure one. I will not discuss here the perspect that recognition may be based in two different processes (however, I consider this an important aspect of recognition, see Engelkamp, 1997a). For my purpose, another aspect of recognition is more important and sufficient, namely that stimuli are re-presented in a recognition test. This feature, that a stimulus that was studied is presented again at test, allows for manipulating in a particular way the similarity of an original item with its correspondent partner item at test.

Again, from a system-oriented approach, one can manipulate independently the conceptual and modality-specific aspects of a test item with regard to its presentation at study. This was done early in a study by Bahrick and Boucher (1968) and recently in a series of studies (e.g., Cooper, Schacter, Ballestreros, & Moore, 1992; Jolicoeur, 1987; Snodgrass, Hirshman, & Fan, 1996; Zimmer, 1995). In all these studies, stimuli were represented identically (same physical features and meaning) or in a physically slightly changed form (same meaning, e.g., the picture of the same chair in a different size) at test. In all these studies it could be shown that physical changes of pictures from study to test that leave the concept unchanged influenced recognition memory. Such findings of physical similarity effects present particularly convincing evidence for a multiple subsystem approach. It is hard to see how a unitary-system approach would explain such effects. Only a system-oriented approach would predict that test items that differ in terms of modality-specific aspects, but are conceptually unchanged, impair recognition performance.

In conclusion, when one wants to study whether we need a system-oriented approach, we have to consider (a) what physical properties the stimuli have, (b) what subjects do with these stimuli (how they encode them), and (c) what they have to recollect at test and which discriminations are required here. In what follows, I will tackle three strategies to find evidence for a system-oriented explanation of the SPT effect.

The first uses *free recall* at test and varies stimuli properties (i.e., modality) at encoding while keeping concepts constant, or it varies the use of modality-specific systems at encoding (again, while keeping concepts constant).

The second strategy uses the double task or *selective interference* paradigm. Again, free recall is a typical task at test. The basic idea of selective interference is that using the same system concurrently leads to noisy traces in this system. Again, modality-specific aspects are at focus because the goal is to demonstrate system-specific interference.

The third strategy uses a *recognition* test as the memory task. This kind of task allows in particular studying congruent and incongruent stimuli at test, whereby congruency is defined along physical properties.

MEMORY FOR ACTIONS: EVIDENCE FOR A SYSTEM-ORIENTED APPROACH IN ACTION MEMORY

Free Recall Studies

Motor performance to pictures and words.   Interestingly, it was already reported by Bahrick and Boucher (1968) that pictures that were only watched were less well recalled than those that were watched and named aloud. Even more interestingly, a strong positive effect of motor behavior at study was observed by Paivio and Csapo (1973) but not even noticed by them. In the framework of the dual code theory, they had their subjects learn pictures and their labels under verbal and visual encoding, respectively. That is, subjects learned the same pictures and words in one experiment under instructions to form images of the referents or to speak their labels internally, and in another experiment under instructions to draw the referents or to write their labels. The differences in free recall were remarkable. Overt behavior improved memory compared with internal processing except for the condition of writing words. The findings are summarized in Table 3.1.

The findings for overt behavior have been replicated by Durso and Johnson (1980), who accidentally used almost the same instructions as Paivio and Csapo (1973).

The important finding of these studies is that overt motor performance enhances recall performance, except when words as stimuli are overtly written. In this case, subjects showed an equal recall for words, no matter whether they were internally spoken or overtly written; in addition, recall was remarkably poor. I assume that this is due to a shallow level of processing in these cases. Internal as well as external verbal reactions to verbal stimuli hinder their conceptual encoding of referential meaning (Zimmer & Engelkamp, 1996). There is a privileged loop from the word entry lexicon to word output lexicon (cf. McLeod & Posner, 1984).

The fact that motor performance in reaction to the to-be-learned items improves recall of these items in the other conditions, however, demonstrates that motor performance is critical for explicit memory performance even if it is not clear whether motor performance improves conceptual and/or motor information, or even other modality-specific information.

TABLE 3.1. Relative Free Recall of Pictures and Words as a Function of Writing and Drawing (in Experiment 1) and of Internal Speaking and Imagining (in Experiment 2 of Paivio & Csapo, 1973)

	Study Material	
	Picture	Word
Drawing (Exp. 1)	.45	.49
Imagining (Exp. 2)	.35	.37
Writing (Exp. 1)	.45	.21
Internal Speaking (Exp. 2)	.37	.21

Motor performance to action phrases.   What could be observed for picture and word recall can also be observed for action recall. In a typical experiment for action recall, subjects are presented with action phrases such as "smoke the pipe," "open the book," "lift the hat," etc. One group of subjects listens to a list of such unrelated action phrases before they recall them. Another group listens to the phrases and additionally performs them without using real objects, or with using real objects, and recalls them. Usually, both groups learn intentionally and are expecting a recall test. The consistent finding in these experiments was that subjects who self-performed the actions retained more action phrases than subjects who learned the phrases only verbally (Cohen, 1981, 1983; Engelkamp & Krumnacker, 1980; Engelkamp & Zimmer, 1983; Bäckman & Nilsson, 1984, 1985). This effect is called SPT effect. It can be considered in analogy to the picture superiority test as an enactment superiority effect.

Although the enactment effect as well as the picture superiority effect are compatible with a multiple systems approach, they are by themselves not convincing evidence for the assumption that the effects are due to modality-specific systems. They can equally be attributed to better conceptual encoding. Indeed, the picture superiority effect has been claimed to be due to better conceptual encoding of pictures than words (e.g., Klatzky, 1980; Marschark & Hunt, 1989), and so the enactment effect has been claimed to be a pure conceptual effect (Helstrup, 1987; Knopf, 1995; Kormi-Nouri, 1995). Therefore, one needs additional evidence to demonstrate that memory after enactment is due to or at least also due to motor information.

It turns out that this is more difficult to manage for action memory than for picture memory. An essential reason for this difference is that the enactment effect is an instructional and not a stimulus effect. The picture superiority effect is based on comparing memory for pictures and words (e.g., Roediger & Weldon, 1987). Hence, a specific stimulus is essential, and correspondingly one can modify the stimulus to explore what properties of a picture influence picture memory. The enactment effect, on the other side, is based on processing identical stimuli, namely action phrases, in different ways. Here one cannot easily manipulate the stimulus properties. Rather, one must manipulate the processing instructions, thereby keeping the action concept constant. The situation is even particularly complicated when enactment of action phrases is compared with a visual condition in which subjects listen to action phrases and at the same time see a model performing the actions. In this case, the stimulus situation and the encoding instructions differ between the visual and the enactment condition.

One of the early questions asked was whether the enactment is in fact a visual and not a motor encoding effect. In this context, three important effects were observed. First, visually imagining someone else performing the denoted actions leads to better memory performance than standard verbal learning of the same action phrases, but to worse memory performance than self-performing them (see Engelkamp & Zimmer, 1985, for a synopsis of experiments). These findings speak against the assumption that whatever may be the reason for the good recall after SPT learning, it cannot be reduced to visual imaginal encoding.

This conclusion is also supported by the second finding, which is more complex. It refers to the situation in which learning by enactment is compared with a situation in which the subjects watch the experimenter or a model performing the actions. This latter situation is also called EPT (for experimenter-performed task). Such a comparison shows that free recall after SPT is sometimes better than after EPTs (Dick, Kean, & Sands, 1989; Engelkamp & Zimmer, 1983; Zimmer & Engelkamp, 1984) and sometimes not (Cohen, 1981, 1983; Cohen & Bean, 1983; Cohen, Peterson, & Mantini-Atkinson, 1987). As Engelkamp and Zimmer (1997) demonstrated, whether a SPT effect can be observed depends on list length and type of design. When lists are sufficiently long, a SPT effect always can be observed. With short lists, a SPT effect can be only observed when SPT and EPT are varied within subjects.

The theoretically important point here is that SPTs and EPTs are influenced differently by certain factors, such as type of design and list length. Whereas, for instance, recall after EPTs suffers from within-subjects to between-subjects learning, recall after SPTs is unaffected from this variation. Similarly, learning by watching someone else performing actions is more strongly influenced by list length than learning by self-performance. Without discussing possible explanations of these differential findings in detail (see Engelkamp, 1998; and Engelkamp & Zimmer, 1997, for a lengthy discussion), it can be concluded that the encoding processes differ in EPTs and SPTs and that the role of visual and motor encoding may be a decisive factor. That is, SPT learning cannot be equated with visual-imaginal encoding.

Thirdly, it could be observed that, although using real objects for enactment improves memory performance compared to enactment with imaginary objects, the presence or absence of objects does not change the size of the SPT effect when SPT and EPT learning is compared (with objects present or absent) (Engelkamp & Zimmer, 1983, 1997). These findings are summarized in Table 3.2.

These findings demonstrate that even visual encoding is not homogeneous, and that visual encoding of perceived static objects must be distinguished from visual encoding of perceived dynamic events such as perceived actions.

Eventually it was observed that recall after SPT learning is independent of whether subjects are blindfolded or not (Engelkamp, Zimmer, & Biegelmann, 1993; Knopf, 1992). Also, this finding speaks against sensory factors as decisive for the SPT effect.

Taken together, these effects show first of all that visual information processing (operationalized as seeing or imagining someone else performing the actions) is not sufficient to produce equally good memory performance as does overt self-performance. Obviously, it is not enough to see an action performed

TABLE 3.2. Relative Performance in Free Recall as a Function of Type of Encoding (EPT, SPT) and Object Status (Objects Present/Absent)

	Type of Encoding		
Object Status	EPT	SPT	SPT effect
Engelkamp & Zimmer (1983)			
Object Present	.39	.53	.14
Object Absent	.30	.45	.15
Object Effect	.09	.08	
Engelkamp & Zimmer (1997)			
Experiment 1			
Object present	.61	.78	.17
Object absent	.43	.60	.17
Object Effect	.18	.18	
Experiment 2			
Object Present	.42	.63	.21
Object Absent	.27	.46	.19
Object Effect	.15	.17	

by someone else. This speaks against the assumption that the SPT effect is caused by activating the visual system. Also, seeing the objects is not decisive for the good memory by enactment. Although the presence and perception of an object that is involved in the action improves recall for the action phrases, this object effect is additive to the effect of enactment proper. This finding not only supports the distinction between a visual and a motor system, but it also supports moreover the idea that one must distinguish between a visual system for static object information that may be involved in picture memory, and a visual system for dynamic event information as provided by seen actions.

Finally, even if the visual perception of one's own enactment does not influence memory of self-performed actions, one may even assume that in a general sense sensory information is not critical for the good memory after enactment. Enactment proper seems to be indispensable.

The assumption that enactment proper is the decisive factor for the good recall after SPT learning is further underscored by experiments that were designed to test whether internal enactment or action planning might be sufficient to generate the SPT effect.

That simply imagining to self-perform actions is not sufficient to induce a comparably good memory as overt enactment could be repeatedly shown (see Ecker & Engelkamp, 1995; Engelkamp & Krumnacker, 1980; Engelkamp & Perrig, 1986; Perrig & Hofer, 1989). There is a clear SPT advantage over imagining self-performing actions. However, it seems to be the case that imagining to self-perform actions and to overtly self-perform actions share process components. This assumption is supported by the finding that subjects are particularly prone to confuse in their memory whether they have performed or only imagined to perform actions when the task is made sufficiently difficult (e.g., Ecker & Engelkamp, 1995; Goff & Roediger, 1998).

Also, planning an action is not sufficient to produce the same memory level as overt enactment. Zimmer and Engelkamp (1984), for instance, studied groups of three subjects under the following conditions. Subjects listened to 54 action phrases. For blocks of 18 phrases, each of the three subjects had the task to watch the other two performing the tasks and to assess the quality of enactment. The other two subjects expected to perform the actions. Actually, however, only one of them was allowed to perform the action. Which one was randomly determined and communicated only after the phrase was presented. In this way, each subject expected to perform 36 phrases but finally performed only 18 of them. The whole study phase was an incidental learning situation. The subjects were made to believe that the purpose of the experiment was to assess action performances. In the unexpected free recall test it turned out that observing others enact and to expect enactment led to equal recall performance and to worse performance than enactment. Although one might like to discuss whether the subjects planned the enactment when they expected to be requested to perform the actions, it is obvious that expectation to perform is not sufficient to produce an SPT-like effect.

In still a different way, Koriat, Ben-Zur, and Nussbaum (1990) induced action planning. They presented their subjects with cards on which four action phrases were printed. The subjects learned with each such card that they were either to perform the actions after presentation or to recall the phrases verbally. Also, these authors observed a clear recall advantage when subjects were instructed to perform over when they were instructed to recall. This "planning" effect was also observed by Koriat, Ben Zur, & Nussbaum (1990) when they used lists of 20 action phrases. Moreover, the "planning" effect was independent of the actual testing mode. It was irrelevant of whether the subjects were tested, in a congruent or an incongruent mode relative to their expectations.

The findings of Koriat, Ben-Zur, & Nussbaum. (1990) could be replicated by Engelkamp (1997b), who included besides verbal learning and planning a standard SPT condition. He observed not only better recall after planning than after verbal learning, but in addition better recall after SPTs than after planning. As with Koriat, Ben Zur, & Nussbaum (1990), these findings were independent of whether testing was congruent or incongruent to the expectations.

The fact that no congruency effect was observed demonstrates that the planning as well as the SPT effect in recall is an encoding and not a retrieval effect. The latter conclusion is underscored by the finding that the SPT effect is not changed when subjects after verbal learning and enactment are unexpectedly tested in a motor mode instead of in a verbal recall mode (Kormi-Nouri, Nyberg, & Nilsson, 1994; Norris & West, 1993). This means that what makes recall so good after enactment is prepared at encoding. It should and cannot be generalized to recognition memory (see further below).

Again it seems likely that action planning and enactment of actions share process components. This assumption is supported by findings that show that the planning effect disappears if action planning and overt enactment are varied within subjects at encoding (Brooks & Gardiner, 1994; Engelkamp, 1997b; cf. also Parks, 1997) and that the combination of enactment with the additional planning to enact at encoding impairs recall compared to enactment only (Engelkamp, 1997b; Schaeffer, Kozak, & Sagness, 1998).

In summary, although it is possible that imagining and self-performing an action and planning actions tap processes that are part of the processes tapped by overt enactment, there are additional processes in the latter case, and these additional processes are decisive for a full-fledged SPT effect.

As with the picture superiority effect, one must look at also what the reasons may be when the enactment effect disappears. In other words, one has to study carefully what factors influence memory under SPT learning and what factors influence memory under the respective comparison or control conditions. We have seen an example for this already when recall after SPTs and EPTs was compared. Type of design and list length influence learning in SPTs and EPTs differently and modified the size of the SPT advantage.

I will report about one more example for a factor that influences differentially SPT learning and the verbal learning control condition. In SPT research, it is well-known that instructions to elaborate action phrases have little effect under SPT learning but have a remarkable effect under verbal learning (Cohen, 1983; Helstrup, 1987; Zimmer, 1984). This instruction to elaborate may abolish the SPT effect by raising the recall level after verbal learning relative to that after SPT learning. The same holds true for the instructions to generate a phrase or an action that is to be performed. Nilsson and Cohen (1988), for instance, presented their subjects under SPT learning objects for which they should name an action phrase that they also had to perform. In a control group, the action phrases (that the other group had generated) were presented and performed. Correspondingly, the subjects under verbal learning generated action phrases to object words. Again, these action phrases were presented to a yoked control group. There was not only no generation effect for the SPT groups (.55 vs. .54), while there was one for the verbal groups (.50 vs. .33), there was in addition no recall differences between the SPT groups and the verbal generation group (cf. also Lichty, Bressie, & Krell, 1988, for the same finding).

The important aspect of these experiments is that efforts to influence recall performances by manipulating the degree of conceptual encoding are successful with verbal learning (as is known from the literature to levels of processing, e.g., Lockhart & Craik, 1990), but are unsuccessful with SPT learning. These findings hint at least to the possibility that recall after SPT does not rely on conceptual information, at least that provided by elaboration and generation instructions. The idea that recall after SPT taps something specific for the motor system remains an attractive assumption.

Selective Interference Studies

The selective interference paradigm has always been considered one of the most appropriate means to demonstrate the necessity of assuming different systems. The basic idea is that a task that uses a specific system (say, the visual) is impaired when the same system is used simultaneously for a second task (due to overwriting), but not when a different system (say, the motor) is used simultaneously. For picture memory, there is ample evidence that a visual and a verbal system should be distinguished (see Engelkamp & Zimmer, 1994a, Chapter 35, for an overview). There is a small number of experiments that tried to demonstrate in selective interference experiments that a motor system should be distinguished from a dynamic visual system. To make the situation less complex, the actions in these experiments were studied without using real objects. Hence, the focus is on the (visual) system for seen and imagined actions on the one hand and on the (motor) system for self-performed actions on the other hand.

Zimmer, Engelkamp, and Sieloff (1984) let their subjects learn 48 action phrases that were presented orally. Either all actions were self-performed, or all were seen when a model performed them, or they were alternating self-performed and seen. This procedure allowed the comparison of memory performance of items under enactment and watching conditions in the context of other enacted or watched items. A disordinal interaction was observed in this experiment. Under SPT learning, subjects recalled more items in the context of watching than in the context of enactment. Under visual learning (seeing the model), more items were recalled in the context of enactment than in the context of watching. Although the items and their conceptual meaning were identical under all four conditions, there were recall differences under SPT learning and visual learning dependent on the encoding of the context items. There was the usual SPT effect in the context of visual interference, but there was an inverse SPT effect (better recall after watching than enacting) in the context of motor interference.

In other experiments, the stability of this selective interference effect and the conditions on which it depends was explored further. One question that was studied was whether similar selective interference effects as under seeing can be observed under imagining another person performing the actions. This question was independently and with a similar procedure studied by Saltz and Donnenwerth-Nolan (1981) and Zimmer, Engelkamp, and Sieloff (1984). In both experiments, the learning material was simple action sentences such as "The teacher opens the door." Subjects in one group had to learn the sentences by taking over the role of the subject and performing the action (without real objects). Subjects in another group were requested to imagine how the subject of the sentence performed the action. The motor interference condition consisted of body-related action phrases (such as "lift your arm") that were to be performed. The visual interference condition was standing pictures of moving persons (e.g., a dancing person) with Saltz and Donnenwerth-Nolan (1981), and video spots of events (e.g., a toppling tower) with Zimmer, Engelkamp, & Sieloff (1984). In both studies, visual distractor items were to be retained for a recognition test. Learning and distracting items were presented alternating in both studies. In both studies, a cued recall test with the subject term as cue was used. The cued recall test was preceded by Zimmer et al. by an additional free recall test. In both studies, an interaction was observed. But the findings differed in detail. The findings are summarized in Figure 3.1.

While Saltz and Donnenwerth-Nolan observed a pattern comparable to Zimmer, Engelkamp, & Sieloff (1984, Experiment 1), SPT learning was more impaired by motor than by visual interference, and imaginal learning was more impaired by visual than by motor interference. Zimmer et al. observed in Experiment 2 only a selective interference for SPT learning, but no such an effect under visual imagining.

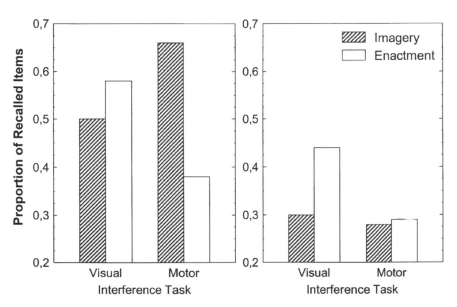

FIGURE 3.1. Cued recall as a function of encoding condition (imagery, enactment) and interference condition (visual, motor) for data from Saltz & Donnenwerth-Nolan (1981) (left), and for data from Zimmer, Engelkamp, & Sieloff (1984, Exp. 2) (right).

In addition to the score for the whole sentence, Zimmer et al. analyzed the recall for the verbs and nouns separately. These separate analyses yielded only a significant interaction for verbs but not for nouns. The interaction effects for verbs corresponds to the one for the whole sentence score. Only SPT learning is selectively impaired.

The inconsistent results of Zimmer, Engelkamp, & Sieloff (1984) and Saltz and Donnenwerth-Nolan (1981) for visual learning motivated Zimmer and Engelkamp (1985) to explore in a further experiment whether the absence of a selective interference effect under visual learning was due to the greater conceptual difference between the learning items (actions) and the distractor items (events). Therefore, Zimmer and Engelkamp (1985, Experiment 1) replaced the learning material under visual learning by event sentences (such as "the milk spills over"). That is, in the SPT group subjects learned action sentences, while in the visual group subjects learned event sentences. The distracting items and the procedure corresponded to Experiment 2 from Zimmer et al. (1984). Memory was tested in free recall. The finding was unchanged. It corresponded to Experiment 2 from Zimmer et al. (1984). There was only a selective interference effect under SPT learning, not under visual learning, and again this interaction pattern was restricted to verb recall. There was no interaction effect for noun recall.

Zimmer and Engelkamp (1985) replicated this pattern again in a second experiment in which, subjects learned action phrases (instead of sentences) in the SPT condition. Both interference tasks were changed. Under motor interference, subjects had to assess the similarity of two movement patterns; under visual interference they had to assess the similarity of two light beams. Again, only a selective interference under SPT learning was observed, and again there was no selective interference effect for visual learning.

To summarize the results: First, the findings of these series of experiments show that in all experiments, a selective interference effect could be observed for SPT learning. A secondary motor task impairs recall after SPTs more than a secondary visual task. Unfortunately, Zimmer et al. (1984) as well as Zimmer and Engelkamp (1985) did not have a control condition. But Saltz and Donnenwerth-Nolan (1981) had one. They also observed that SPT learning was not impaired with visual interference, only with motor interference.

Second, the findings for visual and visual-imaginal encoding show only a selective interference in Experiment 1 of Zimmer et al. (1984) and in the experiment of Saltz and Donnenwerth-Nolan. In three other experiments of Zimmer et al. and Zimmer and Engelkamp, there was no selective interference for visual-imaginal encoding of either action phrases, action sentences, or event sentences.

Third, in the studies of Zimmer et al. (1984) and Zimmer and Engelkamp

(1985), it consistently turned out that the selective interference effect after SPT learning was restricted to verb recall. No interaction between type of encoding and type of interference could be observed for noun recall.

What can be concluded from these results? The selective interference effects after SPT learning and their restriction to verb recall strongly support the assumption that the motor system is decisive in encoding SPTs and recollecting this information. It is particularly interesting to observe that the effect of enactment and its impairment by motor interference is restricted to the verb, that is, the action information of action phrases or sentences. Even a simple event such as acting upon an object is not processed and stored as a homogeneous unit but as a composed unit. And it fits well with the multiple-system approach that it is verb recall and not object recall that is impaired by motor interference.

However, the system-oriented approach is less clearly supported by the results after visual-imaginal encoding. Although the reasons for the inconsistent findings are not quite clear, there are some plausible speculations about why the results were as they were. I will start by giving a possible reason for why Saltz and Donnenwerth-Nolan (1981) observed a disordinal interaction between type of encoding and type of interference. The basic assumption is that the selective interference after visual-imaginal encoding that they observed was due to their specific visual encoding instruction. They instructed their subjects quite explicitly to focus on the whole setting in which the action took place, including many static features such as a specific kind of dressing of the agent. These instructional properties together with the static character of the visual distracting items (standard pictures) may have induced a selective interference in the visual system for static objects.

The main reason why there were no selective visual interference effects in the experiments of Zimmer et al. (1984, except Experiment 1) and Zimmer and Engelkamp (1985) may be seen in the fact that their visual interference task was purely visual except in the first experiment of Zimmer et al. where it was verbal and visual. This feature of the experiments might be critical because the encoding task always required verbal (for the phrases) and visual (when seeing or imagining the action) encoding. Since motor interference was always verbal and motor, there might have been some interference of motor distraction due to the verbal component also with imaginal encoding. However, the pure visual interference was reduced according to the very same logic. There was no verbal interference in this situation. This means that the lack of selective visual interference could be due to a trade-off between verbal interference with the motor distracting task and (pure) visual interference with the visual distracting task. This consideration could also explain the disordinal interaction effect in the first experiment of Zimmer et al. (1984). Only in this experiment a visual distracting task was present that was verbal and visual.

There is, however, one implication of this explanation that also relates to the selective motor interference effects. When in the experiments of Zimmer et al. verbal interference was always a consistent factor contributing to motor interference, but not to visual interference, then this fact could not only be responsible for reducing the visual interference with visual encoding, but also for increasing it with motor encoding. This fact should have led to an overestimation of selective motor interference with SPT learning in these experiments.

Thus, the findings of the selective interference experiments are not sufficiently clear-cut to defend strongly the system-oriented approach. They are at best compatible with such an approach. Therefore, further research on this topic is highly desirable. That more research is desirable becomes clear from a study of Cohen (1989), in which he found only weak selective interference effects using, however, quite different distractor tasks and presenting them in the retention interval (instead of concurrent to the encoding task).

Recognition Studies

Varying conceptual and motor similarity.   It has been consistently observed that recognition is better after SPTs than after verbal learning (Engelkamp & Krumnacker, 1980; Engelkamp, Zimmer, & Biegelmann, 1993; Knopf, 1991; Mohr, Engelkamp, & Zimmer, 1989; Zimmer, 1991). The better recognition performance after SPTs than after VTs is reflected in a greater hit rate as well as often in a lower false alarm rate. Since in these experiments distractors were always conceptually different from the old items, it is likely that the recognition decision is mainly based on conceptual information. In any case, it is possible to make the decision on the basis of conceptual information. In order to test whether motor information contributes to the recognition performance after SPT learning—but not after VT learning—it is necessary to make decisions on the basis of conceptual information difficult and at the same time to vary motor similarity between the items to-be-learned and their distractors. The old/new decision is largely based on conceptual information as long as the conceptual information of a distractor is sufficiently different from the original. Only if conceptual information between an original and its distractor is difficult to discriminate, motor information also should be taken into account in the old/new decision. If conceptual similarity is combined with motor similarity, discrimination should be particularly difficult after SPT learning. It is therefore expected that the motor similarity of distractors impairs recognition after SPT encoding—provided that the distractors are also conceptually similar—but not after VT encoding.

First hints that this expectation is correct were given in an experiment from Zimmer (1984) in which he constructed for each to-be-learned action phrase four distractor phrases. The distractors were constructed in exchanging the object and the verb of the original phrase, respectively, in such a way that the motor

TABLE 3.3. Example of the Construction of Distractors in the
Experiment of Zimmer (1984, Experiment 9)

Original	To Mix the Paint	Motor Similarity
Distractors	to mix the sauce	(motorically similar)
	to shuffle the cards	(motorically dissimilar)
	to stir the paint	(motorically similar)
	to spread the paint	(motorically dissimilar)

movement either was kept unchanged or was changed. Table 3.3 gives an item
to illustrate the construction principle.

Two groups of subjects learned 33 original phrases. One group listened to
the phrases, while the other enacted the denoted actions. In the recognition test,
13 old phrases were presented plus 20 new phrases, five in each of the four
distractor versions. Thus, the subjects saw 33 items in the recognition test, 13
of which were old and 20 of which were new. The results of the recognition
test are shown in Table 3.4.

First, it was observed what is known also from other experiments. Recognition performance was better after enactment than after listening only. Furthermore and more important, there was a different profile of false alarms after
verbal learning and after enactment. Upon closer examination, it can be seen
that this interaction was essentially due to the distractor that had become motorically similar by changing the verb (e.g., "to stir the paint" instead of "to mix
the paint"). After enactment, there were practically no false alarms at all except
for this distractor. Moreover, this distractor produced even more false alarms
after enacting than after verbal learning.

Upon examining this distractor type, one recognizes that its similarity to the
original item is particularly great. The verb is different, but the meaning of the
action is the same. This means that in this case the original item and the dis-

TABLE 3.4. Absolute Number of Errors in Recognition Dependent on Type of
Item. For the Originals, These Were Misses, for the Distractors False Alarms
(after Zimmer, 1984, Experiment 9)

Type of Item	Example	Type of Encoding	
		Enactment	Verbal
Original	to mix the paint	6	18
Distractors			
Motorically Similar	to mix the sauce	3	6
Motorically Dissimilar	to shuffle the cards	1	12
Motorically Similar	to stir the paint	26	19
Motorically Dissimilar	to spread the paint	4	4

tractor are so similar that one may doubt whether the conceptual information of the two differs at all. Therefore, it comes as no surprise that with this type of distractor false alarms were observed more than twice as often as with the other distractor types. That the number of false alarms for this distractor type is even larger after enactment than after verbal learning could be due to the fact that enactment increases the similarity of this distractor type to the original even further.

Engelkamp and Zimmer (1994b) planned therefore in a further experiment to vary orthogonally motor and conceptual similarity between original and distractor. They expected that recognition memory after verbal learning should depend only on conceptual similarity, whereas after enactment it should also depend on motor similarity.

When they tried to construct distractors for the action phrases, it turned out, however, that it was difficult to vary conceptual and motor similarity orthogonally. It was impossible to find a sufficient number of items for which the distractors were conceptually dissimilar but motorically similar. They varied therefore motor similarity only in the context of conceptually similar items, and they included conceptually and motorically dissimilar items as a control. But even when conceptually similar distractors were constructed that were motorically similar and dissimilar, it turned out in a rating experiment that conceptual similarity was rated higher for those pairs of items that were also motorically similar.

In spite of these difficulties, two experiments with this material were conducted. Subjects learned 3×32 action phrases, half by enactment and half under a verbal learning instruction. Half of the phrases that were verbally learned and half of those that were learned by enactment appeared in the recognition test as "old." The other half were distractors corresponding to the three categories described above. That is, items were presented in the recognition test either as originals or as distractors. The expectation was that those distractors that were conceptually and motorically similar to their originals should be harder to reject after SPT than after VT learning, whereas as long as motor similarity was low, there should be no differences after SPT and VT learning or fewer false alarms after SPT learning. For hits, there should be an advantage after SPT learning for all item types because of their better conceptual (and motor) information. I will report only about Experiment 2 because both experiments differed only in stressing literal recognition, and the pattern of results was the same in both experiments.

For hits, there was only a main effect. More hits were observed after SPT (.92) than after VT (.58). For false alarms, there was the expected interaction between task and type of item-distractor similarity. This interaction is summarized in Table 3.5.

TABLE 3.5. False Alarm Rates as a Function of Type of Encoding and Type of Item-Distractor Similarity (after Engelkamp & Zimmer, 1994b, Experiment 2)

	Item-Distractor Similarity		
	M+C+	M−C+	M−C−
VT	.38	.13	.06
SPT	.67	.13	.01

Note:
M+C+ means motorically similar and conceptually very similar.
M−C+ means motorically dissimilar and conceptually similar.
M−C− means motorically and conceptually dissimilar distractors.

The most important finding is that the discriminability between an item and its distractor becomes particularly difficult after SPT learning when the distractor is both conceptually and motorically similar. Distractors that are only conceptually similar to the originals seem to be equally difficult to reject after VTs and SPTs. Dissimilar distractors hardly generate any false alarms in this experiment. The high false alarm rate after SPT learning for conceptually and motorically similar distractors clearly supports the expectations of the system-oriented approach. According to an unitary system approach, there is little reason why false alarm rates after SPTs should increase more than after VTs when the distractors are conceptually and motorically similar. However, until now the effect of motor similarity after SPT learning was only demonstrated for distractors that were highly conceptually similar to the originals. We therefore searched for other possibilities to demonstrate the influence of motor information after SPT learning.

Reactivating motor information at test. A different kind of test to explore whether enactment learning provides motor information in addition to conceptual information is to reactivate the motor information at test, that is, to ask subjects to perform the actions at test before they make their recognition decision. Performing an action again at test should have two different effects on items that were learned under enactment, one when identical items are presented at test and one when (to the originals) conceptually and motorically similar distractors are used at test.

When an identical phrase is re-presented at test, the repeated enactment should enhance recognition performance compared to a verbal test of an identical phrase because not only conceptual information is reactivated but also motor information. That means, in a motor test there is altogether more overlap after enactment than in a verbal test. Therefore, recognition should be enhanced in a motor test. After verbal learning, there is no motor information encoded. Therefore, providing motor information at test should produce no advantage compared to not providing motor information (i.e., using a verbal test) after verbal learning.

When, after learning by enactment, a conceptually and motorically similar action phrase is presented at test, the enactment of such a phrase should make information at encoding and at testing particularly similar, that is, more similar than when there is no enactment at test (as in the experiment of Engelkamp & Zimmer, 1994b, mentioned above). In the latter case, there is less overlap of information between study and test. As a consequence, because of conceptual and motoric similarity to the originals, such distractor items should be particularly difficult to discriminate from their originals and lead to an increased false alarm rate if they are enacted at study and again at test than when not (in a verbal test). For phrases that are learned verbally, no such effect of kind of testing (verbal vs. motor) is expected. Because no motor information is encoded under verbal learning instructions, no impairment is expected when it is provided at test. Both expectations for motor testing after motor learning have been experimentally tested.

Motor testing for "old" items.   First, I will report about experiments in which it was investigated whether originals that occur in the context of conceptually and motorically different distractors are recognized better under motor testing than under verbal testing, but only after enactment learning and not after verbal learning.

Initial experiments of this type were conducted by Perrig and Hofer (1989), although with atypical material and instructions. In their first experiment they used numbers between 10 and 97 as material, and in their second experiment they used letter diagrams as stimuli. They used two encoding conditions. In the imagery conditions, subjects were asked to imagine the acoustically presented items for four seconds and immediately thereafter to imagine drawing the number or letter diagram with their index finger on a sheet of paper. In the enactment condition, subjects were also asked to first imagine the items for four seconds, but then they were requested to actually draw the number and letter diagram with their index finger on a sheet of paper. After the learning phase, there was first an unexpected free recall that was followed by a recognition test. In the recognition test, half of the items were old and half new. The procedure at the recognition test was analogous to that at study. Again, subjects had first to imagine the items (original items and distractors that again were numbers or letter diagrams), and then they either had to draw the items imaginally or actually with their index fingers.

In both experiments, the results did not show a significant interaction between type of encoding and type of test as expected. However, planned comparisons showed no type of test effect after imaginal encoding, but they showed a type of test effect after enactment. There was a better recognition performance if the items were enacted during study *and* test phase than if the items were enacted only during the study phase. Thus, one may assume that the congruity effect is specific for the enactment condition. This finding may be taken as a first hint that by enactment in the learning phase a motor trace is established in memory that can be reactivated and used in the retention test.

However, it must be conceded that in both experiments the interaction effects were clearly not significant. This failure to find an interaction effect might well be due to the fact that Perrig and Hofer used numbers and letter diagrams as stimuli instead of action phrases. These items are rather meaningless and in principle difficult to retain. But the failure to find an interaction effect might be particularly due to the fact that they compared the enactment condition with a condition in which the subjects had to imagine how they themselves enacted. This makes both conditions maximally similar (cf. Anderson, 1984; Ecker, 1995; Goff & Roediger, 1998). According to the multiple system approach, motor imagery must be distinguished from visual imagery. While motor imagery concerns the internal simulation of motor processes, here of self-performing actions, visual imagery of actions refers to the internal simulation of visual processes, here observing somebody else performing actions. In other words, motor imagery is more similar to overt enactment than is visual imagery of actions. These considerations were repeatedly supported by experimental results (Denis, Engelkamp, & Mohr, 1991; Engelkamp, Zimmer, & Denis, 1989). Therefore, the control condition used by Perrig and Hofer (1989) was in a sense highly inappropriate to demonstrate the expected interaction.

Engelkamp, Zimmer, Mohr, and Sellen (1994) therefore applied the same line of reasoning as Perrig and Hofer (1989). However, in their experiment action phrases were to be learned under a verbal learning (control) condition and under an enactment condition. The to-be-learned list contained 80 action phrases. The list was learned under verbal learning instructions by one group and under enactment instructions by another group. In the recognition test, each subject received successively two test lists consisting of 90 phrases each. Each of the two lists contained 10 completely new phrases, 40 old phrases, and 40 distractors that were constructed from old phrases as follows. Half of them were formed by exchanging the verb and leaving the object unchanged, half by exchanging the object and leaving the verb unchanged. Each subject received first a test list under the usual verbal condition, that is, subjects were presented the material phrase by phrase and had to decide whether each one was old or new. With the second test list, the procedure was different: The subjects first had to perform the action upon observing a phrase and then make the recognition decision. Table 3.6 shows the recognition performances under the four conditions that are

TABLE 3.6. Pr Scores as a Function of Type of
Encoding at Study (VT, SPT) and of Type of Test
(Verbal, Motor) (after Engelkamp et al., 1994,
Experiment 1)

Encoding During Learning	Encoding During Test	
	Verbal	Motor
VT	.72	.71
SPT	.85	.93

Note: Pr scores are calculated as proportion of hits minus proportion
of false alarms.

relevant here. Because false alarms were generally rare events, particularly after
learning by enactment, Table 3.6 gives only the Pr scores (hits minus false
alarms).

There was a significant effect of the encoding condition during study. Recognition after SPTs was better than after VTs. This is the usual enactment effect.
And there was a clear-cut interaction between type of encoding and type of test.
This is the enactment-specific congruity effect. Encoding by enactment leads to
better recognition when subjects also enacted during testing than when testing
was only verbal. If the subjects had encoded verbally at study, however, it did
not matter whether the test was verbal or motor.

The pattern of results clearly confirms the expectation that enactment at
test improves recognition performance only after learning by enactment and
not after verbal learning. This pattern was replicated in further (unpublished)
experiments. The finding that enactment at test improves recognition after motor learning reflects the greater information overlap by repeated enactment
compared to verbal testing. The finding that motor testing has no effect after
verbal learning mirrors that only listening to the phrases at study does not
provide motor information. Taken together, the findings show that motor information is encoded by enactment, and it can be used in appropriate memory
tests.

Motor testing for similar distractors.   Next we returned to the hypothesis
that motor similarity (in the context of conceptual similarity between originals
and distractors) should impair recognition performance after enactment compared to verbal tasks. Distractors that are motorically (and conceptually) similar
to a studied item should be more likely to be falsely accepted as old after
learning by enactment than after verbal learning, because in the former but not
in the latter case motor information was encoded during learning. We have seen
above that this holds true for motorically similar distractors that are highly

conceptually similar. We will now test the more specific hypothesis, that the negative effect of motor similarity after learning by enactment is further enhanced when testing is motor. But we also want to replicate the effect of Engelkamp and Zimmer (1994b) because in some other experiments the predicted higher rate of false alarms to motorically similar items after enactment was not observed (Mohr, Engelkamp, & Zimmer, 1989; Zimmer, 1984; cf. also Cohen, Peterson, & Mantini-Atkinson, 1987). In these experiments, the false alarm rates were usually lower after learning by enactment than after verbal learning, but no difference was observed between motorically similar and dissimilar distractors.

There are two possible reasons for these unexpected findings. One is that conceptual similarity is insufficiently controlled for. As repeatedly stated, if distractors can already be rejected because they are conceptually dissimilar, there is no need to take specific movement information into account. The experiment of Engelkamp and Zimmer (1994b) was an effort for better control of conceptual similarity. As the results showed, they ended up with conceptually very similar distractors that were so difficult to discriminate from the originals that the false alarm rate was .38 for verbal learning and extremely high for motor learning (.67). Therefore, one goal was to replicate the finding (interaction) of Engelkamp and Zimmer (1994b) for false alarm rates that are not that high. This means replication with distractors that are conceptually similar but less so as with Engelkamp and Zimmer (1994b).

There is, however, still another reason why no motor similarity effect was observed in the experiments of Mohr et al. (1989) and of Zimmer (1984). When subjects have learned by performing the actions, they have at least two types of motor information, each of which may be sufficient to separate learned items from distractors. So, after learning by enactment, the fact that one remembers having performed the action may already suffice to recognize the item as old. Subjects have no need to take the particular form of a movement into account as long as old items were performed and new items were not, unless the conceptual similarity is so high that the subjects also use the particular form of a movement to make their recognition decision (as with Engelkamp & Zimmer, 1994b) or unless action phrases are also performed at test. Performing items at test forces subjects, too, to resort to information about the form of movements. Thus, information about movement form is a second kind of information that allows separation of old from new items after learning by enactment. This second type of information could have been used in the experiment of Engelkamp and Zimmer (1994b) because the distractors were so difficult to discriminate from originals. This type of information should also be used when the distractors are less conceptually similar but also performed at test.

Thus, in a further experiment of Engelkamp and Zimmer (1995) it was tested (a) whether the interaction between type of encoding and type of distractor could be replicated with conceptually less similar items, and (b) whether this inter-action can be increased if the items are also performed at test. Thus, we expected a three-way interaction between type of encoding, type of testing, and distractor similarity.

Therefore, Engelkamp and Zimmer (1995) selected items for which the dis-tractors were either conceptually and motorically similar or conceptually and motorically dissimilar. This confounding of conceptual and motor similarity was considered as acceptable because it was the central goal to demonstrate that motor similarity for the conceptually and motorically similar items should in-fluence recognition performance more after motor than after verbal learning and particularly so when also testing was motor. The conceptually and motorically dissimilar items thus served as a background to show, first, that similar distrac-tors are more difficult to reject than dissimilar distractors and, second, that this holds more true for learning after enactment and particularly if testing is also motor.

Thus, the three main factors involved in the study were type of encoding during learning (verbal/enactment), type of testing (verbal/enactment), and sim-ilarity of distractor (conceptually and motorically similar/conceptually and mo-torically dissimilar).

Subjects learned 80 action phrases either under verbal or under enactment instructions. For each action phrase, there were two distractors. One was similar and one was dissimilar to the original phrase. Each subject received only one distractor at test. Moreover, each subject received the items at test in two-part lists. For the first part list, recognition testing was verbal, while for the second it was motor. The verbal recognition was always given first to avoid carry-over effects.

There were two additional factors that I will only mention briefly because I will refer to them in discussing the results. One was type of distractor. The distractors were formed from the originals by either changing the verb or the object of the action phrase. For each type of distractor, there was a similar and dissimilar version. The other factor was order of testing. Although each subject was tested either with a similar or a dissimilar distractor, each item was presented twice as original and as distractor within testing. Either the original item oc-curred first or the distractor occurred.

Before I report the results of the false alarm rate, I will briefly mention that the analysis of hits confirmed what was observed in other experiments. There were more hits after learning by enactment than after verbal learning, and this effect was independent of item similarity. This effect replicates Engelkamp and Zimmer (1994b).

More important are the results of the false alarm rates. The most remarkable finding with false alarms is the three-way interaction between type of encoding, type of testing, and distractor similarity (see Table 3.7).

TABLE 3.7. False Alarm Rates as a Function of Type of Encoding (VT, SPT), Type of Testing (Verbal or Motor), and Similarity of Distractor (Similar, Dissimilar) (after Engelkamp & Zimmer, 1995)

Similarity of Distractor	Type of Encoding			
	VT Type of testing		SPT Type of testing	
	Verbal	Motor	Verbal	Motor
Similar	.20	.18	.19	.26
Dissimilar	.03	.05	.02	.02

As Table 3.7 shows, the dissimilar distractors are so seldom falsely accepted that no systematic variance can be observed. Similar items produce as expected more false alarms than dissimilar items, and the rate of these false alarms is increased when testing is motor instead of verbal, but only after learning by enactment.

While this differential increase of false alarms after motor compared to verbal testing was expected after learning by enactment, no differential similarity effect was observed after verbal and motor learning when testing was verbal. This null effect deviates from what was observed by Engelkamp and Zimmer (1994b). They found more false alarms for similar distractors after learning by enactment than after verbal learning, even though testing was verbal. This inconsistent finding could be due to several reasons. I consider two as particularly likely. First, this experiment was much more complex than those of Engelkamp and Zimmer (1994b). In this experiment, there were verb- and object-changed distractors, whereas only verb-changed items were used by Engelkamp and Zimmer (1994b). In this experiment, originals and one distractor were tested within the same subject, and the order of presentation of original and distractor varied. With Engelkamp and Zimmer (1994b) in the recognition test, items were presented either as original or as distractor to a subject. The complex situation of this experiment may have masked the similarity effect under verbal testing.

The other reason is more fundamental. Although efforts were made to control systematically for conceptual and motor similarity, there are no clear-cut criteria for what changes should be considered equivalent. It is very difficult to keep conceptual similarity constant when varying motor similarity, and it is also difficult to control strictly the motor similarity variation. Hence, the experiments might differ accidentally with regard to the success of manipulating the similarity variables. A better method to vary motor similarity while keeping conceptual similarity as constant as possible is therefore needed.

Such a method was realized by Engelkamp et al. (1994) in Experiment 2. The basic idea was to use the same action, that is, the same concept during learning and testing and only to change the form of movement, or leave it unchanged from study to test. This procedure is similar to testing picture recognition for an identical concept either in a congruent or incongruent form (such as same-sized vs. differently-sized). With this logic in mind, the similarity of motor information in study and test was manipulated by having the actions performed either by the same hand or by different hands. Using the same hand to perform the action during study and test should establish more overlap of motor information than using a different hand for study than for test. It was therefore expected that recognition should be better if the same hands were used in the study and test phase than if different hands were used. This finding should occur after learning by enactment; it should not, however, occur after verbal learning. In this case, it should make no difference which hand was used at test.

For action verbs that were performed with either the right or the left hand at study it was clearly the case that their recognition was better when they were tested with the same hand at test than when they were tested with the other hand (cf. Table 3.8).

The analysis of variance was only conducted for hit rates in this study, because false alarms could not be attributed to the different experimental conditions in this experiment that actually had a more complex design than described here.

As mentioned, there was also a verbal learning group. Their hit rates for the one-hand items were independent of whether they were tested with left hand (.66) or right hand (.69), and it was of the same magnitude when testing was verbal (.69).

Thus, this experiment served to demonstrate with strict control of conceptual information to support again the basic hypothesis that learning by enactment provides information about the movement form and that this information is used in recognition memory if motor testing is used. In this experiment, all encoding processes of the enactment group were considered to be equal during study and

TABLE 3.8. Hits of "One-hand" Items as a Function of the Hand Used to Perform the Action at Study and at Test (after Engelkamp et al., 1994, Experiment 2)

Study hand	Test hand	
	Left	Right
Left	.88	.80
Right	.80	.87

test except for the hand used to perform the action. If one agrees that whether one performs an action with the right or left hand the conceptual information of the verb processed does not change, then there should be no effect on recognition dependent on whether one uses the same or different hand to perform an action at study and test unless some information other than conceptual information determines recognition. The results show that there was a hand-congruency effect. Therefore, this effect is attributed to the different motor processes involved in performing actions with different hands.

In summary, recognition experiments demonstrated that motor information is stored with learning by enactment and that it can be used at test. Even if it remains an open question of whether motor information plays a crucial role in verbal testing when the distractors are conceptually different, it seems to be clear that motor information is used under the conditions that testing is also motor. In the case that learning and testing are by enactment, the motor parts of the memory trace seem to be reactivated and to mediate by information overlap the recognition decision. The decision is facilitated (other things being kept equal) if the learned item is identically processed and it is hampered if the processing of the learned item is motorically changed. So far, the conclusion is well supported by experimental evidence.

The situation is a bit less clear if the distractors are conceptually different from the original items, but nevertheless similar. In this case it may depend on the degree of conceptual similarity whether motor information is taken into account or not in the test situation. If the items are enacted at study and test, motor information is obviously taken into account in the recognition decision. This is evidenced by higher false alarm rates for conceptually and motorically similar distractors that are enacted at study and test compared to conditions where learning is motor, but testing is verbal, or where learning is verbal. This pattern was observed for a varying degree of conceptual similarity. An effect of motor similarity after motor learning compared to verbal learning may, however, even be observed if testing is verbal given that the to-be-learned items are highly conceptually similar. In these cases, the ability to discriminate may suffer more under motor learning than after verbal learning compared to a control condition with distractors that are conceptually and motorically dissimilar.

RECONSIDERING THE QUESTION OF A SYSTEM-ORIENTED APPROACH

In the introductory sections, I had outlined what I mean by a system-oriented approach and how it could be experimentally supported (or falsified). I will conclude my contribution in relating the system-oriented approach back to the

reported evidence and in relating it as proposed here to some related proposals
in the literature.

Does the Evidence Support the System-Oriented
Approach?

Could it be demonstrated that the postulated systems and particularly the motor
system contributed independently to memory for action events? I have collected
evidence along three lines, and the outcome can be considered positive.

The first line focused on evidence from free recall studies. The critical question here was whether aspects other than the meaning of actions contribute to
their recall. This approach proved to be more difficult for actions than for objects, but it was nevertheless possible also for actions. Objects or their pictures
can be directly compared with their labels. For objects and their pictures, it not
only could be shown that they are better recalled than their verbal labels (e.g.,
Madigan, 1983; or Paivio, 1986), moreover it could also be demonstrated that
the recall of pictures depended on their physical surface structure, for instance,
colored pictures of objects were better recalled than black and white pictures or
simple line drawings of the objects (e.g., Gollin & Sharps, 1988; Ritchey,
1982).

It is more difficult to make corresponding demonstrations for actions. First,
self-performed actions cannot be directly compared with their verbal labels because subjects must in some way be stipulated to perform the action. Therefore,
in the case of actions, recall is not compared for actions and action phrases but
for action phrases that are listened to and enacted (in SPTs) and for action
phrases that are only listened to (in VTs). For the same reason, perceived actions
(in EPTs) are presented in the context of action phrases. If these necessary
controls are tested, similar recall differences can be observed for actions as for
objects. Not only was memory better for SPTs than for VTs but SPTs were also
better recalled than EPTs, even if only under restricted conditions. This pattern
of findings is in good agreement with the assumptions of a system-oriented
approach.

Also, the manipulation of surface-structure features is more difficult with
actions than with pictures because actions are dynamic events that are physically
more difficult to describe and because they are as behavioral stimuli more difficult to be manipulated in a strictly controlled manner. It is, for instance, difficult to achieve that all subjects perform an action in a specific manner. Nevertheless, it could be observed that perceived as well as performed actions were
recalled better when physical objects were used than when only imaginary objects were used and that, moreover, this object effect was independent of the
SPT advantage over EPTs. This pattern of findings not only supports the distinction between a motor and a visual system, it moreover supports the distinc-

tion between a dynamic visual system (for processing perceived actions) and a static visual system (for processing perceived objects).

Finally, studies were conducted to examine which features of the enactment effect itself can be left out without impairing the SPT recall. Here it was observed that perceiving one's own actions when performing them is not critical for the SPT recall, whereas only planning an action reduces recall for actions, although not to the level of VTs. Thus, the actual execution of an enactment and planning the action both seem to be critical parts of the good recall of SPTs.

Taken together, it was possible to demonstrate (a) what aspects of actions are not specifically influencing memory for self-performed actions, and (b) what aspects may specifically contribute to it. Visually perceiving an object of an action did, for instance, not influence specifically the memory performance after enactment. Also, visually perceiving the action had no specific effect on memory for performed actions. However, to plan or to intend to perform an action seemed to generate part of the specific memory effects that arise by enactment. Thus, it seems justified to assume that planning or intending an action induces part of those processes that enactment proper does induce. Although these results are not (yet) as straightforward evidence for a motor system as those of object memory for a visual system, they are in good agreement with the assumption of a motor system, and they clearly demonstrate that without a system-oriented approach such experiments would not have been designed.

A second kind of evidence for a system-oriented explanation of the SPT effect was sought in selective interference experiments. Unfortunately, the selective interference paradigm has not yet delivered much support for the system-oriented approach in action memory studies, although the logic of these experiments is considered to be particularly straightforward for such an approach. Although throughout all experiments there was a clear-cut selective interference of SPT recall by a distracting motor task, a corresponding selective interference of recall of EPTs or visual-imaginal tasks by visual distractor tasks was not consistently observed. The detailed analysis of the relevant experiments made it clear that there were factors in these experiments that were insufficiently controlled. Most important, the experiments of Zimmer and Engelkamp did not take into account whether visual information processing in the distractor task took place in the context of verbal information processing or not. This, however, seems critical given that both the visual and motor main tasks entailed a verbal component in their experiments. However, a positive aspect of these experiments for a multiple system approach lies in the fact that this approach offers an explanation of why there was the failure to demonstrate selective interference effects after visual-imaginal encoding and that this approach makes clear how better controlled experiments should be designed.

Finally, the finding that the selective motor interference was constrained to the verb recall underlines impressively the assumption that processing object information is not critical for the SPT effect and thereby supports the system approach.

The most convincing evidence for the effects of motor information in the context of action memory comes from the third line of evidence, the manipulation of processing overlap between study and test in recognition experiments. Because in recognition experiments stimuli are re-presented at test, it was possible also to repeat the motor responses produced to the stimuli. This enactment at test allowed to test recognition memory for re-enacting identical actions and for enacting at test actions that were conceptually identical, but varied with regard to the motor response. Thus, the motor response could be identical to the one at learning or show a slightly different movement pattern. Both variations— re-enactment at test as well as motor similarity of the re-enacted motor action to the original action—clearly influenced recognition performance, and it is hard to see how this influence can be attributed to conceptual processes.

So far, the system-oriented approach proved to be useful also in the field of action memory. Still it must be conceded that a "final" proof will not be possible because the system assumption is an assumption to generate and to explain findings. We infer the construct of systems from the findings. And we can never be sure that other sets of assumptions would not also be able to explain the findings. This holds particularly true as long as only a restricted set of findings has to be explained.

Furthermore, there is always the possibility to ascribe any memory effects— be they of pictures or motor movements—to corresponding conceptual processes or any other unspecified processes. However, the problem for such a unitary-process position will be to predict ante hoc such effects as reported in this contribution and to explain them post hoc in a way that allows for generalizations and new predictions.

Related System-Oriented Proposals

At the beginning of this chapter, I sketched the system distinctions that Tulving (e.g. 1985a, 1985b) proposed. The two main systems proposed by Tulving are the semantic and the episodic. Both are characterized by specific states of consciousness that Tulving calls "noetic" and "autonoetic." Autonoetic consciousness refers to memories of autobiographical episodes that occurred at a specific place and time. Noetic consciousness refers to general knowledge about facts that are not place- and time-bound. As I mentioned in my contribution, the system approach that I have proposed here is located in episodic memory because the use of the different informational systems influences episodic memory performance in so-called explicit memory tests such as recall and recognition.

This position of course does not exclude that the informational systems should also be relevant in the context of semantic memory. Semantic knowledge as information is general and independent of the place and time when it was acquired. Therefore, in a typical test of this kind of memory, subjects are asked to verify conceptual predicates. Subjects may, for instance, be asked: "Is a robin a bird?" "Is an apple a fruit?" "Has a tractor larger front than back wheels?" "Is shouting louder than whispering?" etc. The question whether in such tasks modality-specific systems become relevant depends on the specific type of task or question. When the question is categorical, as in the robin- and apple questions, activation of modality-specific information is unlikely. However, this may be different for the tractor-question. Now, the subject might also use his or her visual system to answer the question. Correspondingly, the sound system could be used in the shouting-task (cf. Kosslyn, 1980).

Hence with general knowledge questions, purely conceptual information (as when items have to be conceptually categorized) may be addressed, but the conceptual information may also be enriched by modality-specific information under certain conditions. However, when modality-specific information is addressed and used, a more generic memory trace is internally generated than in an explicit episodic test where a specific memory trace is reactivated. Thus, the informational system approach is also compatible in the context of the semantic memory system proposed by Tulving (e.g., 1985a, 1985b).

There are moreover some "semantic" tasks that make the distinction between semantic and episodic memory less sharp than proposed. This becomes evident when questions refer to referents such as persons or buildings that are unique, but that are not considered as part of an autobiographical episode. When, for example, a person is asked whether building X has a red roof, the person will re-activate his memory of this specific building, including modality-specific features, but the memory trace is not a specific episode in which the building has been seen. There is not a specific viewer-centered perspective that has to be reconstructed at test, according to a foregoing experience. The situation is similar to when one is asked whether, for instance, Prince Charles has a long nose. To answer this question, very likely the face of Prince Charles is activated, but again the viewpoint is not prescribed. That is, the memory traces in the examples are more specific than when questions concerning general knowledge are asked (such as "Have dogs a tail?"), but less specific (and not episodic in a strict sense) than in explicit episodic memory tasks.

What these considerations show is that the distinction of informational systems is independent of the semantic-episodic distinction. The distinction between informational systems makes sense within both the semantic and the episodic system.

Schacter's proposal (1994) comes very close to the system approach proposed here. The main difference to the proposal here is that Schacter confines himself to sensory systems. His focus is on verbal word-form systems and on a visual object-form system (that he calls "structural description system"). He does not consider the question of whether one should postulate also output systems. Nevertheless, the evidence that he considers as support for his system-oriented approach is very similar to the one proposed here. However, he focuses mainly on implicit testing of episodic memory. It is a central question for Schacter (1994) whether the physical aspects of a stimulus in a study episode influence an implicit memory test of this episode. In an implicit memory test, there is by definition no request to recollect an episode. The test is rather like a "semantic" memory task. The subject has, for instance, to assess whether the object that he/she sees is a flower or whether the letter string that he/she sees is a word.

The critical difference between a semantic memory test and an implicit memory test is that in the latter case the stimulus is related to an episode in which the subject experienced this specific stimulus before, even if the subject does not recollect the episode, that is, that he/she is not aware of it. This example makes it once again clear that I use the term episodic differently from other authors (such as Schacter and Tulving) in that I do not consider the autonoetic recollection as a defining attribute.

The interesting point is that many implicit memory tasks react sensitively to changes of the physical properties of the study stimulus. When, for instance, a word was presented in handwriting at study and is presented in printed letters at test, the judgment time is slowed down (e.g., Roediger & Blaxton, 1987). Similarly, when an object stimulus, for instance an apple, is presented at study and in a slightly changed version at test (e.g., in a different form), the reaction time is slowed down (Schacter, Delany, & Merikle, 1990).

In his article, Schacter (1994) not only demonstrates that word-form and object-form information is critical in implicit memory tests, but he also demonstrates that a visual word form and an acoustic word form must be distinguished because changing the modality of a word (acoustic versus visual and vice versa) from study to test reduces the priming effect but does not eliminate it. With this distinction (that is also proposed by Engelkamp, 1991; and by Engelkamp & Zimmer, 1994a), it becomes clear that the verbal system consists already of part systems (visual and acoustic word form systems). It is very likely that other part systems of the verbal system will be isolated in the future when more complex items such as sentences are considered. Altogether, the findings of implicit memory studies show that the assumption of informational systems is also useful to explain implicit memory performance.

It is interesting to notice how Schacter (1994) sees the relation between the implicit expressions of memory supported by the perceptual representation of system (= PRS, this term summarizes the different form-representation systems) and the explicit expressions of memory supported by an episodic system. According to Schacter, "the outputs of PRS subsystems can serve as inputs to the episodic memory" (257), and "a key function of the episodic system is to bind together perceptual with other kinds of information (e.g., semantic, contextual)" (257).

There are several interesting questions that can be addressed to this position, only some of which are dealt with by Schacter. One is the nature of the relation between the semantic memory system and the PRS. Another is what specific implicit memory tasks tap what specific perceptual representational subsystems. This question will become the more urgent to the extent that more perceptual subsystems are identified. Still another question is whether the PRS as expressed in implicit memory tasks and the episodic memory system as expressed in explicit memory tasks are hierarchically organized. For instance, should physical alterations of target stimuli that show effects in explicit memory tests necessarily also show effects in implicit memory tests? Schacter (1994) seems to answer this question positively when he writes: "And indeed, there is some evidence that when explicit tests specifically require access to perceptual information, they exhibit the kind of perceptual sensitivity more often observed with implicit tests" (p. 258).

Recently, however, a couple of experiments were reported that demonstrated that certain physical alterations of target stimuli (such as incongruent size, orientation, or color) consistently showed effects in an explicit recognition memory test, but not in any implicit memory test applied so far (Biederman & Cooper, 1992; Cooper, Schacter, Ballestreros, & Moore, 1992; Zimmer, 1995). These findings do not fit with a hierarchical relation between the PRS and the episodic memory system. In my opinion, the solution lies in analyzing more precisely the specific memory tests used. I spent much space on this aspect in this chapter, and I will not repeat it here. In brief, my message is that only part of the information encoded at study is usually tapped at test and that it depends on the specific test that is used which one is tapped. The specific task used is even more important when implicit rather than explicit tests are applied.

Although Roediger (e.g., 1990), a prominent advocate of a process-orientated approach, considers the process approach an alternative to the system-oriented approach, I will show that his approach may as well be considered a system approach.

The central idea of this approach is that the overlap between processes at study and at test determines the memory performance. This principle, which might be considered as a development of the encoding-specificity principle proposed in the early 1970s (Tulving & Thomson, 1973), is called transfer-appropriate processing, in brief, TAP. It is clear that the assumption of TAP can only be tested when it is specified in advance what processes are encoded at study and which of these encoded processes are tapped at test.

At the beginning stood dissociations between implicit and explicit memory performances. For instance, performance in explicit tests was impaired by amnesia, but performance in implicit memory was not (e.g., Warrington & Weis-krantz, 1968, 1970; Graf, Squire, & Mandler, 1984). Furthermore, some varia-bles, such as levels of processing or generation, seemed to influence performance in explicit memory tests, but not in implicit memory tests, or they even influ-enced them adversely (e.g., Jacoby, 1983; Smith & Branscombe, 1988).

These dissociations were summarized by some researchers (e.g., Squire, 1987) as being due to different memory systems tapped by the two types of tests, namely an explicit, declarative (or episodic) system and an implicit, pro-cedural system, and by others (e.g., Roediger, Weldon, & Challis, 1989) as being due to the processes tapped by these tests, namely conceptually driven processes by explicit tests and data-driven by implicit tests.

Blaxton (1989) demonstrated that it depends on whether a test taps data driven (that is, perceptually based processes) or conceptually driven (that is, meaning-based processes) and not on whether the test is implicit or explicit. This finding was taken as evidence for the process-oriented approach and against the system-oriented approach because the kind of processes used at test (per-ceptual, meaning-based) and not the memory system (declarative/procedural as indicated by type of test) determined memory performance (Roediger, 1990).

Perceptual and meaning-based processes at test, however, are clearly defined by the type of information used and can therefore as well be considered to rely on informational systems. It is evidently just the distinction between perceptual and conceptual information on which some of the system-oriented approaches (e.g., Schacter, 1994) are based. In this sense, the system-oriented approach and the process approach are converging, and there seem to be few differences except for terminology.

A closer look shows that this is not quite the case. Two critical findings remain unexplained when only types of information are considered. The first finding is that some perceptual tests such as size or color influence performance in conceptual explicit tests but not in perceptual implicit tests (e.g., Zimmer, 1995). The second finding is that memory performance of amnesic patients is impaired in explicit tests, but less so or not at all in implicit tests (e.g., War-rington & Weiskrantz, 1970).

The explanation of these findings makes it clear that differences between explicit and implicit memory tests should not be reduced to which of two types of information they tap. In explicit memory testing, it is by definition the case that subjects are required to recollect an experienced episode. That is, some conscious re-experience of an episode is the goal. Achieving this goal obviously means to access an integrated representation of the episode that includes all aspects of the episode, modality-specific as well as conceptual (cf. Schacter, 1994; Snodgrass, Hirshman, & Fan, 1996). This kind of access seems to be impaired by amnesics, and the retrieval process is influenced by all modality-specific aspects of information as well as by conceptual information.

The finding that implicit tests are insensitive to some modality-specific aspects of stimuli such as size or color is more difficult to explain. First of all, with implicit memory tests it seems to depend more on the specific test what informational aspects of an episode are used. The distinction between perceptual and conceptual implicit tests points in this direction. But this classification is not sufficient, as the finding shows that perceptual tests do not react on size, color, etc. It seems more likely that some implicit tests use form information. That is, they only react on those processes from a study episode that are part of form extraction. Correspondingly, they react to changes of stimulus form from study to test, but they do not react on any changes of the study stimulus that are form-irrelevant. Those aspects are color and size, for instance. They do not react either on conceptual processes that occurred at study, for instance, on semantic elaboration (e.g., Jacoby, 1983). It also seems likely that some other implicit tests focus on concept information. They should react to the conceptual aspects of a study episode (e.g., Weldon & Coyote, 1996), but not necessarily on any modality-specific aspects of the episode. Although a complete theory to predict ante hoc what kind of effects can be observed in implicit tests cannot yet be offered, it seems obvious that a system approach is a promising tool in constructing such a theory.

A last comment concerns neural systems. With the technical development of functional brain imaging, much attention has been given to neural systems. There is ample evidence now that activities of specific brain structures are correlated with specific stimuli and/or specific task requirements. PET studies, for instance, show that simply looking at visually presented words activates other brain structures than reading the words aloud or thinking about what the word means (e.g., Petersen, Fox, Posner, Mintum, & Raichle, 1988; Posner & Raichle, 1996). Specific parts of the brain are also involved in processing stimuli of specific modalities and in tasks that require the use of modality-specific information (e.g., Kosslyn, 1994). Thus, the system-oriented approach is also supported by neurophysiological evidence.

Neuroscience has also given some evidence that the activity of specific neural structures is correlated with explicit memory testing. I mentioned already above that explicit memory testing requires to recollect experienced episodes. Achieving this goal means to access an integrated representation of the episode, including all of its informational aspects. This ability to recollect integrated episodes is obviously impaired with amnesics. According to Squire (1992), this integration is achieved by the hippocampus and specific diencephalic nuclei. Tulving, Kapur, Craik, Moscovitch, and Houle (1994) additionally observed that right prefrontal activation is consistently associated with explicit retrieval tasks. These structures are obviously responsible for integrating informational aspects that are represented in distributed neocortical structures (such as color, form, movement) into a holistic representation (e.g., Daum, Gräber, Schugens, &

Mayer, 1996; Heil, Rösler, & Hennighausen, 1996; Squire, Knowlton, & Musen, 1993). Hence the hippocampal system is different from the neocortical informational systems (focused on in this chapter). The hippocampal system is not specialized for the processing of modality-specific information (such as color, form, or movement) but has the function to integrate all the aspects of an experienced episode into an unitary whole that is accessed in explicit recollection. Thus, also neuroscience seems to support the distinction of informational memory systems as well as the specific status of explicit recollection.

REFERENCES

Anderson, J. R. (1978). Arguments concerning representations for mental imagery. *Psychological Review, 85*, 249–277.

Anderson, J. R. (1985). *Cognitive psychology and its implications*. New York: Freeman.

Anderson, R. (1984). Did I do it or did I only imagine doing it? *Journal of Experimental Psychology: General, 113*, 594–613.

Atkinson, R. C., & Shiffrin, R. M. (1968). Human memory: A proposed system and its control processes. In K. W. Spence & J. T. Spence (Eds.), *The psychology of learning and motivation: Advances in research and theory* (Vol. 2). New York: Academic Press.

Bäckman, L., & Nilsson, L. G. (1984). Aging effects in free recall: An exception to the rule. *Human Learning, 3*, 53–69.

Bäckman, L., & Nilsson, L. G. (1985). Prerequisites for lack of age differences in memory performance. *Experimental Aging Research, 11*, 67–73.

Bahrick, H. P., & Boucher, B. (1968). Retention of visual and verbal codes of the same stimuli. *Journal of Experimental Psychology, 78*, 417–422.

Biederman, I., & Cooper, E. E. (1992). Size invariance in visual object priming. *Journal of Experimental Psychology: Human Perception & Performance, 18*, 121–133.

Blaxton, T. (1989). Investigating dissociations among memory measures: Support for a transfer-appropriate processing framework. *Journal of Experimental Psychology: Learning, Memory, and Cognition, 15*, 657–668.

Brooks, B. M., & Gardiner, J. M. (1994). Age differences in memory for prospective compared with retrospective subject-performed tasks. *Memory & Cognition, 22*, 27–33.

Bruce, V., & Young, A. W. (1986). Understanding face recognition. *British Journal of Psychology, 77*, 305–327.

Cohen, R. L. (1981). On the generality of some memory laws. *Scandinavian Journal of Psychology, 22*, 267–281.

Cohen, R. L. (1983). The effect of encoding variables on the free recall of words and action events. *Memory & Cognition, 11*, 575–582.

Cohen, R. L. (1989). The effects of interference tasks on recency in the free recall of action events. *Psychological Research, 51*, 176–180.

Cohen, R. L., & Bean, G. (1983). Memory in educable mentally retarded adults: Deficit in subject or experimenter? *Intelligence, 7*, 287–298.

Cohen, R. L., Peterson, M., & Mantini-Atkinson, T. (1987). Interevent differences in event memory: Why are some events more recallable than others? *Memory & Cognition, 15*, 109–118.

Cooper, L. A., Schacter, D. L., Ballesteros, S., & Moore, C. (1992). Priming and recognition of transformed three-dimensional objects: Effects of size and reflection. *Journal of Experimental Psychology: Learning, Memory, and Cognition, 18*, 43–58.

Daum, I., Gräber, S., Schugens, M. M., & Mayer, A. R. (1996). Memory dysfunction of the frontal type in normal ageing. *NeuroReport, 7*, 2625–2628.

Denis, M., Engelkamp, J., & Mohr, G. (1991). Memory of imagined actions: Imagining oneself or another person. *Psychological Research, 53*, 246–250.

Dick, M. B., Kean, M. L., & Sands, D. (1989). Memory for action events in Alzheimer-type dementia: Further evidence of an encoding failure. *Brain and Cognition, 9*, 71–87.

Durso, F. T., & Johnson, M. K. (1980). The effects of orienting tasks on recognition, recall and modality confusion of pictures and words. *Journal of Verbal Learning and Verbal Behavior, 19*, 416–429.

Ecker, W. (1995). *Kontrollzwänge und Handlungsgedächtnis.* Regensburg: S. Roderer.

Ecker, W., & Engelkamp, J. (1995). Memory for actions in obsessive-compulsive disorder. *Behavioural and Cognitive Psychotherapy, 23*, 349–371.

Ellis, A., & Young, A. W. (1989). *Human cognitive neurospychology.* Hillsdale, NJ.: Erlbaum.

Engelkamp, J. (1990). *Das menschliche Gedächtnis.* Göttingen: Hogrefe.

Engelkamp, J. (1991). Memory of action events: Some implications for memory theory and for imagery. In C. Cornoldi & M. McDaniel (Eds.), *Imagery and cognition.* New York: Springer.

Engelkamp, J. (1994). Mentale Repräsentationen im Kontext verschiedener Aufgaben. In H. J. Kornadt, J. Grabowski, & R. Mangold-Allwinn (Hrsg.), *Sprache und Kognition* (S. 37–54). Heidelberg: Spektrum.

Engelkamp, J. (1997a). *Das Erinnern eigener Handlungen.* Göttingen: Hogrefe.

Engelkamp, J. (1997b). Memory for to-be-performed tasks versus memory for performed tasks. *Memory & Cognition, 25*, 117–124.

Engelkamp, J., (1998). *Memory for actions.* Hove: Psychology Press.

Engelkamp, J., & Krumnacker, H. (1980). Imaginale und motorische Prozesse beim Behalten verbalen Materials. *Zeitschrift für experimentelle und angewandte Psychologie, 27*, 511–533.

Engelkamp, J., & Perrig, W. (1986). Differential effects of imaginal and motor encoding on the recall of action phrases. *Archiv für Psychologie, 138*, 261–273.

Engelkamp, J., & Zimmer, H. D. (1983). Zum Einfluß von Wahrnehmen und Tun auf das Behalten von Verb-Objekt-Phrasen. *Sprache & Kognition, 2*, 117–127.

Engelkamp, J., & Zimmer, H. D. (1985). Motor programs and their relation to semantic memory. *German Journal of Psychology, 9*, 239–254.

Engelkamp, J., & Zimmer, H. D. (1994a). *The human memory. A multimodal approach.* Seattle: Hogrefe.

Engelkamp, J., & Zimmer, H. D. (1994b). Motor similarity in subject-performed tasks. *Psychological Research, 57*, 47–53.

Engelkamp, J., & Zimmer, H. D. (1995). Similarity of movement in recognition of self-performed tasks. *British Journal of Psychology, 86*, 241–252.

Engelkamp, J., & Zimmer, H. D. (1997). Sensory factors in memory for subject-performed tasks. *Acta Psychologica, 96*, 43–60.

Engelkamp, J., Zimmer, H. D., & Biegelmann, U. E. (1993). Bizarreness effects in verbal tasks and subject-performed tasks. *European Journal of Cognitive Psychology, 5*, 393–415.

Engelkamp, J., Zimmer, H. D., & Denis, M. (1989). Paired-associate learning of action verbs with visual-or motor-imaginal encoding instructions. *Psychological Research, 50*, 257–263.

Engelkamp, J., Zimmer, H. D., Mohr, G., & Sellen, O. (1994). Memory of self-performed tasks: Self-performing during recognition. *Memory and Cognition, 22*, 34–39.

Garnham, A. (1985). *Psycholinguistics*. London: Methuen.

Glass, A. L., Holyoak, K. J., & Santa, J. L. (1979). *Cognition*. London: Addison-Wesley.

Goff, L. M., & Roediger, H. L. III. (1998). Imagination inflation for action events: Repeated imaginings lead to illusory recollections. *Memory & Cognition, 26*, 20–33.

Gollin, E. S., & Sharps, M. J. (1988). Facilitation of free recall by categorical blocking depends on stimulus type. *Memory & Cognition, 16*, 539–544.

Graf, P., Squire, L. R., & Mandler, G. (1984). The information that amnesic patients do not forget. *Journal of Experimental Psychology: Learning, Memory, and Cognition, 10*, 164–178.

Harley, T. (1995). *Psychology of language*. Hove: Erlbaum.

Heil, M., Rösler, F., & Hennighausen, E. (1996). Topographically distinct cortical activation in episodic long-term memory: The retrieval of spatial versus verbal information. *Memory & Cognition, 24*, 777–795.

Helstrup, T. (1987). One, two, or three memories? A problem-solving approach to memory for performed acts. *Acta Psychologica, 66*, 37–68.

Hoffmann, J. (1986). *Die Welt der Begriffe*. Berlin: VEB Deutscher Verlag der Wissenschaften.

Homa, D., & Viera, C. (1988). Long-term memory for pictures under conditions of thematically related foils. *Memory & Cognition, 16*, 411–421.

Humphreys, G., & Bruce, V. (1989). *Visual cognition*. Hove: Erlbaum.

Jacoby, L. L. (1983). Perceptual enhancement: Persistent effects of an experience. *Journal of Experimental Psychology: Learning, Memory, and Cognition, 9*, 21–38.

Jacoby, L. L., & Dallas, M. (1981). On the relationship between autobiographical memory and perceptual learning. *Journal of Experimental Psychology: General, 110*, 306–340.

Jolicoeur, P. (1987). A size-congruency effect in memory for visual shape. *Memory & Cognition, 15*, 531–543.

Klatzky, R. L. (1980). *Human memory*. San Francisco: Freeman.

Knopf, M. (1991). Having shaved a kiwi fruit: Memory of unfamiliar subject-performed actions. *Psychological Research, 53*, 203–211.

Knopf, M. (1992). *Gedächtnis für Handlungen: Entwicklung und Funktionsweise*. Habilitationsschrift: Universität Heidelberg.

Knopf, M. (1995). Das Erinnern eigener Handlungen im Alter. *Zeitschrift für Psychologie, 203*, 335–349.

Koriat, A., Ben-Zur, H., & Nussbaum, A. (1990). Encoding information for future action: Memory for to-be-performed versus memory for to-be-recalled tasks. *Memory & Cognition, 18*, 568–578.

Kormi-Nouri, R. (1995). The nature of memory for action events: An episodic integration on view. *European Journal of Cognitive Psychology, 7*, 337–363.

Kormi-Nouri, R., Nyberg, L., & Nilsson, L. G. (1994). The effect of retrieval enactment on recall of subject-performed tasks and verbal tasks. *Memory & Cognition, 22*, 723–728.

Kosslyn, S. M. (1980). *Image and mind*. Cambridge: Harvard University Press.

Kosslyn, S. (1981). The medium and the message in mental imagery: A theory. *Psychological Review, 88*, 46–66.

Kosslyn, S. (1994). *Image and brain. The resolution of the imagery debate*. Cambridge: MIT Press.

Lichty, W., Bressie, S., & Krell, R. (1988). When a fork is not a fork: Recall of performed activities as a function of age, generation, and bizarreness. In M. M. Gruneberg, P. E. Morris, & R. N. Sykes (Eds.), *Practical aspects of memory: Current research and issues*. Chichester: Wiley.

Lockhart, R. S., & Craik, F. I. M. (1990). Levels of processing: A retrospective commentary on a framework of memory research. *Canadian Journal of Psychology, 44*, 87–112.

Madigan, S. (1983). Picture memory. In J. C. Yuille (Ed.), *Imagery, memory and cognition*. Hillsdale, NJ: Erlbaum.

Madigan, S., & Lawrence, V. (1980). Factors effecting item recovery and reminiscence in free recall. *American Journal of Psychology, 93*, 489–504.

Mandler, G. (1980). Recognizing: The judgement of previous occurrence. *Psychological Review, 87*, 252–271.

Marshark, M., & Hunt, R. R. (1989). A reexamination of the role of imagery in learning and memory. *Journal of Experimental Psychology: Learning, Memory, and Cognition, 15*, 710–720.

McCarthy, R. A., & Warrington, C. K. (1990). *Cognitive neuropsychology*. New York: Academic Press.

McLeod, P., & Posner, M. I. (1984). Privileged loops from percept to act. In H. Bouma & D. G. Bouwhuis (Eds.), *Attention and performance, X. Control of language processes*. London: Erlbaum.

Mohr, G., Engelkamp, J., & Zimmer, H. D. (1989). Recall and recognition of self-performed acts. *Psychological Research, 51*, 181–187.

Nelson, D. L. (1979). Remembering pictures and words: Appearence, significance and name. In L. Cermak & F. I. M. Craik (Eds.), *Levels of processing in human memory*. Hillsdale, NJ: Erlbaum.

Nilsson, L. G., & Cohen, R. L. (1988). Enrichment and generation in the recall of enacted and non-enacted instructions. In M. M. Gruneberg, P. E. Morris, & R. N. Sykes (Eds.), *Practical aspects of memory: Current research and issues*. Chichester: John Wiley.

Norris, M. P., & West, R. L. (1993). Activity memory and aging: The role of motor retrieval and strategic processing. *Psychology and Aging, 8*, 81–86.

Paivio, A. (1969). Mental imagery in associative learning and memory. *Psychological Review, 76*, 241–263.

Paivio, A. (1971). *Imagery and verbal processes.* New York: Holt, Rinehart & Winston.

Paivio, A. (1986). *Mental representations: A dual coding approach.* New York: Oxford University Press.

Paivio, A., & Csapo, K. (1973). Picture superiority in free recall: Imagery or dual coding? *Cognitive Psychology, 80,* 279–285.

Parks, T. E. (1997). False memories of having said the unsaid: Some new demonstrations. *Applied Cognitive Psychology, 11,* 485–494.

Pellegrino, J. W., Siegel, A. W., & Dhawan, M. (1975). Short-term retention of pictures and words: Evidence for dual coding systems. *Journal of Experimental Psychology: Human Learning and Memory, 104,* 95–102.

Perrig, W. J., & Hofer, D. (1989). Sensory and conceptual representations in memory: Motor images which cannot be imaged. *Psychological Research, 51,* 201–207.

Petersen, S. E., Fox, P. T., Posner, M. I., Mintum, M., & Raichle, M. E. (1988). Positron emission tomographic studies of the cortical anatomy of single-word processing. *Nature, 331,* 585–589.

Posner, M. I., & Raichle, M. E. (1996). *Bilder des Geistes.* Heidelberg: Spektrum.

Pylyshyn, Z. W. (1973). What the mind's eye tells the mind's brain: A critique of mental imagery. *Psychological Bulletin, 80,* 1–24.

Pylyshyn, Z. W. (1981). The imagery debate: Analogue media versus tacit knowledge. *Psychological Review, 88,* 16–45.

Riddoch, M. J., Humphreys, G. W., Coltheart, M., & Funnell, E. (1988). Semantic systems or system? Neuropsychological evidence re-examined. *Cognitive Neuropsychology, 5,* 3–25.

Ritchey, G. H. (1982). Pictorial detail and recall in adults and children. *Journal of Experimental Psychology: Learning, Memory, and Cognition, 8,* 139–141.

Roediger, H. L. (1990). Implicit memory. *American Psychologist, 45,* 1043–1056.

Roediger, H. L., & Blaxton, T. A. (1987). Effects of varying modality, surface features, and retention interval on priming in word-fragment completion. *Memory and Cognition, 15,* 379–388.

Roediger, H. L., & Weldon, M. S. (1987). Reversing the picture superiority effect. In M. McDaniel & M. Pressley (Eds.), *Imagery and related mnemonic processes.* New York: Springer.

Roediger, H. L., Weldon, M. S., & Challis, B. H. (1989). Explaining dissociations between implicit and explicit measures of retention: A processing account. In H. L. Roediger & F. I. M. Craik (Eds.), *Varieties of memory and consciousness: Essays in honour of Endel Tulving* (pp. 3–41). Hillsdale, NJ: Erlbaum.

Saltz, E., & Donnenwerth-Nolan, S. (1981). Does motoric imagery facilitate memory for sentences? A selective interference test. *Journal of Verbal Learning and Verbal Behavior, 20,* 322–332.

Schacter, D. L. (1990). Perceptual representation systems and implicit memory: Toward a resolution of the multiple memory systems debate. In A. Diamond (Ed.), *Development and neural bases of higher cognitive functions.* Annals of the New York Academy of Sciences (Vol. 608, pp. 543–571). New York: New York Academy of Sciences.

Schacter, D. L. (1994). Priming and multiple memory systems: Perceptual mechanisms of implicit memory. In D. L. Schacter & E. Tulving (Eds.), *Memory systems 1994.* Cambridge: MIT Press.

Schacter, D. L., Delaney, S. M., & Merikle, E. P. (1990). Priming of nonverbal information and the nature of implicit memory. In G. H. Bower (Ed.), *The psychology of learning and motivation*. San Diego: Academic Press.

Schaeffer, E. G., Kozak, M. V., & Sagness, K. (1998). The role of enactment in prospective remembering. *Memory & Cognition, 26*, 644–650.

Schreuder, R. (1987). Word meaning in the mental lexicon: The role of visual, modality-specific representations. In J. Engelkamp, K. Lorenz, & B. Sandig (Eds.), *Wissensrepräsentation und Wissensaustausch*. St. Ingbert: Röhrig.

Seymour, P. H. K. (1979). *Human visual cognition*. London: Collier Macmillan.

Smith, E. R., & Branscombe, N. R. (1988). Category accessibility as implicit memory. *Journal of Experimental Social Psychology, 24*, 490–504.

Snodgrass, J. G. (1984). Concepts and their surface representation. *Journal of Verbal Learning and Verbal Behavior, 23*, 3–22.

Snodgrass, J. G., Hirshman, E., and Fan, J. (1996). The sensory match effect in recognition memory: Perceptual fluency or episodic trace? *Memory & Cognition, 24*, 367–383.

Squire, L. R. (1987). *Memory and brain*. New York: Oxford University Press.

Squire, L. R. (1992). Memory and the hippocampus. A synthesis from findings with rats, monkeys and humans. *Psychological Review, 99*, 195–231.

Squire, L. R., Knowlton, B., & Musen, G. (1993). The structure and organization of memory. *Annual Review of Psychology, 44*, 453–495.

Tulving, E. (1972). Episodic and semantic memory. In E. Tulving & W. Donaldson (Eds.), *Organization of memory*. New York: Oxford University Press.

Tulving, E. (1985a). How many memory systems are there? *American Psychologist, 40*, 385–398.

Tulving, E. (1985b). Memory and consciousness. *Canadian Psychology, 26*, 1–12.

Tulving, E., & Thomson, D. M. (1973). Encoding specificity and retrieval processes in episodic memory. *Psychological Review, 80*, 352–373.

Tulving, E., Kapur, S., Craik, F. I. M., Moscovitch, M., & Houle, S. (1994). Hemispheric encoding/retrieval asymmetry in episodic memory. Positron emission findings. *Proceedings of the National Academy of Sciences, USA, 91*, 2016–2020.

Warren, C., & Morton, J. (1982). The effects of priming on picture recognition. *British Journal of Psychology, 73*, 117–129.

Warren, M. W. (1977). The effects on recall-concurrent visual-motor distraction on picture and word recall. *Memory & Cognition, 5*, 362–370.

Warrington, E. K., & Weiskrantz, L. (1968). New method of testing long-term retention with special reference to amnesic patients. *Nature, 217*, 972–974.

Warrington, E. K., & Weiskrantz, L. (1970). Amnesic syndrome: Consolidation or retrieval? *Nature, 228*, 628–630.

Weldon, M. S., & Coyote, K. C. (1996). Failure to find the picture superiority effect in implicit conceptual memory tests. *Journal of Experimental Psychology: Learning, Memory, and Cognition, 22*, 670–686.

Zimmer, H. D. (1984). *Enkodierung, Rekodierung, Retrieval und die Aktivation motorischer Programme* (Arbeiten der FR Psychologie Nr. 91). Saarbrücken: Universität des Saarlandes.

Zimmer, H. D. (1991). Memory after motoric encoding in a generation-recognition model. *Psychological Research, 53*, 226–231.

Zimmer, H. D. (1995). Size and orientation of objects in explicit and implicit memory: A reversal of the dissociation between perceptual similarity and type of test. *Psychological Research, 57*, 260–273.

Zimmer, H. D., & Engelkamp, J. (1984). Planungs- und Ausführungsanteile motorischer Gedächtniskomponenten und ihre Wirkung auf das Behalten ihrer verbalen Bezeichnungen. *Zeitschrift für Psychologie, 192*, 379–402.

Zimmer, H. D., & Engelkamp, J. (1985). An attempt to distinguish between kinematic and motor memory components. *Acta Psychologica, 58*, 81–106.

Zimmer, H. D., & Engelkamp, J. (1996). Routes to actions and their efficacy for remembering. *Memory, 4*, 59–78.

Zimmer, H. D., & Engelkamp, J. (1999). Levels of processing effects in subject-performed tasks. *Memory & Cognition 27*, 907–914.

Zimmer, H. D., Engelkamp, J., & Sieloff, U. (1984). Motorische Gedächtniskomponenten als partiell unabhängige Komponenten des Engramms verbaler Handlungsbeschreibungen. *Sprache & Kognition, 3*, 70–85.

CHAPTER 4

The Motor Component
Is Not Crucial!

Reza Kormi-Nouri and Lars-Göran Nilsson

In his multiple memory systems view, Tulving (1983) has described episodic memory as unique, concrete, and concerned with personal in the rememberer's past. Episodic memory involves the encoding and subsequent retrieval of memories of personal events. The general framework for episodic memory begins with the witnessing or experiencing of an event and ends with its subjective rememberence. An event that is recorded in the episodic memory system always involves the rememberer, either as one of the actors or as an observer of the event. Episodic memory is characterized by temporal and spatial organization, experiential registration (firsthand or immediate knowledge), deliberate access (conscious effort), self-knowing (aware of his/her identity and existence), and a remembering process (to-be-remembered items).

Memory researchers have primarily used verbal information as the materials to be remembered. Pictures of faces and other nonverbal figures have periodically been used, but the use of verbal materials is dominant. In the beginning of the 1980s a new paradigm in memory research was developed as an alternative to the traditional verbal learning paradigm. This new paradigm of motor memory was simultaneously and independently developed by Cohen (1981), Engelkamp and Krumnacker (1980), and Saltz and Donnenwerth-Nolan (1981). The essence of this paradigm is to have subjects perform minitasks (e.g., roll the ball, break the match) at encoding. Cohen (1981) coined the term "subject-performed task" (SPT) to refer to this type of encoding by means of motor enactment. Memory performance in these motor tasks is compared to memory performance in traditional verbal tasks, in which subjects hear or read the same commands without performing them. The results typically show that memory performance after motor encoding is superior to that after verbal encoding. This superiority, which has been obtained in a variety of experimental settings, is usually referred to as the SPT effect or the enactment effect (see Cohen, 1989, and Nilsson, 2000 for reviews).

Several theories have been proposed to account for the superiority in memory performance after motor encoding as compared to verbal encoding. Cohen (e.g., 1981, 1983) proposed a nonstrategic view of motor encoding. Verbal tasks can benefit from rehearsal, organizational, and associational strategies during presentation of items, whereas such encoding strategies appear to be of little importance in motor tasks. Cohen concluded that motor learning provides an optimal form of encoding, thereby producing a better memory performance than verbal encoding.

Bäckman and Nilsson (1984, 1985) claimed that encoding of motor tasks is nonstrategic in some but not all respects. They proposed a dual conception view of motor encoding: verbal and physical (Bäckman, Nilsson, & Chalom, 1986), and assumed that the encoding of the verbal component is strategic, whereas the encoding of the physical component (weight, color) of motor tasks is nonstrategic (Bäckman, Nilsson, Herlitz, Nyberg, & Stigsdotter, 1991; Bäckman, Nilsson, & Kormi-Nouri, 1993).

Engelkamp and Zimmer (e.g., 1983, 1984) proposed that a special modality for motor programs, in addition to the use of verbal mediation and a visual-sensory modality, can account for the enactment effect. They assumed that motor, verbal, and visual encodings are independent of each other in the sense that they have different representations, codes, and modality-specific properties. Motor encoding is more efficient than verbal and visual encoding, thereby producing the enactment effect.

We argue, however, that motor encoding constitutes a case of episodic memory in the same way that verbal encoding does. But we also propose that the enactment itself contributes to episodic memory. Based on the description of episodic memory outlined by Tulving (1983), we hypothesize that the reason for the superior memory performance after motor encoding, compared to only verbal encoding, is due to better self involvement in the former than in the latter case. For action events, a rememberer has a better awareness and experiential registration of his or her actions than for verbal events. We argue against the motor encoding view, which assumes a special modality for motor programs, in addition to the visual-sensory modality and the verbal mediation (Engelkamp & Zimmer, 1983, 1984, 1985). According to this view, there are independent information-processing systems (motor, visual, and verbal) that allow a separate activating of different representation and information units.

It should be noted that elsewhere we have also argued against the nonstrategic and dual conception views in accounting for the enactment effect (Kormi-Nouri,

Nilsson, & Bäckman, 1994; Kormi-Nouri, 1995). However, it is beyond the scope of this chapter to discuss these issues here.

In this chapter, we propose that there is no need to distinguish between motor and verbal information with respect to modality specification in accounting for the enactment effects. Three different lines of research are presented to support our proposal: (a) lack of retrieval enactment effects, (b) effects of verbal and visual secondary tasks on motor memory, and (c) episodic integration by means of motor encoding.

LACK OF RETRIEVAL ENACTMENT

Based on the Encoding Specificity Principle (Tulving & Thomson, 1973), it can be predicted that enactment at both study and test should result in a better recall performance than a condition with enactment only at one of these stages. More specifically, if action events are encoded in motor codes, then motor cues should lead to a better memory performance than verbal cues. However, several studies have shown that this is not the case (Saltz and Dixon, 1982; Saltz, 1988; Norris and West, 1993; Brooks and Gardiner, 1994; Kormi-Nouri, Nyberg, and Nilsson, 1994). These studies showed that motor encoding does not produce better recall by motor cues than verbal cues. In fact, verbal cues resulted in a better memory performance than motor cues.

Saltz (Saltz & Dixon, 1982; Saltz, 1988) used 12 simple action sentences (e.g., "the workman was digging a hole in the ground," "the doctor fell asleep in the chair") in two encoding conditions: enactment and nonenactment. In the enactment condition, the subjects were told to act out each sentence after they had recited the sentence, which was first read by the experimenter. In the non-enactment condition, the subjects were instructed to recite the sentence twice without any enactment. The subjects were later tested by cueing with the verb phrase of each sentence. During recall, they either were or were not instructed to enact the verb cue before attempting to recall each sentence. The result showed that motoric enactment at encoding doubled recall performance, irrespective of whether enactment of the cues was attempted during the recall phase. Moreover, motoric enactment at retrieval only (i.e., in the absence of encoding enactment) did not improve recall of the sentences.

Norris and West (1993) presented 32 actions involving body parts (e.g., "snap your fingers," "cross your legs") to subjects in two different encoding conditions: enactment and nonenactment, and two different retrieval conditions: enactment and nonenactment (i.e., 2 encoding X 2 retrieval). The result showed that dual enactment (i.e., the combination of motor encoding and motor retrieval) did not reveal an additive effect compared with either single encoding enactment or single retrieval enactment. Here, single motor test (without motor encoding) improved recall of items.

Brooks and Gardiner (1994) used action phrases (e.g., "fly a kite," "beat an egg") involving imaginary objects. They did not have dual enactment condition (i.e., enactment both at encoding and at retrieval). They did compare motor encoding/verbal retrieval and verbal encoding/motor retrieval conditions with verbal encoding/verbal retrieval condition. In Experiment 1, 15 items were used, whereas in Experiment 2, two lists of 12 and 24 items were used. The result showed a typical motor encoding effect but no motor retrieval effect.

Kormi-Nouri, Nyberg, and Nilsson (1994) used different types of items. Experiment 1 (30 items) used body parts (e.g., shake the head), laboratory objects (e.g., look at the door), and external objects (e.g., roll the marble). In Experiment 2 (28 items) external objects were used that were either well-integrated (e.g., write with the pen) or poorly integrated (e.g., lift the glass). Subjects were assigned to different encoding/retrieval conditions: dual enactment (motor encoding/motor retrieval), single enactment (motor encoding/verbal retrieval and verbal encoding/motor retrieval), and no enactment (verbal encoding/verbal retrieval). The results showed an effect of encoding enactment but no additional effect of dual enactment. Moreover, the effect of single retrieval enactment was restricted to items involving body parts.

The data for the above-mentioned studies are shown in Table 4.1. It is important to note that, for SPTs, none of the differences between the two test conditions (i.e., verbal test and enacted test) was statistically significant. Therefore, there is a lack of encoding specificity advantage for the motor encoding/motor test condition over the motor encoding/verbal test condition. Dual modality processing, the combination of motor and verbal processing during encoding and retrieval, results in a recall level that is comparable or higher than single modality processing, motor encoding, and motor retrieval. This indicates that motor retrieval cues are not effective because the stored information is in a verbal rather than in a motor code (see Helstrup, 1986; Nyberg, 1993). If the encoded information had been in motor code, motor cues would have been more effective and an encoding specificity advantage would have been found. The finding that retrieval enactment is effective, as it was for items involving body parts, most likely stems from the increased efficiency of the enactment cue, not because the storage and retrieval formats match.

The results of these studies also show that even though encoding enactment substantially improves memory performance, retrieval enactment is of limited importance. This suggests a fundamental difference between motor processing at encoding and that at retrieval. We believe that the role of encoding enactment is to improve the encoding and the role of retrieval enactment is to increase the accessibility of the information to be retrieved.

TABLE 4.1. Mean Proportion of Correct Recall as a Function of Encoding Condition and Retrieval Condition

	Type of Test	
	Verbal Test	Enacted Test
Saltz and Dixon (1982):		
SPT	.77	.86
VT	.46	.51
Norris and West (1993):		
Organized list		
SPT	.73	.69
VT	.62	.64
Unorganized list		
SPT	.71	.63
VT	.56	.69
Brooks and Gardiner (1994):		
Experiment 1		
SPT	.58	
VT	.49	.49
Experiment 2		
Long list		
SPT	.50	
VT	.40	.38
Short list		
SPT	.61	
VT	.60	.57
Kormi-Nouri et al. (1994):		
Experiment 1		
SPT(body parts)	.80	.70
SPT(external objects)	.76	.70
SPT(laboratory objects)	.56	.66
VT(body parts)	.26	.52
VT(external objects)	.14	.16
VT(laboratory objects)	.18	.26
Experiment 2		
SPT(well integrated)	.93	.87
SPT(poorly integrated)	.60	.49
VT(well integrated)	.73	.69
VT(poorly integrated)	.23	.11

Note: All four studies used younger adults as subjects, and the data presented here are therefore related to this group of subjects. The data for children in the Saltz and Dixon (1982) study, and the data for older adults in the Norris and West (1993) and Brooks and Gardiner (1994) studies were not reported here.

In the Brooks and Gardiner (1994) study, the values are approximations, because the data were presented by figures in this study and there was no access to the original data.

Retrieval enactment may be helpful for memory performance in cases in which enacting improves cue effectiveness. It is possible that such an improvement only occurs for those items that are present at retrieval. Body parts are particularly useful for integration as enactment cues and targets. For example, if the subject is instructed to enact "shake" (cue), it is likely that the subject will shake his or her head and thereby be reminded of the target, "head." In such cases, it is reasonable to assume that retrieval enactment increases the likelihood of the cue leading the subject to the correct target. However, if the subject is instructed to enact "lift" (cue) and the target is "the box," enactment (in the absence of object) should not improve cue effectiveness and may even reduce it.

Although a single retrieval enactment effect (in the absence of encoding enactment) was found only for body parts (Norris, & West, 1993; Kormi-Nouri et al., 1994), the results of these two studies showed that memory performance is highest for motor encoding and verbal test, followed by motor encoding and motor test, verbal encoding and motor test, and verbal encoding and verbal test. Even in the case of body parts, the match between encoding and retrieval (i.e., motor encoding and motor retrieval) did not produce a better memory performance compared to the motor encoding and verbal retrieval condition.

However, Engelkamp, Zimmer, Mohr, and Sellen (1994) found a dual enactment effect. Action events, compared to verbal events, were recognized better in a motor test than in a verbal test. One possible explanation for this inconsistent finding may be that different types of memory tests were used. Engelkamp et al. (1994) used a recognition test, whereas recall tests were used by the other researchers. It is possible that the effect of enactment is more pronounced in recognition tests than in recall tests (see Mohr, Engelkamp, & Zimmer, 1989, and Kormi-Nouri & Nilsson, 1998; but also see Nilsson & Craik, 1990; Nyberg, 1992; and Svensson & Nilsson, 1989, for a contrary view). Since both an action verb and an object noun are present at a recognition test, the effect could be viewed as retrieval integration rather than a simple motor test. The findings of retrieval enactment effects for body-part items in the Kormi-Nouri et al. (1994) and the Norris and West (1993) studies provide support for the notion of retrieval integration for action events. In addition, the results of the study by Kormi-Nouri and Nilsson (1998) provide further support that, in the recognition test, the enactment effect was more striking for well-integrated items than for poorly integrated items. This implies that episodic integration is the source of a better specific information for action events (Kormi-Nouri, 1995).

Another explanation may concern the use of different designs. A between-subjects design with respect to type of test, verbal vs. motor, was used in the studies described. The study by Engelkamp et al. (1994) used a within-subject design. It is possible that, in the Engelkamp et al. (1994) study, the subjects might not be able to retrieve the action and verbal events independently. Although the authors used the fixed order type of testing, first verbal events then action events, this may have caused an advantage of rehearsal in the case of action events. It should also be noted that the presentation time for action events at test was longer than for verbal events.

THE EFFECTS OF VERBAL AND VISUAL SECONDARY TASKS ON MOTOR MEMORY

If motor encoding is processed separately and independently from verbal and visual encoding, as is hypothesized by the motor encoding view (e.g., Engelkamp, & Zimmer, 1983, 1984, 1985), one should expect that the motor task is affected only by a secondary motor task and not by verbal or visual tasks. There are two studies that prove such a prediction wrong. In the first study (Bäckman, Nilsson, & Kormi-Nouri, 1993), it was found that memory for action events deteriorated under divided attention condition, compared to focused attention condition, independently of whether object names (in Experiment 1) or action verbs (in Experiment 2) served as cues. The secondary task used in the divided attention condition was verbal and consisted of backward counting, subtracting 6 and 3, in turn, from a given number, such as 300. The secondary task in the second study (Kormi-Nouri, Nilsson, & Bäckman, 1994) was to monitor the total number of red dots on quickly presented scatterplots. These scatterplots contained differing numbers and configurations of red and black dots. The subjects' task was to count the red dots, holding this number in mind to be added to the number of red dots on subsequent scatterplots. The secondary task was both verbal and visual in nature. Again, in both cued recall conditions (noun cue in Experiment 1, and verb cue in Experiment 2), it was found that memory for action events was affected under the divided attention condition. The data of these two studies are shown in Table 4.2.

Therefore, the results of these two studies show that motor encoding is affected by a verbal or verbal-visual secondary task. This may imply that the processing of a motor information is not independent from verbal or visual information as is assumed in the motor encoding view (Engelkamp & Zimmer, 1983, 1984, 1985).

Contrary to these above findings, there are two studies showing that motor encoding is selectively affected by different interference tasks. In the first study, Saltz and Donnenwerth-Nolan (1981) used action sentences (e.g., the father POLISHED his GUN) as a primary task in different learning conditions; visual, verbal, and enactment. The secondary tasks were also selected in different modalities: visualization, create a mind picture of, for instance, "a baby walking in the living room"; verbalization, repeat the unrelated target verb twice, for instance, "jump," "clap"; and enactment, act out the unrelated target verbs, "jump,"

TABLE 4.2. Mean Proportion of Correct Recall as a Function of Encoding Condition

	Focused Attention	Divided Attention
Bäckman et al. (1993):		
Experiment 1:		
Verb Recall	.71	.41
Color Recall	.61	.43
Experiment 2:		
Object Recall	.49	.35
Color Recall	.28	.24
Kormi-Nouri et al. (1994):		
Experiment 1:		
Verb Recall	.85	.76
Color Recall	.73	.58
Experiment 2:		
Object Recall	.66	.56
Color Recall	.36	.24

"clap." It was found that memory performance was much worse when the primary task and secondary task were learned under the same processing mode than they were learned under different processing modes. More specifically, motor memory, as a primary task, was not affected by visual and verbal secondary tasks; similarly, visual and verbal memory, as primary tasks, were not affected by motor memory as a secondary task. Saltz and Donnenwerth-Nolan (1981) concluded that the enactment facilitation effect is not attributed to visual or verbal processes. This effect is a function of the storage of motoric image or trace that results from the enactment process. In the second study, Zimmer and Engelkamp (1985) examined selective interference for two different types of information: kinematic (e.g., the bridge is collapsing) and motoric (e.g., the father is winding up his watch). The secondary tasks were also similar to the primary tasks, kinematic such as video spots showing moving objects (e.g., swinging metronome) and motoric as in body-related actions, (e.g., scratching oneself). In this study, selective interference was found for motor learned materials but not for kinematic learned materials. Motor learning was worse when the secondary task used was motoric, compared to the condition when motor learning was associated with a kinematic secondary task. It was concluded that kinematic and motoric information belong to two independent memory systems.

The findings of effects of verbal and visual secondary tasks on motor memory are clearly at odds with the findings that motor memory is selectively affected only by motor secondary task. A possible explanation for this discrepancy may be that some studies compared the divided attention with a focused attention condition, no secondary task (Bäckman et al., 1993; and Kormi-Nouri et al., 1994).

The studies by Saltz and Donnenwerth (1981) and Zimmer and Engelkamp (1985) did not use such a control condition. Without this control, one does not know whether motor memory is affected by verbal, visual, and kinematic secondary tasks. The conclusion that motor memory is not affected by verbal, visual, and kinematic secondary tasks is therefore premature. It might be that there are different levels of effects of verbal, visual, and kinematic secondary tasks, compared to motor secondary task, on motor memory. However, claiming that there is no effect at all is simply not accurate.

THE EPISODIC INTEGRATION EFFECTS BY MEANS OF MOTOR ENCODING

In the two previous points, we demonstrated that it is not necessary to assume a special program, code, or representation for motor memory. What makes motor memory so special and distinct from other types of memory (verbal, visual, kinematic) is the "episodic integration effect" (Kormi-Nouri, 1994).

As was noted earlier, we believe that motor memory, like the other types of memory, is episodic memory. Episodic memory is organized in terms of time and space and registered in a self-involved manner. The superiority of motor memory over other types of memory can be explained as a more optimal case of episodic memory. It is reasoned that motor memory increases episodic integration from two different aspects: First, for action events, there is a better integration, interaction, between the environment (i.e., task) and the subject (i.e., rememberer). Subjects are more involved in the learning of motor tasks as compared to verbal tasks. A better self-involvement in action events helps the rememberer to be more aware of his action, self-knowing, thereby leading to a better episodic memory. Second, enactment integrates the components of actions in two ways: within-event integration and between-events integration. As was shown earlier, the effect of enactment is mainly restricted to encoding, but it is not crucial which type of retrieval test is used. Encoding enactment is considered the "glue" that cements the components of actions into a single memory unit or into closely connected memory units. For example, if the action event is "lift the pen," the act of lifting is an attribute of the pen, and the pen becomes a part of the action "lifting." That is, the act of lifting and the pen are registered together, not separately. Enacting a "lifting" motion with the object "pen" upon hearing the sentence should serve to process the event more specifically than merely hearing the sentence. It is proposed that the episodic integration of action events is the source of distinctiveness in the field of action memory (e.g., Bäckman, Nilsson, & Chalom, 1986; Engelkamp, 1990; Helstrup, 1986; Nilsson & Craik, 1990; Norris & West, 1993; Nyberg, 1993; Saltz & Donnenwerth-Nolan, 1981; Zimmer & Engelkamp, 1989).

The mechanism for the episodic integration effect of encoding enactment is not fully understood. It might be the case that enactment is more basic than verbal encoding by being evolutionary older. It is through actions that biological organisms, including man, interact with their environment. It might even be feasible to argue that enactment by such a biological preparedness constitutes the basis for an optimal processing of information. This biological preparedness is set aside when the situation or the task instead requires a verbal encoding.

Kormi-Nouri (1995) examined the effect of semantic integration (i.e., the pre-existing relation between verb and noun for each individual item) at encoding of motor and verbal tasks. Motor and verbal memory was tested in free recall and cued recall with either verbs or nouns serving as cues. It was found that the enactment effect was larger in free recall than in cued recall and was more pronounced for poorly integrated items (e.g., look at the stone) than well-integrated items (e.g., read the book). Not only was the enactment effect larger for well-integrated items in free recall, but it was also larger for poorly integrated items in cued recall. Additionally, there was no difference in efficiency between verb cue and object cue for the motor task, but there was such a differential effect of type of cue for the verbal task. The results of Experiments 2 and 3 are shown in Table 4.3. It should be noted that the Kormi-Nouri study (1995) consisted of a total of four experiments, and the detailed data of all experiments are not reported here.

The conclusion from this study is that motor encoding constitutes an episodic integration by improving item-specific information. The combination of semantic integration (i.e., previously acquired general knowledge of the relation between verb and noun) and episodic integration (i.e., special knowledge of the relation between verb and noun learned at the time of study) provides the best encoding support and consequently the best memory performance for each individual item.

TABLE 4.3. Mean Proportion of Correct Recall across Encoding and Test Conditions

	Free Recall	Cued Recall
Experiment 2 (between-list design):		
SPT-Well Integrated	.49	.87
SPT-Poorly Integrated	.26	.38
VT-Well Integrated	.17	.76
VT-Poorly Integrated	.06	.08
Experiment 3 (within-list design):		
SPT-Well Integrated	.46	.91
SPT-Poorly Integrated	.34	.47
VT-Well Integrated	.16	.81
VT-Poorly Integrated	.09	.12

Kormi-Nouri and Nilsson (1998) examined motor memory and verbal memory with respect to two exceptions (poor integration and cue overlap) from Tulving-Wiseman function (1975). It was found that the enactment effect was higher in recognition than in cued recall (in no-cue overlap conditions). For well-integrated items, the enactment effect was larger in recognition than in cued recall, whereas, for poorly integrated items, it was larger in cued recall than in recognition. The independence between recall and recognition of well-integrated items is more pronounced for encoding enactment. However, for poorly integrated items without encoding enactment, there is a larger dependence between recognition and recall. The results of Experiments 1 and 2 are shown in Table 4.4. The Kormi-Nouri and Nilsson study (1998) consisted of three experiments, and the detailed data of all experiments are not reported here.

These results indicate that encoding enactments provides a functional relation between a verb and noun at the time of encoding. The combination of high semantic and episodic integration (SPT-well integrated items) produces strong integration and thereby independence between recognition and recall. However, VT-poorly integrated items that constitute the lowest degree of integration produce dependence between recognition and recall.

Kormi-Nouri and Nilsson (1999) examined cueing effects of relational and item-specific information after enacted and nonenacted encoding of short sentences (e.g., lift the pen, fold the paper). At encoding, subjects were either informed or not informed about the categorical nature of the nouns used in each sentence. In Experiment 1, the encoding instruction was to remember only the nouns, whereas, in Experiment 2, it was to remember the whole sentence, verb and noun together. At retrieval, subjects were given two tests. In Experiment 1 free recall and verb cued recall were used, and in Experiment 2 categorical cued recall and categorical-verb cued recall were given. Although the results (shown in Table 4.5) revealed a negative effect of intralist verb cueing, the cueing effect

TABLE 4.4. Mean Proportion of Correct Recognition and Recall across Encoding Conditions

	Recognition	Recall
Experiment 1 (no-cue overlap):		
SPT-Well Integrated	.92	.86
SPT-Poorly Integrated	.73	.44
VT-Well Integrated	.58	.78
VT-Poorly Integrated	.53	.15
Experiment 2 (cue overlap):		
SPT-Well Integrated	.92	.87
SPT-Poorly Integrated	.90	.65
VT-Well Integrated	.73	.73
VT-Poorly Integrated	.64	.34

TABLE 4.5. Mean Proportion of Correct Recall as a Function of Encoding and Retrieval Conditions

Experiment 1:	Free Recall	Cued Recall
Without Condition		
SPT	.50	.44
VT	.36	.10
With Condition		
SPT	.58	.48
VT	.43	.15
Experiment 2:	One Cued Recall	Two Cued Recall
Without Condition		
SPT	.49	.50
VT	.37	.28
With Condition		
SPT	.55	.57
VT	.31	.19

Note: In the Without conditions, no information about the categorical cues was given at the study phase, whereas, in the With conditions, such information was given to the subjects.

was different after encoding with enactment than after encoding without enactment. It should be noted that this difference holds true for enactment with real objects (Experiments 1 & 2) but not for enactment with imaginary objects (Experiment 3, not shown here).

In Experiment 1 the inhibitory effect of intralist verb cueing was more striking for verbal tasks than for motor tasks. In Experiment 2 facilitation effects were found for motor task, whereas inhibition effects of intralist verb cueing were observed for verbal task. These dissociative effects of intralist verb cueing for verbal and motor tasks support the episodic integration view of encoding enactment. In line with previous research (Engelkamp & Zimmer, 1994; Knopf, 1991; Kormi-Nouri, 1995; Nyberg, 1993; Saltz, 1988), the findings of the Kormi-Nouri and Nilsson (1999) study reveal that motor encoding can produce a more pronounced item-specific information. Furthermore, in line with Bäckman, Nilsson, and Chalom (1986) and contrary to Zimmer and Engelkamp (1989), the results showed that enactment improves relational processing by integrating the inter-item events. In Experiment 2 the enactment effect was considerably larger for the informed noun category condition, compared to the condition in which the subjects were not informed. Also, whereas motor encoding was positively affected by list structure, verbal encoding was negatively affected.

In a very recent study (Kormi-Nouri, 2000), two experiments systematically compared four SPT conditions involving real/imaginary movement and real/ imaginary object with one verbal condition involving no enactment and no ob-

TABLE 4.6. Mean Proportion of Recall Performance as a Function of Subjects' Viewing Abilities and Type of Encoding

	Encoding Condition				
	VT	SPTrr	SPTii	SPTir	SPTii
Experiment 1					
Sighted	.20	.46	.41	.37	.39
Blindfolded	.22	.46	.44	.35	.39
Experiment 2					
Sighted	.26	.45	.45	.43	.39
Blind	.27	.44	.42	.44	.31

Note: rr= real movement/real object; ri= real movement/imaginary object; ir= imaginary movement/real object; ii= imaginary movement/imaginary object

ject. Sighted subjects were compared with blindfolded and blind subjects. Free recall data showed no difference between the SPT conditions and between the groups of subjects. All SPTs were recalled better than VTs, indicating that the enactment effect is not determined by either movement or object separately, rather both have an effective role and are equally involved for obtaining the enactment effect. The results (shown in Table 4.6) provide no support for the motor encoding and multimodality views but are in line with the episodic integration view.

In sum, we have demonstrated lack of retrieval enactment effects as well as the effects of verbal and visual secondary tasks on motor memory, but we have also demonstrated episodic integration by means of motor encoding. We argue that these experimental findings illustrate that a motor component is not crucial in accounting for the enactment effect. The integration view originally proposed by Kormi-Nouri (1994, 1995) and further elaborated here is more adequate in explaining the empirical effect of a superior memory performance after enactment than after nonenactment at encoding.

REFERENCES

Bäckman, L., & Nilsson, L. G. (1984). Aging effects in free recall: An exception to the rule. *Human Learning,–3*, 53–69.

Bäckman, L., & Nilsson, L. G. (1985). Prerequisites for lack of age differences in memory performance. *Experimental Aging Research, 11,* 67–73.

Bäckman, L., Nilsson, L. G., & Chalom, D. (1986). New evidence on the nature of the encoding of action events. *Memory & Cognition, 14,* 339–346.

Bäckman, L., Nilsson, L. G., & Kormi-Nouri, R. (1993). Attentional demands and recall of verbal and color information in action events. *Scandinavian Journal of Psychology, 34,* 246–254.

Bäckman, L., Nilsson, L. G., Herlitz, A., Nyberg, L., & Stigsdotter, A. (1991). A dual conception of the encoding of action events. *Scandinavian Journal of Psychology, 32*, 289–299.

Brooks, B. M., & Gardiner, J. M. (1994). Age differences in memory for prospective compared with retrospective subject-performed tasks. *Memory & Cognition, 22*, 27–33.

Cohen, R. L. (1981). On the generality of some memory laws. *Scandinavian Journal of Psychology, 22*, 267–282.

Cohen, R. L. (1983). The effect of encoding variables on the free recall of words and action events. *Memory & Cognition, 11*, 575–582.

Cohen, R. L. (1989). Memory for action events: The power of enactment. *Educational Psychology Review, 1*, 57–80.

Engelkamp, E. (1990). Memory of action events and some implications for imagery. In C. Cornoldi & McDaniel (Eds.), *Imagery and Cognition*, pp. 183–219. New York: Spinger.

Engelkamp, J., & Krumnacker, H. (1980). Imaginale und motorische Prozesse beim Behalter verbalen Materials. *Zeitschrift für experimentelle und angewandte Psychologie, 27*, 511–533.

Engelkamp, J., & Zimmer, H. D. (1983). Der Einfluß von Wahrnehmen und Tun auf das Behalten von Verb-Object-Phrasen. *Sprache & Kognition, 2*, 117–127.

Engelkamp, J., & Zimmer, H. D. (1984). Motor program information as a separate memory unit. *Psychological Research, 46*, 283–299.

Engelkamp, J., & Zimmer, H. D. (1985). Motor programs and their relation to semantic memory. *German Journal of Psychology, 9*, 239–254.

Engelkamp, J., & Zimmer, H. D. (1994). *The human memory: A multimodal approach*, pp. 75–79. Seattle: Hogrefe and Huber.

Engelkamp, J., Zimmer, H. D., Mohr, G., & Sellen, O. (1994). Memory of self-performed tasks: Self-performing during recognition. *Memory & Cognition, 22*, 34–39.

Helstrup, T. (1986). Separate memory laws for recall of performed acts? *Scandinavian Journal of Psychology, 27*, 1–29.

Knopf, M. (1991). Having shaved a kiwi fruit: Memory of unfamiliar subject-performed actions. *Psychological Research, 53*, 203–211.

Kormi-Nouri, R. (1994). *Memory for action events: An episodic integration view*. Unpublished doctoral dissertation, University of Ume°a.

Kormi-Nouri, R. (1995). The nature of memory for action events: An episodic integration view. *European Journal of Cognitive Psychology, 7*, 337–363.

Kormi-Nouri, R. (2000). The role of movement and object in action memory: A comparative study between blind, blindfolded and sighted subjects. *Scandinavian Journal of Psychology, 41*, 71–75.

Kormi-Nouri, R., & Nilsson, L. G. (1998). The role of integration in recognition failure and action memory. *Memory & Cognition, 26*, 681–691.

Kormi-Nouri, R., & Nilsson, L. G. (1999). Negative cueing effects with weak and strong intralist cues. *European Journal of Cognitive Psychology, 11*, 199–218.

Kormi-Nouri, Nilsson, L. G., & Bäckman, L. (1994). The dual conception view reexamined: Attentional demands and the encoding of verbal and physical information in action events. *Psychological Research, 57*, 42–46.

Kormi-Nouri, R., Nyberg, L., & Nilsson, L. G. (1994). The effect of retrieval enactment on recall of subject-performed tasks and verbal tasks. *Memory & Cognition, 22,* 723–728.

Mohr, G., Engelkamp, J., & Zimmer, H. D. (1989). Recall and recognition of self-performed acts. *Psychological Research, 51,* 181–187.

Nilsson, L. G. (2000). Remembering actions and words. In F. I. M. Craik & E. Tulving (Eds.) *Oxford handbook of memory* (pp. 137–148). Oxford: Oxford University Press.

Nilsson, L. G., & Craik, F. I. M. (1990). Additive and interactive effects in memory for subject-performed tasks. *European Journal of Cognitive Psychology, 2,* 305–324.

Norris, M. P., & West, R. L. (1993). Activity memory and aging: The role of motor retrieval and strategic processing. *Psychology and Aging, 8,* 81–86.

Nyberg, L. (1992). Examining retrieval component in memory for enacted and non-enacted events. *Umeå Psychological Report, 207.*

Nyberg, L. (1993). *The enactment effect: Studies of a memory phenomenon.* Unpublished doctoral dissertation, University of Umeå.

Saltz, E. (1988). The role of motoric enactment (M-processing) in memory for words and sentences. In M. M. Grueberg, P. E. Morris, & R. N. Sykes (Eds.), *Practical aspects of memory: Current research and issues.* (Vol. 1 pp. 408–414). Chichester: Wiley.

Saltz, E., & Dixon, D. (1982). Let's pretend: The role of motoric imagery in memory for sentences and words. *Journal of Experimental Child Psychology, 34,* 77–92.

Saltz, E., & Donnenwerth-Nolan, S. (1981). Does motoric imagery facilitate memory for sentences? A selective interference test. *Journal of Verbal Learning and Verbal Behavior, 20,* 322–332.

Svensson, T., & Nilsson, L. G. (1989). The relation between recognition and cued recall in memory for enacted and nonenacted information. *Psychological Research, 51,* 194–200.

Tulving, E. (1983). *Elements of episodic memory.* New York: Clarendon Press.

Tulving, E., & Thomson, D. M. (1973). Encoding specificity and retrieval processes in episodic memory. *Psychological Review, 80,* 352–373.

Zimmer, H. D., & Engelkamp, J. (1985). An attempt to distinguish between kinematic and motor memory components. *Acta Psychologica, 58,* 81–106.

Zimmer, H. D., & Engelkamp, J. (1989). Does motor encoding enhance relational information? *Psychological Research, 51,* 158–167.

CHAPTER 5

The Role of Action-Based Structures in Activity Memory

Mary Ann Foley and Hilary Horn Ratner

Memory for simple action descriptions like "lift a spoon" or "close the curtain" is improved when a person enacts the action specified during encoding. Many explanations have been offered to account for why it is that performed actions are remembered better than action descriptions (Bäckman & Nilsson, 1984; Engelkamp & Zimmer, 1994; Cohen, 1989), but what intrigues us about these explanations is what they share in common. Each alternative is a derivative of an explanation offered to account for factors influencing verbal recall. Moreover, the study of performed actions has been influenced by this shared origin, which has served to guide the kinds of questions asked about action memory. Numerous factors have dramatic consequences for verbal memory, including presentation rate, list length, position of items in a list, and list content (e.g., mixed or not with respect to categorical structure). In turn, in the last 20 years, the effect of these kinds of factors on action memory has been the focus of considerable study (for reviews, see Cohen, 1981; Engelkamp & Zimmer, 1994). From our point of view, this approach to the study of action memory has diverted attention away from the study of one of action memory's most distinguishing characteristics, its goal-directed nature. In this chapter, we evaluate these alternative explanations for action memory within the context of our theoretical framework for activity memory, providing evidence for our approach. In the process, we summarize our framework whose central focus is the inherent goal-directed nature of activities (Ratner & Foley, 1994). We close by suggesting new directions for framing questions about activity memory.

THE ADVANTAGE IN MEMORY FOR SELF-PERFORMED ACTIONS

Memory for simple action descriptions like "lift a spoon" or "close the curtain" is improved when a person enacts the actions specified or watches someone else perform the actions during encoding (e.g., Bäckman, 1985; Cohen, 1981; Cohen, 1985; Cohen, Peterson, & Mantini-Atkinson, 1987; Engelkamp, 1986, 1997; Engelkamp & Zimmer, 1985, 1994, 1995; Foley, Bouffard, Raag, & DiSanto-Rose, 1991; Helstrup, 1987; Zimmer, 1984, 1991). When first reported, the effect was referred to as the *Symbolic Enactment* effect because the actions were enacted symbolically (Engelkamp & Krumnacker, 1980), but it has been referred to more recently as the *SPT* effect or the self-performed-task effect (Engelkamp & Zimmer, 1994).

The SPT effect is robust, observed under many encoding instructions and testing conditions. Whether the enactments involve actual objects or substitutes (e.g., gestures, images of objects) (e.g., Engelkamp & Zimmer, 1994), whether recall or recognition is tested (e.g., Cohen, 1989; Engelkamp & Zimmer, 1994), or whether participants have their eyes open or closed during enactment, receiving visual feedback or not (e.g., Engelkamp, Zimmer, & Biegelmann, 1993), the advantage of acting is observed. Moreover, actions can be labeled or not. Although most of the SPT research involves memory for the verbal description of an action, recent studies also show the advantage when action enactment is the only mode of expression during encoding and recall (e.g., Engelkamp, Zimmer, Mohr, & Sellen, 1994).

Explanations for the Enhancement Effect

Many explanations have been offered to account for why performed actions are remembered better than action descriptions, and debate about the persuasiveness of these alternatives continues (e.g., Bäckman, Nilsson, & Chalom, 1986; Cohen, 1989; Engelkamp & Zimmer, 1994). Three explanations have garnered the most attention and empirical support: (1) involvement of automatic or strategic processes, (2) item-specific or relational elaboration, and (3) dual-code, or specific-code, representations.

The first explanation of the SPT effect is that action memory is nonstrategic, whereas memory for words involves intentional encoding. Enacted actions may be remembered better than action descriptions because more strategic, deliberate encoding is needed to remember words, whereas memory for actions may be mediated by more automatic processes. Children have difficulty using mnemonic strategies, and, as a result, memory for words increases with age (e.g., Flavell, 1985). If action memory is nonstrategic, however, then developmental differences should not occur.

Cohen and Stewart (1982) compared recall of words and SPTs for 9-, 11-, and 13-year-old children. Word recall did increase with age; however, no age differences were found for recall of SPTs. When children were questioned about their efforts to learn the items presented, at all ages they reported attempting to memorize the words, but not the actions. Moreover, primacy effects occurred for word recall, but not for actions, indicating that children rehearsed only to facilitate retention of the words. Cohen and Bean (1983) provided further support for the nonstrategic, automatic nature of action memory by showing that learning impaired adults remembered actions, but not words, as well as normal adults.

Unfortunately, the developmental evidence comparing adults and children is contradictory. Although there are instances in which developmental differences in the SPT effect are not observed, in others, children's action memory has been found to improve with age (e.g., Foellinger & Trabasso, 1977; Foley & Johnson, 1985; Johnson, Perlmutter, & Trabasso, 1979; Price & Goodman, 1990; Ratner, Smith, & Dion, 1986). In addition, sometimes young children show better recall of their own actions than those of others (e.g., Baker-Ward, Hess, & Flanagan, 1990) or are able to benefit from memory cues created during acting (e.g., Paris & Lindauer, 1976), but action does not always help children's memory (Foley & Johnson, 1985; Ratner & Hill, 1991), arguing against a critical role of auto-

TABLE 5.1. Summary of Results for Developmental Studies on Action Memory[a]

Study	4	5	6/7	9	11	13	Adults	Findings
Cohen & Stewart (1982)				48.0	47.8	51.8		No SPT[b] age effects
Baker-Ward, Hess, & Flanagan (1990)			35.0	50.0				Age effects (SPT/EPT[c] combined)
Foellinger & Trabasso (1977)		73.0	80.0	85.0	90.0			EPT age effects
Foley & Johnson (1985) (Experiment 1)			28.0	42.7		61.7		Age effects (SPT/EPT combined)
Johnson, Perlmutter, & Trabasso (1979)	54.7			77.1				Age effects (SPT/EPT combined)
Price & Goodman (1990)	57.0	88.0						SPT age effects
Ratner, Smith, & Dion (1986)		8.0					17.1	SPT age effects

[a] Results are given in percentage of correct recall.
[b] SPT is Self-Performed Task.
[c] EPT is Experimenter-Performed Task.

TABLE 5.2. Summary of Results for Enactment Effects in Studies on Children's Action Memory[a]

Study	SPT[b]	EPT[c]	VT[d]	Findings
Baker-Ward, Hess, & Flanagan (1990)	50.0	36.0		6- & 9-year-olds combined; Action effects
Paris & Lindauer (1976)	70.0		31.3	6-year-olds; Action effects
Foley & Johnson (1985) (Experiment 2)	43.0	41.7		6-year-olds; No action effects
	53.0	45.8		9-year-olds; Action effects
	76.8	61.5		Adults; Action effects
Johnson, Perlmutter, & Trabasso (1979)	65.8	66.0		4- & 8- year-olds; No action effects
Ratner & Hill (1991)	30.1	32.2		6-year-olds; No action effects
	40.1	46.8		9-year-olds; No action effects
	42.3	41.7		Adults; No action effects

[a] Results are given in percentage of correct recall.
[b] SPT is Self-Performed Task.
[c] EPT is Experimenter-Performed Task.
[d] VT is Verbal Task.

maticity. In Tables 5.1 and 5.2, summaries are provided of age effects and enactment effects, respectively.

A second explanation relies on the distinction between item-specific and relational processing in verbal memory to account for the SPT effect. Item-specific processing refers to the encoding of information associated with the distinctiveness of each item in a list whereas relational processing refers to the encoding of relationships (e.g., based on similarity) among the items in a list (Hunt & Einstein, 1981). Thus, enactment may enhance memory for verbal descriptions because it contributes to the distinctiveness of an action description *or* because it evokes connections among the actions in the list, perhaps by integrating parts of a sentence into a motorically organized node (e.g., Saltz & Donnenworth-Nolan, 1981). Zimmer and Engelkamp (1985) and Mohr, Engelkamp, and Zimmer (1989) argue that although organization occurs in action memory, it is enhancement of item-specific information that underlies the enactment effect.

Consistent with Zimmer and Engelkamp's claim, Ratner and Hill (1991) examined the integrative role of action in children's and adults' memory and found no evidence that action promotes performance by integrating information. To test the role of integration in children's action memory, Ratner and Hill presented two types of verb phrases, intransitive and transitive, to children and adults for recall. Intransitive verbs encoded actions that do not require objects in their meanings (e.g., sit, dance, walk, leap). If objects appear with these verbs, they are not essential to the meaning of the verb or the action it represents (e.g., sit beside the book). Objects, however, are not optional arguments for transitive verbs (e.g., push, pull, hit, throw) and represent obligatory components of the verb's meaning (e.g., Braine & Hardy, 1982). Consequently, the actions transitive verbs encode are modified to a greater extent by the characteristics of the objects acted on and are integrated more with the action. For example, the action encoded by "pick up" varies considerably, depending on the object that is picked up (e.g., a penny, sand, or a piano). When intransitive verbs appear with objects, the action is not modified across a very wide range. "Sitting" next to a penny or sand or a piano is virtually the same action, regardless of the object the actor sits next to.

If acting improves recall because integration is enhanced, the transitive phrases should have been recalled better than the intransitive phrases, but they were not. Overall, 37 percent of the transitive phrases and 41.3 percent of the intransitive phrases were accurately recalled, exactly opposite to the prediction. When enacting the phrases during encoding and retrieval this difference grew even larger. Participants in an Action-Action condition who carried out the actions during presentation and recall remembered an average of 38 percent of the transitive phrases and 46 percent of the intransitive phrases ($p < .05$). Moreover, participants did integrate the transitive phrases more than the intransitive phrases in their action. Recall was just not influenced by the integration. Integration was defined as a modification of the action in response to the characteristics of the symbolic object. For example, "jump over the puddle" was scored as integrated if the participant propelled his or her body forward rather than up and down. Up-and-down movements would occur if the person were enacting only "jump" without respect to the "puddle." Similarly, "push the refrigerator" was required to include indications of effort (e.g., grunts or resistance against the hands). As predicted, more integration occurred for transitive ($M = 60.3\%$) than intransitive ($M = 39.9\%$) phrases ($p < .05$), but apparently integration did not improve recall.

At the same time, Ratner and Hill also found no evidence that item-specific processing accounted for performance. To examine the role of action elaboration, the number of movements performed for each action was examined. Perhaps more movements were performed for the intransitive than transitive phrases, explaining the difference in recall. Although more movements were carried out when enacting the intransitive ($M = 1.37$) than transitive ($M = .96$) phrases ($p < .0001$), correlational analyses revealed that participants who performed more movements did not recall more phrases ($rs = -.24$ to $.32$, $ps > .10$). Also, there was no increase in movements performed with age; however, older children and adults recalled more phrases than younger children.

A third set of explanations for the SPT effect is based on the notion that actions give rise to multiple codes. When a person performs an action, it is represented both motorically and linguistically. In contrast, when a person observes someone else perform an action, or only hears a verbal description of the action, the corresponding representation is created only linguistically. The dual representation for actions is thought to mediate the recall advantage (e.g., Bäckman, Nilsson, & Chalom, 1986; Cohen, 1989; Engelkamp & Zimmer, 1985; Zimmer & Engelkamp, 1985).

This explanation, however, is weakened by research showing an enhancement effect for self-performed actions in the absence of linguistic codes corresponding to those actions. For instance, adults' memory for dance movements is better if they perform than watch a skilled dancer perform the movements, even though the adults were not aware of the verbal labels corresponding to the ballet and modern dance movements (e.g., Foley, Bouffard, Raag, & DiSanto-Rose, 1991). Furthermore, when dance movements are more elaborate in nature, involving simple or complex sequences rather than isolated movements, the typical enhancement effect is actually reversed. Skilled dancers better remembered dance movements they observed someone else performing ($M = 86$ percent) than those they performed themselves ($M = 74$ percent), a finding inconsistent with a multiple-code view.

Language or Activity Based Explanations?

Interestingly enough, all three explanations offered for the SPT effect have their parallels in the verbal memory literature and could be thought of as derived from these approaches. For example, the absence of developmental differences involving adult/child comparisons in memory for particular kinds of information (e.g., frequency of events) has been used to support the view that these kinds of information are processed automatically (Hasher & Zacks, 1979; Johnson & Hasher, 1987). In addition, when participants are encouraged to focus on individual-item processing, induced by encoding instructions (e.g., rating words for pleasantness) or word list structures (e.g., unrelated word strings), recognition memory is enhanced. Finally, the multiple-entry approach to action memory is reminiscent of the dual-code view invoked to account for the concreteness effect and the picture memory effect. For instance, one explanation for the concreteness effect, or the superior memory for concrete words compared to more abstract ones, is that concrete words evoke both a linguistic and pictorial code for the referents whereas abstract words evoke only a linguistic code (Paivio & Csapo, 1973). Similarly, pictures typically lead to better memory because they evoke both visual and linguistic representations, whereas words are more likely to evoke only one kind of code. Pictures are thought to evoke both conceptual and pictorial representations, augmenting their subsequent recall (Durso & Johnson, 1980; Paivio & Csapo, 1973).

Deriving explanations for the enactment effect from explanations for word memory, however, may shift attention away from the characteristics of actions that are most important in memory. Specifically, from the perspective of activity theories (see Ratner & Foley, 1994), persons are goal-directed processors who carry out actions within the context of larger activities in an attempt to bring about results that satisfy some purpose. Central to this perspective is the goal-directed nature of action and the features of an activity that are organized by a person's goal. Actions in the SPT studies, however, are typically not organized into goal-directed sequences and may strip action of its most important features. In essence, the actions in SPT studies mimic surface features of actions, but do not reflect their goal-directed meanings. SPTs become symbols of actions, rather than actions themselves, perhaps leading more easily to reliance on explanations derived from understanding the recall of words, which are symbols in themselves.

There is another reason that theories of verbal learning may have been used to provide explanations for the SPT effect. Action and action memory traditionally have been considered less conceptually based than other forms of representation and of less significance as individuals grow older (e.g., Piaget, 1952). In theories of cognitive development, action typically represents only the means by which more symbolic knowledge structures are created. These more abstract structures are then seen as replacing rather than complementing the earlier and more primitive action-based representations (e.g., Oppenheimer, 1991). Given the assumption that this process is one of replacement, actions have often been devalued historically and treated as derivative in nature (e.g., Heindel & Kose, 1990). Consequently, analysis of action features may not have been perceived necessary because only the cognitive products supported by action were of interest. Action, however, represents the complex interface between the internal and psychological world and the external and physical world. Action guides understanding of human activity becoming more, not less, central to the individual's developing cognitive system. In addition, new characterizations of cognitive development challenge whether reasoning develops on the basis of perception and action, suggesting instead that representation, perception, and action develop in parallel (e.g., Spelke, Breinlinger, Macomber, & Jacobson, 1992) and independently contribute to changes in cognition.

Nevertheless, at the heart of some dual-code views of action memory emerging from the SPT literature is an effort to assign special status to action information. Engelkamp and Zimmer's (1994, as cited in Engelkamp & Zimmer, 1994) multimodal model of the SPT effect is clearly an attempt to show that the physical aspects of enactment should be central to explanations for action recall. Perhaps, in part, as a consequence of the assumption that conceptual representations replace action representation, many theories of memory ignore the role of the surface features of events in general and the physical aspects of action in particular when accounting for memory performance. Indeed, in an effort to show that enactment effects are mediated by action (i.e., motoric) representations arising from the physical aspects of action, some goal-related but conceptual components of action, such as planning, may have been relegated to play a secondary role in the SPT effect. For example, Zimmer and Engelkamp (1984) asked adults to plan, plan and then perform, or watch someone else perform simple actions. Planning alone and watching led to similar levels of recall (about 26 percent), considerably lower than the level reported for planning and enacting (about 44 percent). This pattern led Zimmer and Engelkamp to conclude that the enactment effect cannot be "reduced" to planning, or more generally, to a conceptually based explanation.

CONTRIBUTIONS OF PLANNING TO ACTIVITY MEMORY

Zimmer and Engelkamp's emphasis on motoric codes in the enactment effect represents an important step forward. This explanation emphasizes the features of actions, rather than the features of words, in the enactment effect. Nevertheless, the explanation does not go far enough because it does not emphasize the features of activities. Activities are composed of actions that are goal-directed, performed in order to accomplish some other purpose, and these goals specify features which in turn are important in influencing activity memory. One of these features is planning, which contributes to activity memory, not because it is conceptual or symbolic, but because it is related to the actor's goal. In order to emphasize action in enactment effects, it is not necessary to de-emphasize conceptual information.

Ratner, Smith, and Bazzy (1987) asked five-year-olds and adults to make clay together. For some actions in the activity, participants only planned what would happen (i.e., deciding what actions were needed to accomplish a subgoal pictorially represented). For other actions, participants performed the actions. Half of each type of action, planned and performed, was carried out by the child and the other half by the experimenter. If the motoric components of actions are critical in the SPT effect, then an advantage in memory for actions that were performed by the participants themselves would be expected. Any effects of planning might augment the advantage in recall of self-performed actions, but actions planned but not performed should not be recalled as well as those both planned and performed. However, this was not the case. Rather, the critical factor influencing recall was whether or not the individual had been directly involved in planning. Self-planned actions were better recalled than other-planned actions regardless of who carried them out.

Similarly, Bender and Levin (1976) showed that when young children are explicitly told to plan interactions involving toys, their memory is better than other children not given planning instructions. Kindergarten children were asked (a) to play with some toys and plan to play with others, (b) to play with some toys and resist playing with others, or (c) to plan to play with toys or to imagine playing with them (without reference to planning). Memory for the imagined actions was much worse for children who were simply told to imagine playing with the toys, leading Bender and Levin to conclude that planning supports memory. This work also suggests that planning and imagining are distinctly different cognitive operations. Along similar lines, Zimmer and Engelkamp (1996) reported that enactment of action descriptions led to better memory than simple imitation of enactments, suggesting, again, that intentional planning is an important component of enactment effect.

Planning may not be the only "prospective process" that contributes to memory. Anticipation of actions may also influence how and how well information is remembered. In a set of collage-making studies we have carried out (e.g., Foley, Ratner, & Passalacqua, 1993; Foley & Ratner, 1998a), children made collages, alternating placement of the collage pieces with a female adult. On a surprise memory test, children identified who contributed particular pieces to the collage, themselves or the person with whom they interacted. Preschoolers' falsely claimed they contributed pieces to the collage that the adult actually contributed, but they rarely claimed the experimenter contributed pieces that the children contributed themselves. When preschoolers were actively involved in making decisions about the collage-making activity (i.e., selecting their own pieces and coordinating their placement), their overall level of confusion about individual contributions was much less. Furthermore, outcome effects interacted with decision making, affecting the overall levels of errors. When adults controlled the selection and directed the placement of collage pieces, preschoolers who made identifiable collages were more confused than those who made abstract ones, but when these operations were under children's control the effect of collage type, or outcome was reversed with greater confusions following the creation of abstract collages rather than identifiable ones.

We interpreted preschoolers' misattribution bias to claim responsibility for the actions of the adult as an indication that anticipations about the actions of another person as well as anticipations about one's own actions influence activity memory. As children observe another individual initiate his or her actions, they may imagine themselves doing, thinking, or feeling as the other person acts, thinks, or feels. Later on, when asked to identify who performed the action, they may mistakenly claim that they did because they become confused between the representation of the actual action with the representation of their anticipation.

Similarly, after learning in which rooms to place furniture in a dollhouse, preschoolers are more likely to claim they placed objects actually placed by an adult if they first learned where to place the objects in a collaborative context (Ratner, Foley, & Gimpert, 2000). Again, we interpret these memory errors as evidence for the role of anticipations in children's memory for actions. As when making the collage with an adult, we argue that children anticipate the way in which they would place the furniture pieces into the dollhouse while watching the adult place her pieces, and later mistakenly think they placed the pieces themselves. In noncollaborative contexts in which children have no opportunity to observe the adult, errors are low and children are no more likely to say that they carried out the adult's action than they are to say that the adult carried out their action. Several studies support the role of these anticipatory processes in activity memory (Foley et al., 1993; Foley & Ratner, 1998b; Ratner, Foley, & Gimpert, 2000), but the important point here is that collectively these studies highlight the role of planning and anticipation in memory.

Why these apparent contradictions about the role of prospective processing in action memory? In the SPT studies, there is typically no goal guiding the enactment of the simple actions except the goal to meet the experimenters' requests to perform the actions. In contrast, in the clay-making studies, the Bender and Levin study, the collage studies, and the dollhouse study, each action was performed for the purpose of accomplishing some goal.

In source-monitoring studies as well, the effects of goal-related processing are apparent. For example, in early source monitoring studies, adults and children were asked to perform simple actions not unlike those included in the SPT studies. On a surprise memory test, they were asked to remember who performed each action, one type of source-monitoring task. Not only were both age groups quite good at reporting the source of each action, but when a mistake was made there was no systematic pattern in the error rates, as in the collage and dollhouse studies. Adults and children were just as likely to mistakenly claim they performed an action that was performed by someone else as they were to claim the reverse (e.g., Foley, Johnson, & Raye, 1983; Foley & Johnson, 1985). But when there is an activity goal, such as in the collage and dollhouse studies described earlier, biases in source monitoring errors emerge.

The SPT effect may not be "reducible" to planning because planning is relatively irrelevant to carrying out the actions in an SPT task. Without goals directing and organizing the actions, motoric features may be important in supporting memory because there are no other features available. But this does not mean that planning does not play an important role in activity memory. When characteristics of actions derived from their goal-directed nature are present, these features may become more critical, unless the motoric aspects of the action are centrally related to the goal of the action, such as in the case of dance or sports. Again, processes that are based both on action and on conceptual thinking are undoubtedly important in activity memory.

A THEORETICAL FRAMEWORK FOR ACTIVITY MEMORY

Action enactment effects can be conceptualized in at least two ways. Action enactment can be added to the list of factors known to affect memory for verbal materials, such as descriptions of actions. Or action enactment can be an object of study in itself. From our point of view, although the SPT effects were initially reported within the context of the study of verbal descriptions, efforts to explain these enhancing effects clearly suggest that action memory is deserving of more prominence. If the goal is to account for enactment effects, then extant theoretical explanations for the SPT effect fall short as explanatory mechanisms because of their failure to include consideration of the goal-directed nature of action memory.

Our *Activity Memory Framework*, in contrast, begins with a consideration of the goal-directed nature of actions (Ratner & Foley, 1994). Our survey of activity theory (Ratner & Foley, 1994) examined both behavioral and cognitively based perspectives, including those of European origin (e.g., Barsalou, 1991; Heckhausen & Beckman, 1990; Kruglanski, 1996; Leontiev, 1978; Savitsky, Medvac & Gilovich, 1997). On the basis of action descriptions within these theories, we identified four principle features of activities that are specified by the goal(s) of the actor(s) and should influence memory: (1) prospective processes (i.e., anticipations and plans that guide the activity), (2) outcome(s) of actions and activities, (3) relational structures (i.e., the sequence of acts that may lead up to the outcome(s)), and (4) the retrospective activations of related and past activities.

These features lead to a set of questions about action memory that are very different from those raised in theoretical approaches to the study of the SPT effect, in particular, and action recall, in general (Ratner & Foley, 1994). For example, questions concerning the number of actions in a list would become of interest only in relation to the links (if any) among the actions temporally ordered. Presumably as the number of actions in a list increases, the opportunity for affecting their relational structure increases.

At first glance, it might appear that our framework is simply a more elaborate version of other multiple entry views of memory. Activity features could influence memory because they add perceptual, motor, or conceptual codes to the representation of an activity, rendering the activity more memorable (Bäckman, Nilsson, & Chalom, 1986; Cohen, 1989; Engelkamp & Zimmer, 1985). However, we argue that feature effects are not simply reducible to elaboration effects. Rather, they influence memory because they are related to the actor's goals above and beyond the perceptual, conceptual, or motoric representations resulting from their enactments. We share the view with these dual code explanations for the SPT effect that action-based structures complement other kinds of information. Our view departs from multiple code views, however, because of a shift in focus. Rather than focusing on the kinds of information that may be represented in action memory (e.g., visual, auditory, motoric), we focus on the goal-directed nature of actions. As a result, although motoric information may indeed be represented in action memory, if it is, its importance is tied to its connection with the purpose and/or outcomes of the actions. Before elaborating on the kinds of questions that emerge from our framework, each feature will be described in brief.

Prospective Processes

Prospective processes include both complex and deliberate plans to produce outcomes and anticipations of outcomes that may be more automatic. Both anticipations and plans related to goals may occur before or during the activity. In SPT studies, as well as many of our own, the plans have been coincident with the enactment. But in our studies, the actions have been performed in the context of goal-directed activities that guide requests to perform the actions (e.g., making collages, making clay, or completing other science-like projects). Regardless of the temporal relationship between planning and enacting, our framework predicts that the qualities of the plans and anticipations should influence memory. These qualities include the goal guiding the activity, the level of effortful involvement of the actor, or the presence and type of symbolic markers. In a new study just completed, we have convincing evidence for the importance of goals. Preschoolers were asked to trace and imagine tracing pictures of objects; when those activities occurred in the context of listening to a story involving the pictures, children were subsequently much more confused about which pictures they actually traced and which they only imagined tracing (Ratner, Foley, & Gimpert, 2000).

Children are certainly not alone in their tendency to claim undue responsibility for the outcomes of social exchanges. For example, cryptomnesia effects, or acts of inadvertent plagiarism, indicate that adults generate responses they believe to be original to them when actually the responses were expressed by someone with whom they were interacting. As Marsh and his colleagues have shown, adults will claim they generated responses actually generated by others (Brown & Murphy, 1986; Marsh & Bower, 1993; Marsh & Landau, 1995; Marsh, Hicks, & Bink, 1998). These errors can be interpreted as evidence that adults covertly anticipate what others are likely to say, later taking credit for the utterances, forgetting their responses were only anticipations. Thus, the role of recoding processes mediating anticipations in adults and children alike is worthy of systematic exploration.

Relational Structure

Acts are related to one another to compose an interconnected sequence (e.g., Nelson, 1986; Ratner & Foley, 1994; Wertsch, 1985). At least two organizations are available for conceptualizing relational structure. Acts can be organized in a linear way, ordered in time, with no goal- or outcome-related connections (e.g., Mandler, 1984). Or they may be organized hierarchically, reflecting culturally defined motives, personally defined goals, or the operations giving rise to the actions themselves. In either case, our framework leads to the expectation that relational structure will affect memory for actions as well as for the agent of those actions. And, indeed, we review a considerable body of work that is consistent with this view (Ratner & Foley, 1994). By way of illustration, acts that are most causally related to the goal of a script are remembered best by three to five year olds as well as older individuals (e.g., Nelson & Gruendel, 1981). Further, younger children can reproduce the hierarchical structure of a repeated event, although more of the structure emerges with greater experience (Ratner, Smith, & Padgett, 1990).

Outcomes

Activities involve people engaged in purposeful actions, acting on objects, and with each other, to achieve some result or outcome. As a reflection of an actor's goals, outcomes should be well remembered and they are. Memory for the outcomes of actions is remarkably good whether actions are actually enacted (e.g., Ratner, Smith, & Dion, 1986) or described as part of a story (e.g., Mandler & Johnson, 1977). The perceptual coherence of an outcome also influences whether action source (i.e., who performed which action) is well remembered (Foley et al., 1993) and how well the overall activity is recalled (Ratner, Bukowski, & Foley, 1992; Ratner, Foley, & McCaskill, in press).

Even SPT effects are influenced by outcomes, perhaps because outcomes are more relevant to isolated actions than plans. For example, Smyth (1991) showed that movements that lead to some outcome (e.g., pick up a ball) are remembered better than those that involve no outcome at all (e.g., point to a ball). Similarly, Ratner and Hill (1991) found that children recalled more actions if the actions resulted in an observable outcome during encoding. Visible changes in state also enhance source-monitoring performance. Young children are quite confused about what they traced and what they imagined tracing unless the actual tracing activities produced visible consequences (Foley et al., 1983).

Finally, actions that produce no outcomes but share surface features with actions that do produce outcomes are remembered poorly. Ratner and Foley (1996) presented children with two types of actions. In one version of the action an outcome was produced, but in another version no outcome occurred. For example, children played with a puppet suspended on strings in a box. In one version of the action, children pulled the strings and the puppet moved (outcome). In the other version of the action, children pulled the strings, but the puppet did not move (no outcome). Children were more likely to recall the action, "pull the strings," when the puppet moved.

By considering outcomes and prospective processes as distinct features in our model, we certainly do not intend to suggest that their effects are independent. The anticipation of an action (or the planning of that action) and its outcome make clear the complexity of action, indicating that activity memory cannot be "reducible" to any one feature. An outcome may be anticipated and match the representation for this anticipation, or it may be unanticipated. When not anticipated, outcomes can evoke surprise or confusion. When complex activities are the focus of study, the functional significance of the activity should figure prominently, binding the effects of outcomes and plans in intriguing and significant ways.

Retrospective Processes

Retrospective processes involve the activation of any aspect of a past instantiation of a present enactment (e.g. Foley, Santini, & Sopasakis, 1989). So, when symbolically showing an adult how to play with toys, a child may think of her own version of the toy or think about an occasion in which she played with that toy. These reflections may also be represented in memory, later serving as retrieval cues or as cues for discriminating the source of memories. For example, if a child remembers what she thought about when pretending to play with a toy guitar, she may be better able to remember that she only pretended to use that toy (Foley, Harris, & Hermann, 1994). Retrospective processes are included in all models of memory (e.g., associative, information processing, connectionist) and are labeled in various ways (e.g., inter-item associations, script-based associations, knowledge effects). Although retrospective processing is simply another kind of memory entry, our decision to identify it as a separate feature calls attention to the timing of its occurrence. In particular, we are interested in the retrospective processing that occurs as an activity unfolds. Here it may play an important role in modulating attention among the other three features of actions.

Perhaps one reason that enactment enhances recall is because it is more likely to evoke retrospective processing. When children are asked to imagine their parents performing actions that involve the use of two objects (e.g., scissors and newspaper), they often report thinking about occasions in which their parents used these objects at home (e.g., "I thought of my mom cutting out the picture for me"). Recall is better for those words that evoked this sort of retrospective processing (Foley, Belch, Mann, & McLean, 1999).

CONNECTIONS BETWEEN THE ACTIVITY MEMORY FRAMEWORK AND OTHER MODELS

Our framework is not unique in its suggestion that reflection processes, such as prospective and retrospective processes, may create "entries" in memory representations for events. We know that perceptual events, including action, trigger internally-based ones (e.g., implicit associative responses), and these internally-based events also give rise to memory representations that are sometimes mistaken as memories for actual events. Both words and implicit responses to the words as well as symbolic actions (e.g., Deese, 1959) and inferences about instruments of actions (Paris & Lindauer, 1976) are thought to be represented in memory. Consider the resurrection of Deese's paradigm for the study of implicit associative responses for the study of false memories (Roediger & McDermott, 1995) as a case in point. More recent developmental memory models share this point of view. For example, Reyna & Brainerd's (1995) fuzzy-trace theoretical model is consistent in its suggestion that events have multiple representations in memory—one version more generic in form and the other more specific in its relationship to the actual event. Many factors determine which of these representations are accessed, including the purpose in remembering and the nature of the questions guiding the act of remembering (Brainerd & Reyna, 1995; in press; Reyna & Brainerd, 1995; Reyna & Kiernan, 1994; 1995). Clearly, then, models of memory emanating from the study of verbal materials have long acknowledged that the consequences of reflection may be represented in memory.

Moreover, Marcia Johnson and her colleagues have argued that the kind of operations giving rise to these reflective processes (e.g., relatively automatic vs. more effortful processing) are also represented in memory (Johnson, 1983, 1992; Johnson & Chalfonte, 1994; Johnson, Foley, Suengas, & Raye, 1988; Johnson, Hastroudi, & Lindsay, 1993; Johnson & Raye, 1981; Johnson, Raye, Foley, & Foley, 1981). These "entries" about reflective processes include search processes rendering solutions to word problems, imaginal processes resulting in the creation of images, and reflective processes involved in reminiscing (Johnson, 1983; Johnson et al., 1993). Indeed, over 15 years of research on source monitoring ability, or the ability to distinguish between the sources of memory (e.g., perception vs. imagination), confirm this aspect of Johnson's theoretical framework. This kind of evidence has led Johnson to propose a more elaborate version of a multiple-entry model (MEM), characterized by three kinds of subsystems of representation: sensory, perceptual, and reflective (Johnson, 1983).

According to the MEM model, reflective processing includes reflections about ongoing experiences (e.g., noticing commonalities between events) as well as reactivations of information not currently available to consciousness). In brief, these reflective processes may go beyond the immediate consequences of perception and include the processes mediating the manipulation of information, the anticipation of events, and the consideration of alternative perspectives about the interpretation of events. These reflective processes may vary from the relatively automatic activation of information to more deliberate acts and are referred to as "supervisor" and "executive" functions. Supervisor functions are thought to mediate plans and outcome assessments, whereas executive functions are thought to mediate more effortful cognitive acts (e.g., such as those guiding problems solving and memory searches). The important point for present purposes, however, is the notion that the occurrence of cognitive operations also leads to potential "entries" in the representational system.

In our theoretical framework, reflective activity also figures prominently. We place particular emphasis on the perspective a person adopts during anticipation. A shift in the perspective adopted can affect source-monitoring for both adults (Foley et al., 1991) and children (Foley & Ratner, 1998a; 1998b) alike. Moreover, these perspectives are linked to goals guiding children's activity in both individual (Ratner et al., 2000, Experiment 1) and collaborative contexts (Foley et al., 1993; Foley & Ratner, 1998b, Experiments 2 and 3).

We assign separate status to prospective and retrospective processes, either of which could be deliberate or automatic in kind (Ratner & Foley, 1994). Within a developmental context, our distinction is particularly important because the emergence of these two kinds of processes appears to follow different time-courses (Ratner & Foley, 1994). Equally important, our approach calls attention to the importance of considering the content of these processes (e.g., type of plan, focus of the anticipation) and the context from which it arises (e.g., shared vs. solitary activities) (e.g., Foley & Ratner, 1998b). What is critical in our approach, however, is the relation between the consequences of reflection and the goal motivating the action or activity. The contribution reflective processes make to activity memory occurs not because of an additional, or complex, conceptual code, but because of the relation between the information and the goal of the activity. Indeed, the effect of any feature on memory cannot be explained solely in terms of the additional enhancement it provides. We argue that if the feature is centrally related to the goal of the activity, then its effect will be greater than if the feature is peripheral to the actor's goal.

For example, both multiple-entry models of memory and our model predict that actions leading to visible consequences of an action would be better remembered, and indeed they are (Foley, Aman, & Gutch, 1987). A multiple-entry model might explain these effects by suggesting that the actions themselves give rise to motoric codes based on kinesthetic cues associated with the production of the actions as well as visual cues associated with the consequences following enactments. Visual consequences could be effective cues because they provide external markers of an action; however, the presence (or absence) of visible consequences alone does not fully capture an explanation for the outcome effects. The nature of the outcome figures prominently in the effects, in part, because of its relationship to the goal of the activity.

If outcomes were important only because of the external markers provided, other markers, such as objects, would be expected to lead to the same effects. Yet interactions with physical objects do not necessarily influence memory performance as visible consequences of actions do. For instance, 3- and 4-year-olds were more confused than older children when asked to remember whether they really played with a toy or used a toy substitute. The toy substitutes were objects (e.g., blocks, tubes) or gestures (e.g., pantomiming the use of the objects with the hands). Young children's confusions were comparable for the two kinds of substitutes, despite the fact that only one involved object manipulation. Specifically, children were more likely to claim that they actually played with a toy when they only pretended to do so (on average, committing 2.00 errors out of a possible 8) than they were to claim that they used a substitute when they actually played with a toy (Foley, Harris, & Hermann, 1994). On average, they committed 2.00 and .94 errors, respectively (out of a possible 8). However, this difference was comparable for the two types of toy substitutes, that is, gestures and toy substitutes, with means equal to 1.06 and .94, respectively.

Similarly, in studies of the ability to discriminate between memories for real and imagined activities, the presence of physical props (colorful cardboard cutouts) does not enhance performance. Children (four, six, and eight year olds) drew pictures and imagined themselves drawing other pictures. Drawing and imagining occurred in the presence or absence of the colorful cutouts. Developmental differences were found in the ability to discriminate real from imagined activities in that 4-year-olds performed worse than the two older groups, as summarized in Table 5.3, but at no age did performance depend on the presence of the props (Harris & Foley, 1993). Thus, neither the mere presence of physical objects (Harris & Foley, 1993) nor their manipulation (Foley, Harris,

TABLE 5.3. Proportion Source Monitoring Score

	Age of Participant		
	4 yrs	6 yrs	Adult
Prop Absent	.80	.95	.99
Prop Present	.80	.95	.99

& Hermann, 1994) facilitates performance, suggesting that visible consequences are more than physical markers of activities. Visible consequences associated with actions appear important because they are the products of children's action and not because they are contiguous with events, reminding children that the events occurred.

This point is further supported by the results of the Ratner and Foley (1996) study. In that study actions with outcomes were remembered better than actions without outcomes; however, this difference occurred only when the child performed the actions. Half the actions were carried out by the child and the other half were performed by the experimenter. When recalling the actions performed by the experimenter, actions with outcomes were recalled no better than actions without outcomes. Thus, the visible consequences created by outcomes in themselves were not important in supporting memory; it was the relation between the outcome and the actor, mediated by his or her goal, that was critical for improved recall.

WHAT IMPLICATIONS DOES THE ACTIVITY MEMORY FRAMEWORK HAVE FOR ACTION MEMORY RESEARCH?

Our Activity Memory Framework is an invitation to raise broader questions about the basis for enactment effects that emphasize persons as goal-directed agents. Questions that reflect the purposive nature of voluntary actions shift the focus from quantitative to qualitative characteristics of the activity. For example, rather than asking whether the length of action lists influences memory, we might ask whether and when a list can be integrated into a sequence and recalled more effectively. Indeed, memory performance does improve if isolated actions can function as part of a goal-directed sequence (e.g., Fivush, Pipe, Murachver, & Reese, 1997; Hutton, Sheppard, Rusted, & Ratner, 1996). Similarly, will the number of actions required to complete an activity be less important in influencing memory than the qualities of a product created or less important than the person for whom the activity is performed? Will the characteristics of visible outcomes, such as the cues they leave behind, be more important than their mere presence?

More broadly, with its emphasis on person(s) and goal(s), the Activity Memory Framework provides a useful heuristic for examining the complex ways in which goals may influence activity memory in more applied contexts. We know that young children exhibit virtually no confusion about who did what when there is no goal guiding their actions (Foley & Johnson, 1985). Yet, young children are very confused about action source following the completion of a shared activity (Foley & Ratner, 1998a; Foley, Querido, & Ratner, 1997; Ratner et al., 2000). Because young children share their lives and activities with so many social partners, confusions may be more likely in real life contexts. Are there some contexts or situations that promote confusion and others that reduce it? Are there some types of social partners that are more likely to create confusion? To what extent does the other person's goals also influence children's reports? While participating in a shared activity, such as reading a book together, what will the consequences be for the child when asked to report what happened if the person with whom the child interacts works to deceive him or her (e.g., by convincing the child that someone performed actions the person did not perform)? To what extent will the goals of the person asking the questions affect the child's performance?

These are but a few of the intriguing questions that call for attention once a neglected but central feature of enactments, their goal-directed nature, is restored to a position of prominence. We offer the Activity Memory model as a framework to help generate a new set of questions about memory for actions.

REFERENCES

Bäckman, L. (1985). Further evidence for the lack of adult age differences on free recall of subject-performed tasks: The importance of motor action. *Human Learning, 4*, 79–87.

Bäckman, L., & Nilsson, L. G. (1984). Aging effects in free recall: An exception to the rule. *Human Learning, 3*, 53–69.

Bäckman, L., Nilsson, L. G., & Chalom, D. (1986). New evidence on the nature of the encoding of action events. *Memory & Cognition, 14*, 339–346.

Baker-Ward, L., Hess, T., & Flannagan, D. (1990). The effects of involvement on children's memory for events. *Cognitive Development, 5*, 55–69.

Barsalou, L. (1991). Deriving categories to achieve goals. In G. H. Bower (Ed.), *The psychology of learning and motivation: Advances in research and theory* (Vol. 27, pp. 1–64). New York: Academic Press.

Bender, B. G., & Levin, J. R. (1976). Motor activity, anticipated motor activity and young children's associative learning. *Child Development, 47*, 560–562.

Braine, M., & Hardy, J. (1982). On what case categories there are, why they are, and how they develop: An anagram of *a priori* considerations, speculation, and evidence from children. In E. Wanner & L. R. Gleitman (Eds.), *Language acquisition: The state of the art* (pp. 219–239). New York: Cambridge University Press.

Brainerd, C. J., & Reyna, V. F. (1995). Autosuggestibility in memory development. *Cognitive Psychology, 28*, 65–101.

Brainerd, C. J., & Reyna, V. F. (1998). When events that were never experienced are easier to remember than events that were. *Psychological Science, 9*, 484–490.

Brown, A. S., & Murphy, D. R. (1989). Cryptomnesia: Delineating inadvertent plagiarism. *Journal of Experimental Psychology: Learning, Memory and Cognition, 15*, 432–442.

Cohen, R. L. (1981). On the generality of some memory laws. *Scandanavian Journal of Psychology, 22*, 276–281.

Cohen, R. L. (1983). The effect of encoding variables on the free recall of words and action events. *Memory & Cognition, 11*, 573–582.

Cohen, R. L. (1989). Memory for action events: The power of enactment. *Educational Psychology Review, 1*, 57–80.

Cohen, R. L., & Bean, G. (1983). Memory in educable mentally retarded adults: Deficit in subject or experimenter? *Intelligence, 7*, 287–298.

Cohen, R. L. Peterson, M., & Mantini-Atkinson, T. (1987). Interevent differences in event memory: Why are some events more recallable than others? *Memory & Cognition, 15*, 109–118.

Cohen, R. L., & Stewart, M. (1982). How to avoid developmental effects in free recall. *Scandanavian Journal of Psychology, 23*, 9–16.

Deese, J. (1959). On the prediction of occurrence of particular verbal intrusions in immediate recall. *Journal of Experimental Psychology, 58*, 17–22.

Durso, F. T., & Johnson, M. K. (1980). The effects of orienting tasks on recognition, recall and modality confusion of pictures and words. *Journal of Verbal Learning and Verbal Behavior, 19*, 416–429.

Engelkamp, J. (1986). Differences between imaginal and motor encoding. In F. Klix & H. Hagendorf (Eds.), *Human memory and cognitive capabilities*. Amsterdam: Elsevier, North-Holland.

Engelkamp, J. (1997). Memory for self-performed tasks versus memory for performed tasks. *Memory and Cognition, 27*, 117–124.

Engelkamp, J., & Krumnacker, H. (1980). Imagery and motor processes in the retention of verbal materials. *Zeitschrift für experimentelle und angewandte Psychologie, 27*, 511–533.

Engelkamp, J., & Zimmer, H. D. (1985). Motor programs and their relation to semantic memory. *General Journal of Psychology, 9*, 239–254.

Engelkamp, J. & Zimmer, H. D. (1994). *The human memory: A multimodal approach*. Seattle: Hogrefe.

Engelkamp, J., & Zimmer, H. D. (1995). Similarity of movement in recognition of self-performed tasks and of verbal tasks. *British Journal of Psychology, 86*, 241–252.

Engelkamp, J., Zimmer, H. D., & Biegelmann, U. E. (1993). Bizarreness effects in verbal tasks and subject-performed tasks. *European Journal of Cognitive Psychology, 5*, 393–415.

Engelkamp, J., Zimmer, H. D., Mohr, G., & Sellen, O. (1994). Memory for self-performed tasks: Self-performing during recognition. *Memory & Cognition, 22*, 34–39.

Fivush, R., Pipe, M. E., Murachver, T., & Reese, E. (1997). Events spoken and unspoken: Implications of language and memory development for the recovered memory debate. In M. A. Conway (Ed.), *Recovered and False Memories* (pp. 34–62). New York: Oxford University Press.

Flavell, J. H. (1985). *Cognitive Development*. Englewood Cliffs, NJ: Prentice-Hall.

Foellinger, D., & Trabasso, T. (1977). Seeing, hearing and doing: A developmental study of memory for actions. *Child Development, 48*, 1482–1489.

Foley, M. A., Aman, C., & Gutch, D. (1987). Discriminating between action memories: Children's use of kinesthetic cues and visible consequences. *Journal of Experimental Child Psychology, 44*, 335–347.

Foley, M. A., Belch, C., Mann, R., & McLean, M. (1999). Self-referencing: How incessant the stream? *American Journal of Psychology, 112*, 73–96.

Foley, M. A., Bouffard, V., Raag, T., & Disanto-Rose, M. (1991). The effects of type of imagery and type of movement on memory for dance. *Psychological Research, 53*, 251–259.

Foley, M. A., Harris, J., & Hermann, S. (1994). Developmental comparisons of the ability to discriminate between memories for real and memories for symbolic enactments. *Developmental Psychology, 30*, 206–217.

Foley, M. A., & Johnson, M. K. (1985). Confusions between memories for performed and imagined actions: A developmental comparison. *Child Development, 56*, 1145–1155.

Foley, M. A., Johnson, M. K., & Raye, C. L. (1983). Age-related changes in confusion between memories for thoughts and memories for speech. *Child Development, 54*, 51–60.

Foley, M. A., Querido, J., & Ratner, H. H. (1997). Who found Waldo—you or me? Paper presented at the Eastern Psychological Association Meetings, Washington, DC.

Foley, M. A., & Ratner, H. H. (1998a). Children's recoding in memory for collaboration: A way of learning from others. *Cognitive Development, 13*, 91–108.

Foley, M. A., & Ratner, H. H. (1998b). Distinguishing between memories for thoughts and deeds: The role of prospective processing in children's source monitoring. *British Journal of Developmental Psychology, 16*, 465–484.

Foley, M. A., Ratner, H. H., & Passalacqua, C. (1993). Appropriating the actions of another: Implications for children's memory and learning, *Cognitive Development, 8*, 373–401.

Foley, M. A., Santini, C., & Sopasakis, M. (1989). Discriminating between memories: Evidence for children's use of spontaneous elaborations. *Journal of Experimental Child Psychology, 48*, 146–169.

Harris, J., & Foley, M. A. (1993). An investigation of preschoolers' ability to discriminate between memories of real and memories of imagined events. Unpublished manuscript.

Heckhausen, H., & Beckmann, J. (1990). Intentional action and action slips. *Psychological Review, 97*, 36–48.

Helstrup, T. (1987). One, two or three memories? A problem-solving approach to memory for performed acts. *Acta Psychologica, 66*, 37–68

Heindel, P., & Kose, G. (1990). The effects of motoric action and organization on children's memory. *Journal of Experimental Child Psychology, 50*, 416–428.

Hunt, R. R., & Einstein, G. O. (1981). Relational and item-specific information in memory. *Journal of Verbal Learning and Verbal Behavior, 20*, 497–514.

Hutton, S., Sheppard, L., Rusted, J. M., & Ratner, H. H. (1996). Structuring the acquisition and retrieval environment to facilitate learning in individuals with dementia of the Alzheimer type. *Memory, 4*, 113–130.

Johnson, L., Perlmutter, M., & Trabasso, T. (1979). The leg bone is connected to the knee bone: Children's representation of body parts in memory, drawing and language. *Child Development, 50*, 1192–1202.

Johnson, M. K. (1983). A multiple-entry modular memory system. In G. Bower (Ed.), *Advances in the psychology of learning and motivation* (Vol. 17, pp. 81–123). New York: Academic Press.

Johnson, M. K. (1992). MEM: Mechanisms of recollection. *Journal of Cognitive Neuroscience, 4,* 268–280.

Johnson, M. K., & Chalfonte, B. L. (1994). Binding complex memories: The role of reactivation and the hippocampus. In D. L. Schacter & E. Tulving (Eds.), *Memory systems 1994* (pp. 311–350). Cambridge: MIT Press.

Johnson, M. K., Foley, M. A., Suengas, A. G., & Raye, C. L. (1988). Phenomenal characteristics for perceived and imagined autobiographical events. *Journal of Experimental Psychology: General, 117,* 371–376.

Johnson, M. K., Hastroudi, S., Lindsay, D. L. (1993). Source monitoring. *Psychological Bulletin, 114,* 3–28.

Johnson, M. K., & Raye, C. L. (1981). Reality monitoring. *Psychological Review, 88,* 67–85.

Johnson, M. K., Raye, C. L., Foley, H. J., & Foley, M. A. (1981). Cognitive operations and decision biases in reality monitoring. *American Journal of Psychology, 94,* 37–64.

Kruglanski, A. W. (1996). Goals as knowledge structures. In P. M. Gollwitzer & J. A. Bargh (Eds.), The psychology of action: Linking cognition and motivation to behavior (pp. 599–618). New York: Guildord.

Leontiev, A. N. (1978). Activity, consciousness, and personality. Englewood Cliffs, NJ: Prentice-Hall.

Mandler, J. (1984). *Stories, scripts, and scenes: Aspects of schema theory.* Hillsdale: Erlbaum.

Mandler, J., & Johnson, N. (1977). Remembrance of things parsed: Story structure and recall. *Cognitive Psychology, 9,* 111–157.

Marsh, R. L., & Bower, G. H. (1993). Eliciting cryptomnesia: Unconscious plagiarism in a puzzle task. *Journal of Experimental Psychology: Learning, Memory and Cognition, 19,* 673–688.

Marsh, R. L., Hicks, J. L., & Bink, M. L. (1998). Activation completed, uncompleted and partially completed intentions. *Journal of Experimental Psychology: Learning, Memory and Cognition, 24,* 350–361.

Marsh, R. L., & Landau, J. D. (1995). Item availability in cryptomnesia: Assessing its role in two paradigms of unconscious plagiarism. *Journal of Experimental Psychology: Learning, Memory and Cognition, 21,* 1568–1582.

Mohr, G., Engelkamp, J., & Zimmer, H. D. (1989). Recall and recognition of self-performed actions. *Psychological Research, 51,* 181–187.

Nelson, K. (1986). *Event knowledge: Structure and function in development.* Hillsdale, N.J.: LEA.

Nelson, K., & Gruendel, J. (1981). Generalized event representations: Basic building blocks of cognitive development. In M. E. Lamb & A. L. Brown (Eds.), *Advances in developmental psychology* (pp. 131–158). Hillsdale, NJ: Erlbaum.

Oppenheimer, L. (1991). The concept of action: A historical perspective. In L. Oppenheimer & J. Valsiner (Eds.), *The origins of action: Interdisciplinary and international perspective* (pp. 1–35). New York: Springer-Verlag.

Paris, S. G., & Lindauer, B. (1976). The role of inference in children's comprehension and memory for sentences. *Cognitive Psychology, 8,* 217–227.

Paivio, A., & Csapo, K. (1973). Picture superiority in free recall: Imagery or coding? *Cognitive Psychology, 5*, 176–206.

Piaget, J. (1952). *The origins of intelligence in children.* New York: International Universities Press.

Price, D., & Goodman, G. (1990). Visting the wizard: Children's memory for a recurring event. *Child Development, 61*, 684–680.

Ratner, H. H., Bukowski, P., & Foley, M. A. (Apr. 1992). Now you see it, now you don't: The role of action and outcome in children's event memory. Paper presented at the conference on Human Development, Atlanta, Ga.

Ratner, H. H., & Foley, M. A. (1994). A unifying framework for the development of children's activity memory. *Advances in Child Development and Behavior, 25*, 33–105.

Ratner, H. H., & Foley, M. A. (Aug. 1996). Children's activity memory: When are self-actions remembered better than others' actions? Paper presented at the International Congress of Psychology, Montreal, Canada.

Ratner, H. H., & Foley, M. A. (Apr. 1997). Children's collaborative learning: Reconstructions of the other in the self. Paper presented at the Biennial Meetings of the Society for Research in Child Development. Washington, DC.

Ratner, H. H., Foley, M. A., & McCaskill, P. (in press). Understanding children's activity memory: The Role of Outcomes. *Journal of Experimental Child Psychology.*

Ratner, H. H., Foley, M. A., & Gimpert, N. (2000). Person perspectives on children's memory and learning: What do source-monitoring failures reveal? In K. P. Roberts & M.Blades (Eds.), *Children's Source-monitoring.* Mahwah, NJ: Erlbaum p. 85–114.

Ratner, H. H., & Hill, L. (1991). The development of children's action memory: When do actions speak louder than words? *Psychological Research, 53*, 195–202.

Ratner, H. H., Smith, B., & Bazzy, D. (Apr. 1987). The role of planning and acting in memory for events. Paper presented at the meeting of the Society for Research in Child Development, Baltimore, MD.

Ratner, H. H., Smith, B., & Dion, S. (1986). Development of memory for events. *Journal of Experimental Child Psychology, 41*, 411–428.

Ratner, H. H., Smith, B., & Padgett, R. J. (1990). Children's organization of events and event memories. In R. Fivush & J. A. Hudson (Eds.), *Knowing and remembering in young children* (pp. 65–93). Cambridge: Cambridge University Press.

Reyna, V. F., & Brainerd, C. J. (1995). Fuzzy-trace theory: An interim synthesis. *Individual Differences, 7*, 1–75.

Reyna, V. F., & Kiernan, B. (1994). Development of gist versus verbatim memory in sentence recognition: Effects of lexical familiarity, semantic content, encoding instructions, and retention interval. *Developmental Psychology, 30*, 178–191.

Reyna, V. F., & Kiernan, B. (1995). Meaning, memory and the development of metaphor. *Metaphor and Symbolic Activity, 10*, 309–331.

Roediger, H. L. III, & McDermott, K. B. (1995). Creating false memories: Remembering words not presented in lists. *Journal of Experimental Psychology: Learning, Memory & Cognition, 21*, 803–814.

Saltz, E., & Donnenwerth-Nolan, S. (1981). Does motoric imagery facilitate memory for sentences? A selective interference test. *Journal of Verbal Learning and Verbal Behavior, 20*, 322–332.

Savitsky, K., Medvec, V. H., & Gilovich, T. (1997). Remembering and regretting: The Zeigarnik effect and the cognitive availability of regrettable actions and inactions. *Personality and Social Psychology Bulletin, 23*, 248–257.

Smyth, M. (July 1991). *Pick and point: Action memory with and without specific interactions with objects.* Paper presented at the International Conference on Memory, Lancaster, England.

Spelke, E. S., Breinlinger, K., Macomber, J., & Jacobson, K. (1992). Origins of knowledge. *Psychological Review, 99*, 605–632.

Wertsch, J. (1985). *Vygotsky and the social formation of mind.* Cambridge: Harvard University Press.

Zimmer, H. D. (1991). Memory after motoric encoding in a generation-recognition model. *Psychological Research, 53*, 226–231.

Zimmer, H. D., & Engelkamp, J. (1985). An attempt to distinguish between kinematic and motor memory components. *Acta Psychologia, 58*, 81–106.

Zimmer, H. D., & Engelkamp, J. (1996). Routes to actions and their efficacy for remembering. *Memory, 4*, 59–78.

CHAPTER 6

What Is the Meaning of a Memory-Systems Approach?

Comments on Engelkamp

Lars-Göran Nilsson and Reza Kormi-Nouri

The notion that memory can be divided into different systems is relatively new. When Tulving (1972) made the distinction between episodic and semantic memory he paved the way for a more elaborate conceptualization, in which memory systems was a key term (Tulving, 1983, 1984, 1985). Tulving's view of memory and the use of this key term has later been refined and developed in many steps (e.g., Tulving, 1993), and the term has been discussed and adopted by many others (e.g., Weinberger, McGaugh, & Lynch, 1985).

The memory-systems approach has now also been adopted by Engelkamp (this volume) for memory research in general, but for research on memory for enacted events in particular. However, it is not immediately transparent to us what Engelkamp means by his version of the systems approach. Is it the same thing as memory systems as proposed by Tulving and others, or is it something new?

When going through the memory literature long before that of modern times, it soon becomes clear that proposals of different kinds of memory are strongly related to the use of different types of materials to be remembered. It goes without saying that many students of memory have observed different phenomena with different types of to-be-remembered information that their subjects have been presented with. Apparently, when people have observed that memory functions differently for different types of materials, it has been convenient to assume that different mechanisms or different forms of memory are responsible.

Probably the first one to point this out in a theoretically meaningful way was Paivio (1969), in proposing his dual code model with a visual and a verbal code. However, many before him proposed different kinds of memory dependent upon what type of materials the subject was trying to remember. This approach, to propose different functional and/or structural mechanisms for different types of materials, was also common in applied settings, often related to ideas in everyday psychology. For example, it is not uncommon to say that some people are good at remembering faces, others are good at telephone numbers, with implicit assumptions that the kind of memory that is responsible for faces and telephone numbers, respectively, varies in efficiency between individuals.

Philosophers, psychologists, and others have thus been interested in the issue of different forms of memory for a long time. It is, however, beyond the scope of this commentary to present an overview of this. The interested reader should consult Schacter and Tulving (1994) for such a review.

ENGELKAMP'S MEMORY SYSTEMS

Engelkamp (this volume) begins his argument by stating what he does not mean by his systems approach. Obviously, Engelkamp does not mean the same thing as the multi-store approach as proposed by Atkinson and Shiffrin (1968) and others (e.g., Melton, 1963; Waugh & Norman, 1965). Moreover, he explicitly states that the distinction by Tulving (1972) in terms of episodic and semantic memory is not in line with his thinking either. As it seems, Engelkamp wants to narrow the domain of systems to episodic memory only. He states that he is interested in the autonoetic feature of episodic memory but then at the same time says that he does not care whether episodic information is conscious or not. What Engelkamp is interested in seems to be the kind of information that different systems can handle within episodic memory. Apparently, he thinks that something is missing in the concept of episodic memory, since it does not take into account the nature of the to-be-remembered information within this system.

The systems that Engelkamp proposes to have different functions within episodic memory are based on Paivio's (1969) notion of verbal and visual codes. In addition to these code systems, Engelkamp also proposes an action code system. These three code systems are said to be specialized for the representation and processing of information. The type of information in each system is assumed to depend on the physical appearance of stimuli and on the pattern of movement that is produced. Hence, the systems are modality specific and differ only with respect to the sense modality in which the information is processed. It makes a difference whether the information within episodic memory is verbal or nonverbal, visual or acoustic, sensory or motor, or conceptual. General sup-

port for this view is taken from data showing a superior memory performance
for information presented in one mode than in another. Thus, in much the same
way that Paivio used the picture superiority effect as evidence for his dual code
theory, Engelkamp is using the enactment effect as evidence for the notion that
there are different memory systems for information that is encoded by means
of enactment as compared to information that is encoded without enactment.
The problem with such an approach, however, is that it does not say anything
about why there is a superior memory performance after enactment than after
verbal encoding. By saying that the enactment system is more efficient does not
mean that an explanation is offered. The critical question is why the enactment
system is more efficient. It does not seem that the systems approach proposed
by Engelkamp can account for this.

  With respect to the influence from Paivio (1969, 1971), Engelkamp parts
company on one critical account. In contrast to Paivio, Engelkamp claims that
there is an inherent relation between an object and its label. Engelkamp agrees
with other code theories (e.g., Glass, Holyak, & Santa, 1979; Seymour, 1979)
when claiming such an inherent relationship.

  The main field of application of Engelkamp's theory is certainly that of memory for enacted events, although the theory has a more general flavor too. With
respect to interpreting data from action memory experiments, Engelkamp feels
a need to make a distinction between input and output systems. Engelkamp states
that memory after enactment benefits from an action output system, whereas
memory for verbal, nonenacted materials and pictures benefits from a verbal
and a visual input system, respectively. This distinction between input and output
systems is not clear to us, and we do not think that it is in line with the principle
of parsimony.

  Moreover, by considering action memory as an output system, one might
also mean that the enactment effect should be related more to the retrieval phase
than to the encoding phase. However, this does not seem to be the case in the
action memory literature. The main body of research in this field has been
conducted in the domain of encoding enactment; only a few studies have been
conducted in the domain of retrieval enactment. As summarized by Cohen
(1989) and Engelkamp and Cohen (1991), there is an overwhelming amount of
evidence for enactment effects in the first category of experiments, but no such
evidence in the second category (e.g., Brooks & Gardiner, 1994; Kormi-Nouri,
Nyberg, & Nilsson, 1994; Saltz & Dixon, 1982).

  Another point relating to this conceptual problem with input and output systems and the actual data from encoding and retrieval manipulations of enactment
is the statement by Engelkamp that episodic information (including motor actions) can be reflected in both explicit memory tests and implicit memory tests.
Although Engelkamp states that he is particularly interested in autonoetic consciousness in his framework as a means for the individual to become aware of

his or her own identity and existence in subjective time, he also states that he does not believe that episodic information, if it is remembered, is dependent on autonoetic consciousness. In saying this, Engelkamp paints a seemingly paradoxical and rather complex picture. This means, among other things, that episodic information can be reflected in both explicit memory tests and implicit memory tests. It makes little sense, we think, to argue that episodic information may be both conscious and unconscious, unless the mechanisms for this are specified.

Thus, in sum at this stage, one may say that the systems approach of Engelkamp consists of systems within episodic memory. These systems differ with respect to the information they can handle. Some systems are more efficient than others, and this is why there is a superior memory performance, when such a system has been responsible for the processing of the to-be-remembered information rather than a less efficient system. We are concerned that such an approach may not take us any further than being merely descriptive. It is quite obvious that Engelkamp's use of the term memory system is different from the way the term is used in previous research. We are therefore also concerned that the use of the term memory system in this way may lead to semantic confusions and unnecessary controversy. Our view is that the field is drifting more and more toward a descriptive side and further away from explanation, the more new ways of defining memory systems are invented. We think that Engelkamp is contributing to this development when launching memory systems the way he does.

CRITERIA FOR IDENTIFYING MEMORY SYSTEMS

How should memory systems be defined? What is required in terms of criteria, when someone wants to identify a given form of memory as a memory system? Tulving (1984) has specified some principles that can be applied for distinguishing potentially different memory systems. Schacter and Tulving (1994) recently set up some basic criteria for being able to state that one is dealing with different memory systems. The remaining part of this chapter will be used for evaluating Engelkamp's systems approach vis-à-vis these criteria.

According to Tulving (1984), memory systems can be distinguished on the basis of, first, different behavioral and cognitive functions and the kinds of information they process. Second, a given memory system should operate according to laws and principles that are different from those determining the operation of another system. Third, different systems should be based on different neural substrates. Fourth, different memory systems should develop at different stages of the phylogenetic and ontogenetic development. Finally, different memory systems should have different formats in representing stored information. On the

basis of these five principles, Schacter and Tulving (1994) specified three formal
criteria for distinguishing between memory systems, to be used by anyone who
is interested in avoiding semantic confusion and controversy.

These three criteria are class-inclusion operations, properties and relations,
and convergent dissociations. By class-inclusion operations is meant that an
"intact memory system enables one to perform a very large number of tasks of
a particular class or category, regardless of the specific informational contents
of the tasks" (Schacter & Tulving, 1994, p. 15). For one thing, this means that
modality of presentation of information and type of information cannot be distinguishing features of a memory system. Moreover, it means that a given brain
state should affect all memory functions equally if they are subserved by a given
system, and differently than nonmemory functions and those memory functions
subserved by other memory systems. With respect to episodic memory this
means that the encoding, storage, and retrieval of any type of information (e.g.,
verbal, pictorial, and motor) constitute operations that are class inclusive. Encoding, storage, and retrieval are no doubt objectively identifiable as separate in
the sense that different variables can affect these operations differently. However,
this does not preclude the fact that they are all included in a class of operations
that are necessary for episodic memory.

The property-and-relations criterion means that any given memory system
must be described in terms of a property list. The identity of a given system
should be possible to determine on the basis of this list. The relation between
a particular system and other systems should also be possible to specify on the
basis of this list. The relational aspect of this criterion means that some properties identifying one given system also may be on another list identifying another system. That is, the property lists of separate systems may include some
features that are similar and others that are different. According to Schacter and
Tulving (1994) the properties of any system should include rules of operation,
kind of information, neural substrates, and statements of what the system is for.

The third criterion, convergent dissociations, specifies that there should be
dissociations between task performances when different memory systems contribute differently to the performance in these tasks. It is explicitly stated that it
is not sufficient to demonstrate a single kind of dissociation between the performance of two memory tasks. Different dissociations must be converging in
the same direction to be able to postulate that one is dealing with different
memory systems; there must be dissociation of different kinds, observed with
different tasks, in different populations, and using different techniques (Schacter
& Tulving, 1994). Converging evidence for different memory systems can be
based on "functional dissociations on tasks alleged to tap different systems,
neuropsychological dissociations that involve contrasts between spared and impaired performance in relevant potential populations, or stochastic independence

between tasks that are sensitive to the operation of different systems" (Schacter & Tulving, 1994, p. 18).

An evaluation of Engelkamp's systems approach on the basis of these three criteria suggests, to us at least, a clear picture that the systems that Engelkamp is proposing are not to be referred to as systems. With respect to the first criterion it is quite clear that the encoding and retrieval of enacted and nonenacted events should be subserved by a single episodic memory system rather than two different memory systems. It has been demonstrated many times that enactment at encoding produces a higher degree of performance than nonenactment. Merely a difference in performance level does not preclude that both enactment and nonenactment are subserved by a single episodic memory. Higher efficiency of the potential motor code system should be the likely candidate property producing this superiority in memory performance. However, merely efficiency would not qualify as a critical property according to the second criterion. According to the third criterion one would expect converging dissociations between performances in the task of enacted encoding and the task of nonenacted encoding. It is true that results have been obtained showing different data patterns for enactment and nonenactment conditions, but it is equally true that striking similarities in data patterns have been observed in conditions of enacted and nonenacted encoding. Again, merely a difference in performance level between enacted and nonenacted encoding would not be sufficient. Interactions with other task variables or population properties are required. Considering one data domain where interactions have been obtained might be illustrative. It was suggested some time ago that no age deficits should be obtained after enacted encoding, whereas the typical age deficit should be obtained in conditions of nonenacted encoding (Bäckman & Nilsson, 1984, 1985). Although such results have indeed been obtained, several studies have failed to demonstrate such an interaction with age of the subjects (e.g., Cohen, Sandler, & Schroeder, 1987; Nilsson & Craik, 1990).

In conclusion, we argue that the systems proposed by Engelkamp do not qualify as separate memory systems. Episodic memory is very different from other memory systems that have been proposed, for instance, semantic memory, procedural memory, perceptual representation system, and short-term memory. The main difference between episodic memory and these other systems is that it makes it possible for a person to "travel" through subjective time. Episodic memory allows the individual to re-experience, through autonoetic consciousness, previous experiences, and it allows the individual to project this experience into the future. The function of episodic memory is to make this possible independently of whether the particular experience to re-experience or to project into the future is a verbal experience, a pictorial experience, or a motor experience.

A given event may be encoded in many different ways. For example, it may be encoded in a deep and elaborate fashion or in a shallow fashion, or it may be encoded by giving more or less emphasis to the verbal components, to the pictorial components, or to the motor components of the event. In this way it may be easier to re-experience a given event dependently on how it was encoded, and in a similar manner, it may be easier to project an experience into the future dependent on type of encoding, but the ease with which these re-experiences and projections can be made does not make episodic memory any more different than the other memory systems in this fundamental way of mental travel in subjective time through autonoetic awareness. According to our view, it is possible to do this mental travel in subjective time for verbal experiences, pictorial information, and motor information.

REFERENCES

Atkinson, R. C., & Shiffrin, R. M. (1968). Human memory: A proposed system and its control processes. In K. W. Spence & J. T. Spence (Eds.), *The psychology of learning and motivation* (pp. 89–195). New York: Academic Press.

Bäckman, L., & Nilsson, L. G. (1984). Aging effects in free recall: An exception to the rule. *Human Learning, 3*, 53–69.

Bäckman, L., & Nilsson, L. G. (1985). Prerequisites for lack of age differences in memory performance. *Experimental Aging Research, 11*, 67–73.

Brooks, B. M., & Gardiner, J. M. (1994). Age differences in memory for prospective compared with retrospective subject-performed tasks. *Memory & Cognition, 22*, 27–33.

Cohen, R. L. (1989). Memory for action events: The power of enactment. *Educational Psychology Review, 1*, 57–80.

Cohen, R. L., Sandler, S. P., & Schroeder, K. (1987). Aging and memory for words and action events: Effects of item repetition and list length. *Psychology and Aging, 2*, 280–285.

Engelkamp, J., & Cohen, R. L. (1991). Current issues in memory for action events. *Psychological Research, 53*, 175–182.

Glass, A. L., Holyoak, K. J., & Santa, J. L. (1979). *Cognition.* London: Addison-Wesley.

Kormi-Nouri, R., Nyberg, L., & Nilsson, L. G. (1994). The effect of retrieval enactment on recall of subject-performed tasks and verbal tasks. *Memory & Cognition, 22*, 723–728.

Melton, A. W. (1963). Implications of short-term memory for a general theory of memory. *Journal of Verbal Learning and Verbal Behavior, 2*, 1–21.

Nilsson, L. G., & Craik, F. I. M. (1990). Additive and interactive effects in memory for subject-performed tasks. *European Journal of Cognitive Psychology, 2*, 305–324.

Paivio, A. (1969). Mental imagery in associative learning and memory. *Psychological Review, 76*, 241–263.

Paivio, A. (1971). *Imagery and verbal processes.* New York: Holt, Rinehart & Winston.

Saltz, E., & Dixon, D. (1982). Let's pretend: The role of motoric imagery in memory for sentences and words. *Journal of Experimental Child Psychology, 34*, 77–92.

Schacter, D. L., & Tulving, E. (1994). What are the memory systems of 1994? In D. L. Schacter & E. Tulving (Eds.), *Memory systems 1994* (pp. 1–38). Cambridge: MIT Press.

Seymour, P. H. K. (1979). *Human visual cognition.* London: Collier Macmillan.

Tulving, E. (1972). Episodic and semantic memory. In E. Tulving & W. Donaldson (Eds.), *Organization of memory.* (pp. 381–403). New York: Academic Press.

Tulving, E. (1983). *Elements of episodic memory.* Oxford: Clarendon Press.

Tulving, E. (1984). Multiple learning and memory systems. In K. M. J. Lagerspetz & P. Niemi (Eds.), *Psychology in the 1990's* (pp. 163–184). Amsterdam: Elsevier.

Tulving, E. (1985). How many memory systems are there? *American Psychologist, 40*, 385–398.

Tulving, E. (1993). Human memory. In P. Andersen, Ö. Hvalby, O. Paulsen, & B. Hökfelt (Eds.), *Memory concepts 1993: Basic and clinical aspects* (pp. 27–45). Amsterdam: Excerpta Media.

Waugh, N., & Norman, D. (1965). Primary memory. *Psychological Review, 72*, 89–104.

Weinberger, N. M., McGaugh, J. L., & Lynch, G. (Eds.) (1985). Memory systems of the brain. New York: Guilford Press.

CHAPTER 7

What Does It Mean That the Motor Component Is Not Crucial?

Comments on Kormi-Nouri and Nilsson

Johannes Engelkamp

The goal of Kormi-Nouri and Nilsson is to argue "that there is no need to distinguish between motor and verbal information with respect to modality-specific information accounting for the enactment effects." In order to support this argument, they demonstrate: (a) lack of retrieval enactment effects, (b) effects of verbal and visual secondary tasks on motor memory, and (c) episodic integration by means of motor encoding.

One central aspect of their contribution is that they "argue against the motor encoding view" of Engelkamp and Zimmer (1983, 1984, 1985). Although it is true that we claim that motor encoding is involved in SPT learning, we do not claim that other types of encoding (e.g., verbal and visual) are irrelevant. This aspect has been stated more explicitly in more recent publications (e.g., Engelkamp, 1990, 1997; Engelkamp & Zimmer, 1994). I will comment on this point because it may create unnecessary misinterpretations. I will refer in my comments to Engelkamp and Zimmer (1994) because it is published in English, whereas the two other books are only available in German (although an English version of my 1997 book appeared in 1998 with Psychology Press under the title *Memory for actions*).

The following assumptions of our multimodal approach to memory are ignored or misunderstood by Kormi-Nouri and Nilsson:

1. We clearly distinguish between item-specific and relational information.
2. We consider relational information to be conceptual, whereas we assume that item-specific information consists of conceptual *and* modality-specific information.
3. Central is our assumption that a part of explicit episodic memory is always conceptual; however, it can be enriched by modality-specific information.

As to the enactment effect, which is discussed by Kormi-Nouri and Nilsson, we have tried to show in our research that it also relies on motor information. We do not claim that it is exclusively due to motor information. To give just two quotes from our book:

> The idea that conceptual information contributes to the enactment effect does not contradict the multimodal theory. On the contrary, in this model conceptual information plays a particular role under enactment. (Engelkamp & Zimmer, 1994, p. 245)

> in the multimodal theory it is assumed that enactment also enhances conceptual encoding. This holds true insofar as performing an action focuses information processing on those aspects which are relevant for action. This means that enactment also improves item-specific conceptual encoding processes. . . . In addition, the multimodal theory claims that enactment also provides specific motor information and that this information contributes substantially to the enactment effect. (Engelkamp & Zimmer, 1994, p. 226)

Thus, our goal was and is to demonstrate that the enactment effect cannot be explained by *only* assuming an enriched conceptual information.

LACK OF RETRIEVAL ENACTMENT

On this background, the question arises of whether the lack of retrieval enactment effects excludes the possibility that motor information contributes to the enactment effect. Kormi-Nouri and Nilsson argue that "if action events are encoded in motor codes, then motor cues should lead to a better memory than verbal cues," according to the encoding specificity principle. The assumption that an encoded component should necessarily lead to an effect of encoding specificity is too unspecific. It is important to ask whether the encoded component will be used in the specific test applied. It is known, for instance, that learning words underwater improves later free recall underwater compared to recall on land (Godden & Baddeley, 1975), but it does not influence recognition selectively (Godden & Baddeley, 1980). Also, the studies of verbal overshadowing show that a specific encoded aspect (here the visual encoding of nonverbal stimuli) does show its influence during test depending on type of test used (Brandimonte, Schooler, & Gabbino, 1997).

Hence, the critical question is whether one can find conditions under which motor encoding leads to an encoding specificity effect. It is not enough to show conditions under which the effect does not show up. As to motor encoding, Kormi-Nouri and Nilsson summarize that there is a lack of retrieval enactment effects. That means that there is no recall difference after motor encoding when the test is verbal and when it is motor. However, Engelkamp, Zimmer, Mohr, and Sellen (1994) found an encoding specificity effect after motor encoding when a recognition test was used. This result is considered a "single inconsistent finding" with no theoretical impact by Kormi-Nouri and Nilsson. In my opinion, both findings should be taken seriously. One finding is that there is no encoding specificity effect for motor encoding when a recall test is used, *and* the second effect is that there is an encoding specificity effect for motor encoding when a recognition test is used. In this context, I would like to note that Engelkamp et al. not only observed "that actions (compared to verbal events) were recognized better in a motor than in a verbal test." This finding refers to their Experiment 1. In their Experiment 2 they demonstrated, moreover, that the advantage of motor testing after motor encoding was reduced when the action at test was performed with the other hand than at study. A similar finding, namely a decrease in recognition memory, with motorically similar distractors, was observed when subjects performed actions during recognition (Engelkamp & Zimmer, 1995). This encoding specificity effect with motor encoding in a recognition test as well as the decrease of this effect with motorically similar distractors is clear evidence for what Kormi-Nouri and Nilsson expected if a motor code is involved in motor encoding. There is little reason to give these findings less weight than the lack of an encoding specificity effect in recall.

There is still another aspect of the findings reported by Kormi-Nouri and Nilsson on which I would like to comment. In discussing the encoding specificity of SPTs, they refer to a study by Brooks and Gardiner (1994). This study does not contribute to the encoding specificity question after motor encoding, because these authors have not included a motor test after SPT learning. Here, Table 1 in chapter of Kormi-Nouri is misleading the reader.

However, it is true that Brooks and Gardiner (1994) had a verbal and a motor test after verbal learning and could not observe an advantage of motor over verbal testing. However, it should be mentioned that the learning conditions were different, depending on the two testing conditions. It was the goal of Brooks and Gardiner (1994) to replicate an effect of Koriat, Ben-Zur, and Nussbaum (1990) who had shown that learning action phrases with the intention to perform the actions at test (so to speak, planning to perform actions) led to better recall than learning the same action phrases with the intention to recall the phrases verbally. Brooks and Gardiner (1994) were unable to replicate the finding of Koriat et al. (1990). However, Engelkamp (1997) could not only replicate the findings of Koriat et al. (1990)—enhanced recall for to-be-performed items over for to-be-recalled items when subjects had learned phrases—but he could also demonstrate why Brooks and Gardiner (1994) could not replicate the findings of Koriat et al. (1990). Taken together, from these findings it can be concluded that enactment at study (SPT) and planning to enact at test seem to have something in common that makes both different from verbal encoding. It is likely that this common aspect is related to a motor code.

In sum, the demonstration that there is no encoding specificity effect after SPT learning in recall does not speak against the motor encoding view, whereas, that there is such an encoding specificity effect after SPT learning in recognition speaks in favor of a motor encoding view.

THE EFFECTS OF VERBAL AND VISUAL SECONDARY TASKS ON MOTOR MEMORY

Kormi-Nouri and Nilsson argue: "If motor encoding is processed separately and independently from verbal and visual encoding, as is hypothesized by the motor encoding view (e.g., Engelkamp & Zimmer, 1983, 1984, 1985), one should expect that the motor task is affected only by a secondary motor task and not by verbal or visual tasks."

The main problem with this argument is that it ignores the assumption that verbal, visual, and motor encoding may take place independently in SPTs. We assume that using these different codes may occur independently of each other. However, we allow for their occurring together in learning action phrases by enactment. For instance, when real objects are used in SPTs, we claim that the visual code is activated by perceiving the objects and influences memory independently of the motor code that is activated by enactment (see Engelkamp & Zimmer, 1994, Chapter 4.3, and Engelkamp & Zimmer, 1997). Furthermore, we distinguish a system for static visual information for processing object information from a system for dynamic visual information for perceiving actions (see Engelkamp and Zimmer, 1994, Chapter 4.6). Of course, we also assume that the verbal system is always activated when action phrases are learned, be it by listening to them in verbal tasks (VTs), by listening to them and perceiving the experimenter-performed tasks (EPTs), or by listening to them and self-performing the actions in subject-performed tasks (SPTs) (see Engelkamp & Zimmer, 1983, 1994). Taken together, from assuming independent encoding systems it does not follow, as Kormi-Nouri and Nilsson assume, that the motor task (SPTs) should be affected only by a secondary motor task and not by verbal or visual tasks.

However, they are correct in pointing to the fact that the findings of selective interference paradigms are inconsistent. However, in discussing these inconsistencies it might be worthwhile to take the following aspects of interference experiments into account.

First, interference may be due to the attention-demanding properties of the tasks used. This type of interference is called central interference. It is likely, for instance, that the secondary task of counting backward in steps of threes and sixes is attention-demanding and invokes central interference with VTs as well as with SPTs (e.g., Bäckman, Nilsson, & Chalom, 1986; Engelkamp & Zimmer, 1996). Besides central interference, there may be interference due to the fact that main and secondary tasks use the same code system and that this common use lowers the discriminability of memory traces in that system. This type of interference is called structural interference. It is this type of interference that Kormi-Nouri and Nilsson discuss in their contribution. However, in interpreting interference effects as structural, one has to make sure that central interference is controlled.

Furthermore and particularly important in the context of selective motor interference studies, one must carefully control which code systems are involved in the main task (here SPTs) and in the secondary task (e.g., counting dots or watching video spots of events). Assuming, for instance, that SPTs with real objects are used, this task means that the verbal system is involved (subjects listen to or see phrases), that the static visual system is involved (subjects perceive objects), that the dynamic visual system may be involved (subjects perceive themselves performing the actions), that the motor system is involved (subjects enact), and, of course, that the conceptual system is involved (subjects understand the meaning of the phrases). Hence, verbal, static visual, dynamic visual, motor, and conceptual secondary tasks should lead to structural interference with SPTs.

What these considerations make clear is that the selective interference experiments with action phrases must be better controlled than they have been controlled in the past. Hence, as Engelkamp (1997, p. 69) has summarized, the findings of the selective interference experiments with action phrases do not allow unequivocal interpretations, because the experiments were unsufficiently controlled. However, the multimodal theory as proposed by Engelkamp and Zimmer (1994) makes it clear how such a control could be achieved.

To summarize, the observation of Kormi-Nouri and Nilsson, that the findings of selective interference experiments with SPTs are inconsistent, is correct, however, this situation allows so far no unequivocal conclusion against the assumption that SPTs involve motor encoding (see Engelkamp, 1997, pp. 66–70, for a detailed discussion).

THE EPISODIC INTEGRATION EFFECTS BY MEANS OF MOTOR ENCODING

In their first two sections, Kormi-Nouri and Nilsson tried to show that assumptions following from a motor encoding view do not hold true and that therefore this theoretical position must be wrong. In the last section, they argue for the episodic integration view as a proposal to explain encoding by enactment by only assuming unitary conceptual encoding processes. Their central assumption is that "subjects are more involved in the learning of motor tasks as compared to verbal tasks. A better self-involvement in action events helps the rememberer to be more aware of his action (self-knowing), thereby leading to better episodic memory." The problem with this position is that "self-involvement" and "better awareness" of actions in SPTs have not been demonstrated directly. For this purpose it would be necessary to vary "self-involvement" and "awareness" at encoding independently of type of encoding (SPT, VT). If self-involvement and awareness can only be realized by enactment, then the explanation is not more than a paraphrase of the memory advantage of SPTs and VTs.

The presentation of data relating to the size of the SPT effect and pre-experimental associations between verbs and nouns in the to-be-learned phrases does not clarify the episodic integration process either. To point just to one problem: The finding that the enactment effect was larger for well-integrated items (= high association between verbs and objects) than for poorly integrated items (= low association between verb and objects) in free recall and that the opposite finding was observed in cued recall (with noun or verb as cue) remains unexplained. The conclusion and assumption that episodic integration (by SPT learning) and high pre-experimental verb-noun association provide the best encoding support does not explain this dissociation. If this assumption holds true, the SPT effect should be larger for highly associated verb-noun phrases than for poorly associated phrases in free recall as well as in cued recall. However, this is not the case.

The situation becomes even more complicated when Kormi-Nouri and Nilsson make the additional assumption that "enactment integrates the components of actions in two ways: within-event and between-events integration." This assumption is particularly hard to understand because Kormi-Nouri and Nilsson say nothing in their contribution about the question that between-event integration is improved by enactment. Whereas it is at least plausible to assume that enactment helps to integrate the individual actions (see also Engelkamp, 1995, for such a view), it is harder to see why associations between unrelated actions (relational encoding among actions) should be supported by enactment.

To conclude, the episodic integration study of Kormi-Nouri and Nilsson does not present evidence for a purely conceptual encoding view nor does it present evidence against a motor encoding view.

REFERENCES

Bäckman, L., Nilsson, L. G., & Chalom, D. (1986). New evidence on the nature of the encoding of action events. *Memory & Cognition, 14*, 339–346.

Brandimonte, M. A., Schooler, J. W., & Gabbino, P. (1997). Attenuating verbal overshadowing through color retrieval cues. *Journal of Experimental Psychology: Learning, Memory & Cognition, 23*, 915–931.

Brooks, B. M., & Gardiner, J. M. (1994). Age differences in memory for prospective compared with retrospective subject-performed tasks. *Memory & Cognition, 22*, 27–33.

Engelkamp, J. (1990). *Das menschliche Gedächtnis*. Göttingen: Hogrefe.

Engelkamp, J. (1995). Visual imagery and enactment of actions in memory. *British Journal of Psychology, 86*, 227–240.

Engelkamp, J. (1997). *Das Erinnern eigener Handlungen*. Göttingen: Hogrefe.

Engelkamp, J., & Zimmer, H. D. (1983). Zum Einfluß von Wahrnehmen und Tun auf das Behalten von Verb-Objekt-Phrasen. *Sprache & Kognition, 2*, 117–127.

Engelkamp, J., & Zimmer, H. D. (1984). Motor program information as a separable memory unit. *Psychological Research, 46*, 283–299.

Engelkamp, J., & Zimmer, H. D. (1985). Motor programs and their relation to semantic memory. *German Journal of Psychology, 9*, 239–254.

Engelkamp, J., & Zimmer, H. D. (1994). *The human memory. A multimodal approach*. Seattle: Hogrefe & Huber.

Engelkamp, J., & Zimmer, H. D. (1995). Similarity of movement in recognition of self-performed tasks. *British Journal of Psychology, 86*, 241–252.

Engelkamp, J., & Zimmer, H. D. (1996). Organisation and recall in verbal tasks and in subject-performed tasks. *European Journal of Cognitive Psychology, 8*, 257–273.

Engelkamp, J. & Zimmer, H. D. (1997). Sensory factors in memory for subject-performed tasks. *Acta Psychologica, 96*, 43-60.

Engelkamp, J., Zimmer, H. D., Mohr, G., & Sellen, O. (1994). Memory of self-performed tasks: Self-performing during recognition. *Memory & Cognition, 22*, 34–39.

Godden, D., & Baddeley, A. D. (1975). Context-dependent memory in two natural environments: On land and under water. *British Journal of Psychology, 66*, 325–331.

Godden, D., & Baddeley, A. D. (1980). When does context influence recognition memory? *British Journal of Psychology, 71*, 99–104.

Koriat, A., Ben-Zur, H., & Nussbaum, A. (1990). Encoding information for future action: Memory for to-be-performed versus memory for to-be-recalled tasks. *Memory & Cognition, 18*, 568–578.

CHAPTER 8

Why Do Actions Speak Louder than Words?

Action Memory as a Variant of Encoding Manipulations or the Result of a Specific Memory System?

Hubert D. Zimmer

INTRODUCTION: A SUMMARY OF THE POSITIONS

In the preceding chapters of this book, a long series of empirical data was presented that provided grounds for the suspicion that action memory is something specific. Most of the reported experiments demonstrated excellent memory performances for actions when they were self-performed, and such performance levels were usually not achieved with other types of encoding. Furthermore, some manipulations of the encoding conditions, known for being effective in verbal memory, did not show similar effects in SPT, whereas some other effects occurred only if the actions were performed during study. Taking these results as a whole, performing actions during study must be considered a specific encoding condition that differs from standard verbal encoding. However, considering performance as a unique encoding operation does not necessarily take into consideration that actions are remembered by a specific memory system; on the contrary, this point is controversial, as demonstrated by the contributions to this book.

In this closing chapter, I want to deal with these controversial aspects by way of comparison, and I want to evaluate the arguments that support the different positions. Before I discuss and relate these positions, I want to briefly repeat the central assumptions held by the authors and summarize the arguments they put forward in support of their positions.

Automatic Retrieval of Prospective Memory for Actions

Guynn, McDaniel, and Einstein investigated *memory for event-based, to-be-performed actions*. Specific for this type of memory is that subjects have to remember, at the right time, to perform the target action without an additional prompting. As a consequence, in the prospective memory task, people are not in a retrieval mode when they work on the memory task. It is actually the opposite. Participants perform a different action, and they are supposed to (incidentally) remember what to do when the critical event occurs and then have to interrupt the ongoing behavior in order to perform the target action. The memory situation is therefore comparable to a dual task situation. Due to the necessity of remembering something without an explicit retrieval prompt, the authors see a parallel between the prospective memory task and the involuntary remembering condition. In terms of theory, they contrast a "familiarity plus search" model with an "automatic associative activation" hypothesis and argue in favor of the latter attempt. They suggest that the target event (an item) is processed by the hippocampal component, which automatically activates the to-be-performed target action. This action is then delivered to a working memory that schedules and monitors all ongoing actions. Although the to-be-performed target action was retrieved, in the extreme case, an overload of this working memory would lead to the omission of actions due to the limited capacity of this memory.

From the perspective of these authors' opinion, the main bottleneck for prospective memory performances is the association between the target event and the target action. In support of their position, they mention that: (a) manipulations of features of the target item that influence its memory were ineffective (e.g., its familiarity, its frequency of presentation); whereas in contrast (b) manipulations of the association between the target event and the action influenced prospective memory performances; (c) the response latencies were low when the target actions were performed; and (d) dividing attention during encoding impaired prospective memory, whereas dividing attention during retrieval did not. Only elderly subjects showed a reduced probability for performing the target actions if the participants had to solve an additional task during retrieval. The authors attributed this latter effect to scheduling problems. Additionally, they speculated that two different part systems might contribute to the memory of retrospective and prospective actions. Retrospective memory is supported by a frontal (retrieval) component that is involved in an active search for memory entries, while *prospective memory is supported by a different frontal component that controls the execution (scheduling) of actions that are automatically re-trieved by the hippocampal system.* However, it should be mentioned in paren-theses that both tasks also share some components, such as the hippocampal component, which causes the automatic retrieval of items, both in prospective and retrospective memory tasks.

The Contribution of Motor Components to Action Memory

The chapters that follow dealt with memory for performed actions. First, En-gelkamp presented his *motor-system explanation of SPT memory*. He postulated that episodic memory is supported by independent sub-systems that represent different contents. He distinguished the representation of the items' meaning from the representation of their surface features. The latter are the acoustic and visual word forms and the respective nonverbal input representations. Most no-tably, he also *attached importance to the representations of the output modali-ties*, that is, performing actions. His general claim was that, in addition to input features, surface features of output are elements of memory traces. Therefore, memory is a function of three factors: (a) the stimulus modality that determines the used entry (input) or output system, (b) the automatic and strategic encoding operations, and (c) the demands of the memory task, that is, what kind of in-formation is necessary to solve the task. According to Engelkamp, the fact that, in memory experiments, effects of the surface qualities were rarely observed is a consequence of the inadequate testing procedure that was used in most of the experiments. Usually, it was sufficient to remember the meaning of the item in order to solve the memory task, but it was not necessary to take into account surface features. If, however, subjects were required to distinguish old and new items on the basis of surface features, feature similarity became relevant, and memory of these features could be shown. In summary, in Engelkamp's view, *the specific quality of SPT is that the to-be-learned actions were overtly carried out during encoding* and, with this enactment, *motor components of the actions got part of the memory trace.*

In support of his position, he cited the excellent memory performances if the actions were performed during study. These effects were also observed, in com-parison to a visual condition, even if the visual input was eliminated. This demonstrates that pure performance is capable of enhancing memory without additional input information. Second, he reported selective interference experi-ments. A motor secondary task during encoding impaired SPT memory more than a visual secondary task. Finally, Engelkamp presented a series of studies in which the similarity of movements, between study and test, influenced rec-ognition in SPT but not in VT. Re-performing the same action during testing increased memory, and performing a slightly different action hampered memory only if the actions were performed during study. Additionally, if SPT distractor items were closely related in their meanings to the study items, the similarity of the movements increased the rate of false alarms. On the basis of these results, Engelkamp postulated that a "movement" trace, represented within a motor system, contributes to SPT memory.

SPT Memory as a Variant of Conceptual Encoding

Kormi-Nouri and Nilsson contradicted Engelkamp's position. They argued that the *motor component is not crucial* for SPT memory. *The subject-performed task is only a variation of encoding conditions* that should be handled within the traditional episodic memory models. SPT is only another variation of processing, as it is also manipulated, for example, in the levels of processing research. The fact that memory in SPT is increased was explained by these authors using the assumption of a higher self involvement in SPT than in VT, an increased awareness, and an increased experiential registration of the self-performed action. Due to the identical function of SPT memory and VT memory, these authors consider episodic memory as a unitary system, independent of the modalities of the to-be-remembered items.

In support of their position, Kormi-Nouri and Nilsson first reported several experiments which demonstrated that retrieval enactment is not memory effective. In the authors' view, from a system approach, one should expect that performing during retrieval is also memory efficient. At least in SPTs, memory performances should be higher when subjects also enacted during retrieval than when they did a verbal recall (the principle of encoding specificity). However, whereas SPT processing during study had a large effect on memory compared to VT, the same manipulation, during testing, did not influence free recall performances. The authors assumed that motor retrieval cues were ineffective because "the stored information was in a verbal rather than in a motor code."

Next, they discussed the selective interference experiments. They made two points against these experiments. First, they claimed that the data did not show independence, and, second, they questioned the significance of the reported results for a specific motor interference. On the one hand, memory for performed actions was impaired by an additional load of central processing capacity. The authors concluded that both performances are the result of the same memory system because the same task also interfered with verbal memory. If SPT processing had been done by an independent system, divided attention should not have impaired memory. On the other hand, Kormi-Nouri and Nilsson pointed out the fact that in most of the interference studies only control groups with secondary tasks were included. Therefore, one could not decide whether SPT memory was unimpaired or only less impaired, for example, by a non-motor secondary verbal task. They interpreted both results as speaking against a motor system explanation.

If motor components did not contribute to memory in SPT, it remains to be explained why SPT memory is better than VT memory. The authors' alternative to explain the SPT memory advantage is an *integration hypothesis*. Performing actions should lead to a better integration between the environment (i.e., the task) and the subject (i.e., the rememberer), perhaps because performance, from an evolutionary standpoint, is older than verbal encoding. Enactment is considered the "glue" that generates single memory units. In support of this position, it was reported that the SPT effect was higher in free recall than in cued recall and that it was higher for less integrated than for well-integrated action phrases. This integration is the item-specific component of SPT encoding. Additionally, they reported results that, in their view, had shown an enhanced relational processing of items in SPT.

Actions as Goal Directed Behavior

In the next chapter, Foley and Ratner discussed *retrospective action memory* in the broader context of *activity memory*. In this perspective, they first questioned the validity of some of the features postulated for action memory. They reported results (developmental effects) that contradict the non-strategic learning assumption made by certain authors for SPT. Furthermore, they did not find effects of the richness of physical features (number of movements) or effects of integration of physical features (transitive versus intransitive verbs) in free recall of executed actions. This non-effect is a contradiction to the item-specific integration hypothesis. Finally, they did not find effects of the availability of labels for the remembered actions, whose effect is incongruent with a dual encoding explanation (verbal and nonverbal codes). In the authors' view, this result also contradicts a motor component explanation because these authors interpreted the "motor-system explanation" as a variant of a dual encoding model. As a further shortcoming of SPT research, they stated that verbal memory, for the performed actions, is usually tested, neglecting other nonverbal types of knowledge about the actions.

As an alternative, the authors suggested to view SPTs as a variant of goal-directed activities, although this is a strongly reduced case. Characteristic of these activities is that subjects perform them with the intention of influencing the environment in order to reach their goals. Actions and also SPTs are interfaces between the subject's inner and outer worlds. Foley and Ratner emphasized that, although this goal-directed aspect is usually minimized in the laboratory context of SPTs, it is of great importance for everyday actions. Therefore, SPT only mimics surface features of actions. However, it does not represent the full action. Nevertheless, *SPTs are generally processed as goal-directed actions, and this should cause their memory effect.* From this point of view, actions have at least four aspects: (1) they have prospective features, that is, they are planned and the probable outcomes are anticipated by the agents; (2) the real execution produces an overt outcome that is perceived as the result of the self-performed activity and therefore caused by the actor. (3) actions have an inner structure, that is, a sequence of part actions (in-order-to relations); and (4) the present action spontaneously elicits reflections about the present and similar past actions. All these aspects contribute to action memory.

In support of their position the authors reported results from memory experiments, several of which were carried out with children. In these experiments, it was shown that planning contributed to SPT memory, that actions with real outcomes were recalled better than actions without outcomes, and that source memory (whether the action was really performed or not) was impaired if the actions' results were anticipated. Additionally, Foley and Ratner discussed that all results of the reflective processing of self-performed actions, for instance, noticing its results, its effectiveness, one's own mood during performance, etc., led to memory entries. This effect resembles their position to other multiple-entry models, in which the richness of encoding is mentioned as relevant for increased memory performance of SPT (e.g., Bäckman & Nilsson, 1984). However, in contrast to these explanations, the authors emphasized that it is not the number of features that cause the increased memory performance, but it is the fact that all of these processes *evaluate the action's outcome and its consequences in relation to the goal of the action*, where the process differs from discerning the same features in isolation.

A TASK ANALYSIS OF SPT

In order to discuss and evaluate the different approaches that were suggested to explain memory for actions, I will begin with a task analysis (cf. also Norman, 1988), and then I will use this as a background for the evaluation of the different positions. A subset of the relevant part processes of a subject-performed task is illustrated in Figure 8.1.

For an analysis of the involved processes, I want to take a concrete example: suppose that the to-be-performed action is "to tear the paper." Upon verbal command, participants have to go through a sequence of processes when they perform the action "tear the paper." *The main steps in performing actions are: lexical-semantic processing, formation of volition, movement and motor programming, execution and monitoring, and evaluation.*

At the *lexical-semantic stage*, subjects have to process the phrase in order to understand what they are being requested to do. In this first step, the components

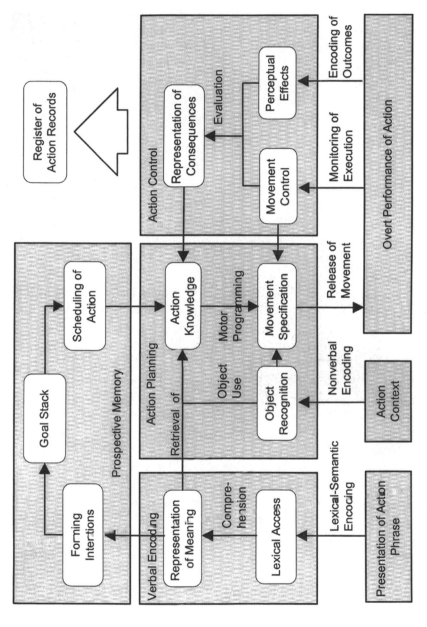

FIGURE 8.1. An illustration of part processes that are involved in the encoding and the control of actions in subject-performed tasks.

157

of the phrase make contact with a verbal lexicon (cf. Figure 8.1), and then the meaning of the denoted action has to be analyzed to find out what to do. This might lead to a representation like TEAR (patient: PAPER). If the meaning was completely broken down, in the example, this would lead to a representation like: goal: cutting; recipient: the paper; means: by the movement of tearing; starting condition: intact sheet of paper; final condition: smaller pieces (e.g., Aebli, 1980; Gentner, 1981; Norman & Rumelhart, 1975; Österreich & Köddig, 1995). Under SPT, semantic processing is focused on the action component of the phrase. This has two consequences. The first is that other associated aspects of the item's meaning, which are possible and which in other contexts might be intended by the speaker, are not activated, for example, "the paper is made unreadable" or "the paper is destroyed because the actor is angered by it." It is even possible that these meanings are actively suppressed. The second consequence is that the motor representation, the program that enables its execution and that is associated to this action, is additionally activated (see below). By the activation of this motor representation, information about the movement component of the action is made available (Engelkamp & Zimmer, 1984). The representation of the output components feeds back activation into the semantic representation.

The second stage is the *formation of volition*. Actions that should be executed must be intended. Even in the laboratory task, participants must form, at least in general, the intention to carry out the action in order to plan its execution (cf. Heckhausen & Beckman, 1990). Subjects don't perform each action that pops into mind. Only actions that are actual goals or actions receive this status because they are linked to goal actions that will eventually be performed (Österreich & Köddig, 1995). Usually actions receive this status by the way that subjects intend to perform a specific action. I assume that a consequence of forming the intention to perform a specific action is that the action receives the specific status of being a "to-be-executed action." Another consequence is that, after its execution, the respective action is tagged as "already performed." All to-be-executed actions constitute the goal stack. At this point in the action planning sequence, the action is either immediately executed as in SPT tasks, or it is delivered to the "to-be-performed under suitable conditions" list of actions as in prospective memory tasks.

Therefore, in some way, *prospective memory* is always involved if actions are to be performed (cf. Fig. 8.1). In the prototypical prospective memory task, participants have to wait for some time or they have to wait for a specific signal in order to proceed (cf. the chapter by Guynn et al.). In the SPT task, subjects can immediately execute the action. Obviously, compared to the SPT task, the prospective memory task has additional features, for instance, the intended actions have to be memorized and retrieved at the right time. Subjects therefore have to additionally encode the target item, which is the cue for executing the target action. However, this component is, in my view, not the important feature of a prospective memory task; on the contrary, it is similar to a retrospective memory task. The core quality of the prospective memory task is that there are actions having the specific status of to-be-performed, that is, they have the goal status, and this feature is shared by prospective memory tasks and SPT tasks.

In my view, the volitional stage as a whole makes it necessary to postulate the existence of two memory structures: a goal stack that temporarily holds a list of the to-be-performed actions, and an action register that temporarily stores which actions were already performed.

The next step is *movement programming*. When the phrase is understood and the action should be performed, the actor has to access his or her memory in order to retrieve the kind of movement that needs to be performed. It is likely that the same programming is partially done if the performance of actions is only covert (imagined), but not overt (cf. Heuer, 1985). In the example, he or she has to remember what kind of movement has to be carried out when something is torn. I assume that this planning process implies access to stored knowledge about movements. Humans have available knowledge about known actions, for instance, action schemata (Vallacher & Wegner, 1987), which enables them to perform the actions. We called the entries in this knowledge base motor programs (Engelkamp & Zimmer, 1994) to emphasize that they are related to overt action and muscle movements. These programs are thought of as "functional states that dispose the organism to carry out particular movements or classes of movements" (Rosenbaum, 1991, p. 114). Therefore, with the suggestion of motor programs, one should not necessarily associate low-level muscle commands, although their existence would not contradict our idea. What is assumed, however, is that this knowledge is specific to motor actions, that it is necessary to carry out actions, and that the performance of actions is hampered if this representation is impaired (cf. Rothi, Ochipa, & Heilman, 1997). I assume that, when the action is planned, some kind of motor program is accessed, and this enables the performance of the sequence of operations necessary to prepare the execution of the action.

During the planning process, the forthcoming movement is prepared and the movement elements are assembled. It is assumed that this preparation is partially done before the overt action is started. If real objects are present, not only is the intended action relevant but also other environmental information (cf. Figure 8.1). Most prominent are the available action elements and tools. The actors have to pay attention to this information in order to act successfully. The tools specify which type of movement is possible. The specific features of the objects restrict the manner in which the action can be performed. These features determine the concrete movement parameters, for example, force, velocity, spatial extent, etc. This specification of the actual movement is *motor programming* in the narrower sense. It enables the smooth execution of overt movements.

At some time in the planning process, the *execution* is released, the movement is carried out, and the execution is *monitored*. The person moves her or his hands in opposite directions to tear wrapping paper from a present or to pretend to tear a fictitious paper. Usually, in a SPT experiment, the actor can immediately perform the action and start the enactment of the movement as soon as he or she knows what to do. In this phase, the muscles have to be enervated, and the action has to be completely specified. Even if all specifications of an action have not been done during planning, when the action is executed, the parameters must be specified. The execution therefore guarantees the complete instantiation of a motor action.

When the action is carried out, the overt performance is monitored. If it was not successful, if the paper was too durable, the execution would be corrected and the action would be performed in a more forceful way. During monitoring, additional information about the action is processed and thereby encoded, for example, outcomes, obstacles, movement parameters, etc. Due to the fact that feedback is essential for actions because it indicates success or failure, it may automatically be integrated into the representation of the action. The additional information would enrich the action record. These features, however, are not always available. They depend on the specific conditions of the task, (with or without objects, with opened eyes or with closed eyes, whether subjects enact in a social context or individually). Furthermore, because SPT is often realized without objects, the additionally available information is extremely limited. There are no observable outcomes, and the movement parameters do not need to be specified with regard to environmental details. Nevertheless, one might speculate that the goal-movement-outcome sequences, in some sense a closed loop, is the core element of a motor action.

Finally, the actions are *evaluated*. The actor classifies the actions as successful or not. Dependent on the importance of the goal and the outcome, and dependent on the emotional predisposition of the actor, he or she will show an affective reaction to this outcome. If the action failed, he or she may redesign subgoals, and a different action will be performed to reach the goal. In the experiments, all actions are usually successful that reduce the subjective value of success and also prevent negative emotional reactions. I do not know about experiments, for instance, in which the paper could not be torn. In SPT tasks, the evaluation is therefore strongly reduced, but in everyday actions this might be different (cf. the chapter by Foley & Rattner).

This task analysis reveals a lot of processes that are elicited by the instruction to perform actions during encoding, and that do *not exist* in the same way if actions are encoded under verbal task conditions. We have to expect that the results of some or even nearly all of these additional processes become a member of the memory record of the item in a subject-performed task. All of these additional components can therefore, in principle, contribute to the memory performances of performed actions because all aspects belong to SPT processing. From this point of view, it is not surprising that SPT memory is different from VT memory. Additionally, viewing this list of part processes involved in actions, one can immediately recognize that the different approaches presented in this book seek to explain SPT memory by focusing on different aspects. In taking this diversity seriously, apart from some specific aspects, a real contradiction or a conflict between pairs of explanations does not exist until one of these components is considered as the only critical one that can exclusively explain the SPT advantage, and the other components are declared as irrelevant. In principle, therefore, the different approaches can coexist, and one has to (empirically) decide under which condition which component is relevant for memory, and which one is not.

However, the task analysis of SPT experiments, and of action memory in general, should not end with encoding. We also have to take into account *the retrieval situation* when memory is tested. Except for prospective memory and recognition, in the preceding chapters, little was said about retrieval aspects.

Prospective memory has very specific retrieval conditions. In these tasks, participants have to retrieve the target action(s) whenever the target item is perceived while they are working on a different task. This retrieval has to be started either voluntarily when the critical item is recognized (it interrupts the ongoing task) or the retrieval process is automatically released without conscious control. In one sense, the retrieval process itself can therefore be seen as the critical memory performance. In prospective memory tasks, the item content is always available; subjects usually know what to do if they are asked, but this content is sometimes not accessed at the right moment. In retrospective memory this is different. In this task, for some of the to-be-remembered items, no memory traces exist. Therefore, retrospective memory is confined by the availability and the accessibility of the items, whereas prospective memory is confined by the accessibility of items. In everyday prospective memory, the difference between these two tasks might be less extreme because not only one but several actions are to be performed, and therefore remembering what the to-be-performed target actions are is difficult.

In *retrospective memory*, retrieval has a different role. In this case, subjects are explicitly instructed to make a retrieval attempt. Most often, they are required to *recall* the items, that is, they have to list the names of the actions. Participants should do this without additional support or they receive associated cues (e.g., category names) to aid retrieval. In free recall, subjects have to generate items, and, therefore, the availability of *retrieval paths* (relational information) is important, which can be used by an automatic or intentional *search* process. However, in addition to this search based recall, an *automatic retrieval* is possible, in which process items are directly accessed and pop into conscious memory without intentional search. Finally, in other memory tasks, persons are requested to give the missing part of the actions in *cued recall*. They are required to name the used object, given the verb as cue, or to name the action itself (the verb), given the noun. In the latter task, intra-item connectivity is relevant, and this information is item-specific information from the list's perspective. Finally, a *recognition* task can be performed, in which case subjects have to decide whether the presented action was studied before or not. Usually this task is an old-new-recognition task. Subjects have to decide whether the presented action was included in the study list or not. In SPT, subjects have at least one additional information available to help them reach decisions in this task. All old items but none of the new items were performed. This might enable the good memory performances in recognition. The more specific information about the manner of the performance was seldom tested in SPT experiments. Considering all of these differences while testing memory, it is clear that one should take into account the specific testing condition if one is searching for an explanation of SPT memory.

CRITICAL COMPONENTS OF PROSPECTIVE MEMORY FOR ACTIONS

Before I discuss the individual components of subject-performed tasks, I want to deal with prospective memory. Therefore, I want to start by saying a few words about those aspects that are additionally necessary in prospective memory as well. Guynn et al. restricted their analysis to event-based actions, so that I can also leave out time-based actions.

In event-based actions, in principle, *two* memory items exist: the target event that is the signal to proceed, and the target action itself, which is to be performed. The participant processes the target event in a stream of other events. When it is presented, he or she has to retrieve the to-be-performed target action, and this action has to be experienced as something that should be performed now. The ongoing action has to be interrupted, and she or he has to carry out the target action. A break in this chain, at any place, would prevent the execution of the target action. If the target event is overlooked because it is not appropriately encoded, if the event does not elicit the target action, or if the target action is not experienced as something that has to be performed now the prospective memory task is missed.

Guynn, McDaniel, and Einstein are right in pointing out that an important bottleneck of prospective memory is the association between a target event and the target action because it is always critical that the target action is accessible. I also agree that the retrieval of the target action can usually be classified as an automatic retrieval. Subjects do not check any (familiar) item to see whether it is a target event or not, and they do not constantly search for possible target actions. Therefore, the prospective memory performance should be a function of the effectiveness by which the automatic retrieval process, elicited by the target event, is able to bring the target action into consciousness. The prospective memory task is therefore comparable to the automatic retrieval in a paired-associate-learning task, and, in fact, the same factors seem to influence both tasks (cf. e.g., McDaniel, Robinson-Riegler, & Einstein, 1998). The necessity to construct new associations is especially apparent in those cases in which the to-be-performed action is not related to the denoted action, for example, to push a button when the word "waving" is presented. The tasks used in the experiments of Guynn et al. were of this type.

However, in accepting this automatic component, one should not overlook that other retrieval possibilities are available as well. The existence of the automatic component does not exclude the possibility of an intentional search for to-be-performed actions. Subjects can intentionally scan their memory to find out what they have to do, and then the situation is more similar to that of free recall. This might not occur in the laboratory situation realized by Guynn et al., but for everyday actions it is common. Specific cues might not directly retrieve to-be-performed actions, but they elicit a memory check to see whether all intended actions were performed, for instance, when leaving the office or when closing an order list. Therefore, prospective and retrospective memory tasks share a lot of features in the retrieval component because the automatic as well as the deliberate retrieval possibilities exist in prospective memory just as in retrospective memory.

Nevertheless, in one aspect, retrieval in prospective memory differs from retrieval in retrospective memory. In prospective memory tasks, persons have *two competing tasks*. They work on a cover task, in order to simulate the everyday situation of ongoing activities, and additionally they should perform the target action when the target event occurs. Retrieval of the target action is therefore not the participants' main task (for exceptions see e.g., Engelkamp, 1997; West, 1986). Retrieval in prospective memory is similar to a secondary task. During processing of the target event, the retrieved target action has to take over action control against the resistance of the ongoing action, which has to be interrupted. In my view, this dual task condition particularly causes some of the specific effects of prospective memory. A conflict resolution is always necessary to "decide" which of the competing productions is executed. It is probably this component that Guynn et al. discussed as a specific working memory, which is less effective for elderly than for younger people, and it could be this component that causes impaired prospective memory if the frontal lobes are damaged (Shallice & Burgess, 1991; Shimamura, Janowsky, & Squire, 1991). Due to this competition for action control in prospective memory, there is also a trade-off between the control of the primary (cover) task and one of the prospective memory tasks (cf. Ellis & Nimmo-Smith, 1993). The more effort participants invest in the primary task and the better processing is focused on this task, the better competing actions should be inhibited. As a consequence, counterintuitive performances in prospective memory should be reduced with an increase of effort in the main task. Otherwise, reducing the effectiveness of action control might increase the likelihood of performing a prospective target action if the action is automatically retrieved. If subjects are not very effective in inhibiting competing, usually irrelevant actions in everyday contexts, a target action in a prospective memory task might have a better chance to take over action control.

A further peculiarity of prospective memory is related to this conflict of productions or action goals, and in my view this aspect is not yet sufficiently explained by the automatic retrieval idea. A target action, in prospective memory, has a specific quality that distinguishes this representation from all other representations of actions, as well as from action representations in a retrospective memory task. Although in both tasks the same *action content* is retrieved, for instance, "making a phone call," in the prospective task, making a phone call must be additionally experienced as an *intended* action. It is not sufficient that the content is retrieved; it must also be undertaken as an actual goal. Of course, not all actions that come to mind are performed. What has to be added is the volition to perform it (cf. Figure 8.1). That the item's content is automatically retrieved therefore does not explain how the item is receiving its status as an actual goal. We have to explain what distinguishes goals from non-goals (cf. Heckhausen & Beckman, 1990).

We can consider different solutions to this problem. Goals might be kept active in a *goal stack* (Anderson, 1983) that would keep these items permanently in a working memory (cf. Goschke & Kuhl, 1993). One might think that the frontal component discussed by Guynn et al. is such a working memory. However, this is not the case. The authors discussed that an action is delivered to the frontal component by automatic retrieval, from which it follows that the action was not previously contained in this memory. The assumed frontal component only schedules actions that already compete for action control. However, a specific version of this frontal component would operate in the intended way. The scheduling component must hold the target action(s), like a goal stack, and the automatically retrieved target action hits this entry, which effects results in the execution of the action. The "working memory" would then be the reference list of actual action goals that is used to control the execution.

Another possibility is that *target actions are retrieved*, as in explicit memory, and participants become aware of the action. Each conscious action is checked as to whether it is a member of a goal list, similar to what happens in recognition, when the item has to be recognized as a member of a study list. Like in recognition, this latter process can be thought of as a two-component process: a familiarity process and/or an active retrieval of relevant knowledge that, in this context, could be a kind of a goal marker. Solving a prospective memory task might then be described as a two-step process. A specific content is brought into consciousness by automatic retrieval, and the participant becomes aware of this item as a goal action due to its familiarity or its distinctness (uniqueness). If this happens, the ongoing action is interrupted and the target action is performed. These two possibilities, to control for prospective memory, might co-exist. They might represent *different types of action control, a direct specification of actions, and a conscious control.*

Obviously, whether retrospective and prospective memory are the same or not cannot be decided in an all or nothing fashion. Some components are shared by both memory tasks. The action content has to be retrieved, either by a search process or by an automatic retrieval of the target action. Then the actions have to be recognized either as a member of the study list or a member of the goal set. However, there are also differences. In prospective memory, the memory task is a secondary task that has to be performed apart from the main task. A retrieved action must get the status of an actual action goal, and the action impulse of the target action must be strong enough to interrupt the primary task. This aspect is unimportant in retrospective memory. Due to these characteristics of prospective and retrospective memory, the trade-off between inhibition of concurrent tasks and focusing on the main task operates in opposing directions. A very efficient inhibition of concurrent tasks usually enhances performances in retrospective memory, but it might reduce event based prospective memory. Additionally, the effectiveness of a scheduling component becomes relevant, as discussed by Guynn et al. This component is not important in retrospective memory because usually the only task participants have is remembering. In contrast, in prospective memory, scheduling is one of the most important components for memory. After this short discussion of prospective action memory I want to deal with the components of retrospective action memory.

THE COMPONENTS OF THE SPT ADVANTAGE: A CRITICAL EVALUATION

Actions as Achievement Situations and as Social Events

The preceding discussion concerning prospective memory, and especially the arguments and results put forward by Foley and Ratner in Chapter 5, emphasized the specific importance of action goals. *If an intended action is performed a goal always exists that the actor is willing to achieve.* This aspect is particular to actions and has several consequences.

First, actions can be *successful* or they can fail with all the positive and negative emotions of the actor. For everyday actions, these effects are very likely important components that contribute to memory. We know that emotions influence memory (Christianson, 1992), and similarly the emotional reaction to the self-performed action should change memory performances. The same is true for *self-involvement*, which also enhances memory. Subjects think about self-relevant actions more often; they evaluate the action's outcomes more carefully, and they consider possible reasons for success or failure. These reflections, cf. Johnson's multiple-entry model discussed in Chapter 5, should also become part of the memory record. All of these (part) processes are able to enhance memory of actions due to the fact that this information elaborates the memory entry of the action. The results of monitoring actions, as well as subjects' consideration regarding success and failure, should therefore also contribute to action memory.

For this reason, Foley and Ratner are probably right when they state that effects caused by goals and self involvement are relevant for the memory of activities. Activities are complex actions that, in principle, could fail, and they are often difficult sequences of part actions in which each action is based on the outcome of the previous one. The actor can attribute success or failure in these activities to his or her own effort. Furthermore, due to the fact that other people usually take part in the activities as well, these peoples' social reaction to the actor's behavior reinforces this action or punishes it. The results presented in Chapter 5 confirm that these components influence memory. We therefore have to recognize the effects of goals, of success, of failure, as well as of social contexts on memory for activities and on memory for everyday actions. However, these topics are not an issue in SPT research.

It is therefore questionable whether these aspects are essential characteristics of every action, including SPTs, or whether they are a *surplus of activities performed in social contexts*. Most subject-performed tasks either do not show these features or show them in a merely rudimentary way. Therefore, these features probably do not explain the memory advantage observed in SPT studies. SPTs are small actions that are very simple. Usually, there is no chance of failing, and the only emotional reaction might be that participants are ashamed of the overt enactment in public. After a few actions, even this feeling is lost, and subjects are quite relaxed. Moreover, in SPT studies, the experimenter usually takes precautions to avoid that participants have such emotional reactions. Therefore, the emotional components should be fairly unimportant for SPT memory, although they clearly contribute to memory for everyday activities. The same is true for the success that subjects experience in the performance of the action. The actions are so simple that nobody would be proud of the successful execution of the action (for another influence of success on action memory cf. the section "The Episodic Integration effects by Means of Motor Encoding" in Chapter 4). In addition, in subject-performed tasks, actors have only a minimal social context, namely the experimenter, because the action is performed alone in the laboratory. Even the necessity of monitoring is reduced because often no real objects were given to the subjects. Instead of the absence of all these components, memory is enhanced if subjects performed the actions during study.

Taking these differences between activities and SPTs into account, I suspect that the encoding of the actions' outcome and the self-involvement of the participants are not very likely to explain the memory advantage for SPT as compared to VT. Although all these features are relevant for memory of everyday activities, and also for laboratory studies that simulate components of these situations, simply performing, as done in SPT studies, must enhance memory by mechanisms other than these goal-specific effects discussed by Foley and Ratner. In principle, the authors present this argument themselves when they state "that actions in SPT, mimic surface features of actions, but do not reflect their goal-directed meanings." If the authors are right in this respect, then the effects based on evaluating goal-directed aspects cannot be relevant for memory in SPT.

Nevertheless, it is too hasty to infer from this position that any influence of the subjects' reflections on SPT memory can be ignored in general. If such processes were enabled by the experimental conditions, they influenced memory. For example, if actions are performed with real objects, monitoring processes and evaluations of the action's outcome contribute to action memory, probably because these results are automatically integrated into the memory record. However, these effects do not properly represent the SPT effect. In contrast, they contribute to SPT memory above and beyond the effects that are more closely tied to performance itself. As the effects of objects in SPT demonstrate, the encoding of object information enhances memory (Engelkamp & Zimmer, 1983, 1996; Nyberg, Nilsson, & Bäckman, 1991). However, the SPT effect, that is, the effect of enactment, is strong and of the same size, even if no objects were given to the subjects, which demonstrates that performance per se is memory efficient. Interestingly, the effects of objects were lowered if the objects were not really used in the actions, and if the actions did not produce real outcomes, although the objects were still physically present (cf. penultimate section of the chapter by Foley & Ratner). One might interpret this latter result as support for the assumption that additional perceptual information is most memory efficient if the "objects" were *relevant* for the action, either as instruments, patients, or outcomes.

Focusing Processes on Performance

A further consequence of the fact that actions are goal directed was already mentioned as we discussed prospective memory. There I speculated that concurrent actions, which do not contribute to the same goal, are inhibited in order to maximize the effectiveness of the actor. This behavior has three consequences: (1) the processing of item meaning is focused on the action denoted by the phrase; (2) all items on the study list are certainly processed and participants do not skip processing any of the items; and finally (3) each item is conceptually encoded because participants have to know what to do, independent of the subjects' encoding strategies or efforts.

The fact that, in SPT, thinking is oriented to the action goal and performance determines the kind of information that is processed during encoding. In the context of actions, it is less likely that phrases are interpreted in different ways. On the contrary, thinking is focused on the core meaning of the target item. The subjects' task is to understand which action the phrase is referring to, and then they are required to perform this action. This is a clear goal for processing, and it is not obvious why participants should do something else. Therefore, further processes, such as organization, elaboration, and others, are usually not directly supported by performance. On the contrary, all types of processing are time consuming, and therefore, within the limited encoding time, there is a trade-off between these two classes of processing, action relevant and non-relevant processes. *The information on the action is processed at the expense of other information* because the performance of the action can be controlled by the experimenter (it is visible). As a consequence, performance enhances item-specific information, but it does not increase relational information (cf. the results reported in Chapter 1 and Zimmer & Engelkamp, 2000.) Establishing episodic relational information (Engelkamp, 1998), that is, *new* relations between unrelated items, is especially hindered by performance (e.g., Engelkamp, Mohr, & Zimmer, 1991).

The next effect is also caused by the fact that actions had to be overtly performed. *The overt enactment supports the control of attention or mental processing.* The overt performance can be controlled by the experimenter, and this guarantees the processing of each item. The necessity to perform each action helps subjects attend to each action and avoid losing some items due to inattentiveness. *Performance is an environmental support for cognitive processing*, and this might, in part, explain why differences in the individual effectiveness of mental processing are less important in SPT than in VT. Those people who need such support, such as elderly people (Craik, 1983), should benefit more from this quality than those who do not need this support. These differential benefits of different groups of subjects equalize memory performances. However, this advantage is lost if the memory task gains from additional processes, especially relational processing. For example, if the material is organized and the study list is rather long, memory is enhanced if people have good retrieval paths. Therefore, with such lists, the effectiveness of mental processing is relevant again, because performance directs processing to the item itself, but it does not trigger these further processes. This would explain, for example, why under these conditions aging effects occur again (for instance, Brooks & Gardiner, 1994). The environmental support of performance is therefore only effective if the information that was processed during the carrying out of the action, because it was action relevant, is also that kind of information that is helpful in solving the memory task.

Finally, performance supports mental processing in a third way because subjects have to know what to do. During the planning of the action, participants have to understand what the meaning of the verbal command is, and this causes the semantic processing of each item. Therefore, *conceptual processing is a necessary component of SPT*. This aspect is often overlooked when it is discussed, whether the memory advantage of SPT is a conceptual effect or something else. In order to perform an action, on verbal command, it is obligatory to process the command's meaning in order to know what is to be done (cf. Figure 1). Therefore, in a subject-performed task, conceptual information is processed, and this information should contribute to memory. Due to this effect, the instruction to perform an action implicitly is also an instruction for conceptual processing. This explains why levels of processing effects are reduced in SPT compared to VT (Nilsson & Craik, 1990). There is conceptual encoding, which also has a task that orients subjects to the verbal surface of the items (Zimmer & Engelkamp, 1999). However, one should consider the possibility that the content of conceptual processing is a different one in SPT than in VT.

For SPT, in my view, one should therefore not ask whether processing is exclusively conceptual or "motor." It is always both! Carrying out actions on verbal commands always includes conceptual processing, and therefore, in SPT, actions cannot be performed without conceptual processing. The fact that conceptual information is processed when actions are performed was never denied when the contribution of motor information to memory was claimed (cf. the comment by Engelkamp). Therefore, it is not a contradiction to the motor-component view if divided attention during encoding impairs memory (cf. Chapter 4). In this respect, Kormi-Nouri and Nilsson are correct in stating that SPT is a conceptual encoding task. However, this is only part of the effect. The influence of divided attention on memory performances only demonstrates that voluntary encoding processes also contribute to memory in SPT, but it does not say anything about the contribution of other processes, for instance, motor processes, to SPT memory.

Item Integration by Performance

Kormi-Nouri and Nilsson explained the SPT effect using an item-integration hypothesis (Kormi-Nouri, 1994). Three components were mentioned as relevant: (1) a better integration between the environment (the task) and the subject, (2) a better within-event integration, that is, an integration of the components of actions, and (3) an enhanced between-event integration.

The first argument is very similar to the suggestion of a *higher ego-involvement* in actions than in verbal tasks as it was already discussed under the goal-oriented perspective. Therefore, I do not want to discuss this aspect further. The new aspect, mentioned by the authors, that humans might have a specific "biological preparedness" to integrate actions will be discussed later. However, before continuing, I would like to make one additional remark to clarify the restrictions involved in the integration of information in the context of actions. We know that SPT does not enhance memory of the action's context, that is, information about the environment in which the action was performed (e.g., Koriat, Ben-Zur, & Druch, 1991). The assumption that performance enhances the integration of the environment is therefore only valid if the action itself is taken as the environment and not the environment in which the action is carried out.

The second aspect of the integration hypothesis is more relevant here because we had not yet discussed this aspect in more detail. The authors postulated that *performance is the "glue" "that cements the components of actions into a single memory unit."* Similar suggestions were already made earlier in the course of SPT research. Engelkamp and Perrig (1986) investigated sentence memory, in cued recall, with the idea that performance enhances the strength of connections between sentence elements that are functionally related in performing the actions. Zimmer (1986) demonstrated that, in SPT, sentences with common words did not show a FAN effect (in VT they did) if the two sentences denoted actions with different movements and these movements were performed. He presumed that the involved different motor programs divided the representations of the sentences into two unique and separate memory tokens. Furthermore, the item-specific effects, discussed in Chapter 1, are interpreted in a comparable way. The postulation that performance enhances integration is, therefore, to a large extent, the same as saying that performance enhances item-specific information and generates unique memory entries. Most researchers on action memory, including myself, therefore will agree on this point. However, the really interesting question remains unsolved by this statement. What is the mechanism (the glue) that connects these elements?

Kormi-Nouri and Nilsson assumed that it is the fact that the action (the movement) and the object, for instance, lifting and the pen, are registered together and not separately. What does this mean? One possibility is that *performance helps delineate episodes*. The goal to perform the denoted action indicates the beginning and the end of the episode, that is, from presentation of the sentence up to the completion of the action. All aspects between these two points belong to the same episode. The actions clearly cut the flow of events into pieces that are the to-be-remembered items. This clear separation would make the entries of the individual items more distinct. Using this, performance would help to generate tokens in memory. One could say it guides perception, and, with this, it indirectly contributes to the integration of the memory components. I am not aware of any research that has been done specifically to test this idea, but it is an interesting aspect that merits more attention.

However, it is also possible that performance not only defines episodes but also contributes more directly to the generation of tokens. *Carrying out an action may actively bind together the components involved in the action.* The motor program, or an action schema (Norman, 1981), which is activated to perform the action, could have this integrative capability. The action plan for lifting something has a "slot" for the object that is lifted, and when these actions are performed the movement parameters have to be adjusted to the features of the used objects. This specification integrates the object into the movement (cf. Figure 8.1). The action programs might therefore be the units that clump and bind together the components of actions. Zimmer (1986) interpreted his effects in this way. If such schemata or programs bind the components of actions together, then the item-integration hypothesis does not contradict the motor interpretation of the SPT effect. On the contrary, the integration could be interpreted as an effect of the activation of motor programs that occurs when actions are performed during study.

The empirical results, in support of the within item integration, are ambiguous. In cued recall, Kormi-Nouri and Nilsson reported higher SPT effects for poorly integrated items than for well integrated items (look at the stone versus read the book). In these experiments, the integration was manipulated by the pre-experimental association between the verb and the noun. However, this procedure makes it difficult to distinguish between semantic and episodic memory because subjects could name the correct target as the most likely associate, even if they did not remember the episode. In fact, for well integrated items, with both encoding operations, subjects' performance scores were very high so that differences in the size of the SPT effect made a clear-cut interpretation impossible. Additionally, in this experiment, verbal associations were manipulated, the association of the noun and the verb, rather than the availability of motor programs or action schemata,

More critical, therefore, is another result that was reported by Foley and Ratner (cf. Ratner & Hill, 1991). They observed that sentences with transitive verbs that require objects (e.g., push the refrigerator) were *not* recalled better than intransitive sentences (e.g., sit beside the refrigerator). This would mean that free recall does not profit from item integration. In contrast, if the actions were (re)performed during recall, the manner in which the movements were carried out indicates that for transitive verbs, object information was available to the subjects. The actions were specified, taking into account the specific features of the objects. For example, subjects pretended to push something with their hands that was difficult to move, as if the object was a refrigerator. This effect was stronger for the better integrated transitive verbs than for the intransitive verbs. This latter effect indicates: (a) that movement-specific information is part of the memory trace; (b) that it is remembered, if this kind of information has to be specified during testing, for example, because the actions were to be performed again; and (c) that this effect is stronger if an object is obligatory for the action. Therefore, the results in recall and re-performance do not correspond to each other. Nevertheless, it seems likely that in some way performance enhances the integration of the action elements. However, further experiments are necessary to decide which mechanism integrates components during performance, and how this integration contributes to recall.

Between-Item Integration in SPT

From the viewpoint of Kormi-Nouri and Nilsson, the third component that should be enhanced by performance is *between-item integration*. As Engelkamp has already stated in his comment, based on the assumption that the functional role, which objects have for actions, integrates verbs and objects, it is not implied that relational information should also be enhanced by performance. Actually, in several experiments, evidence was found against the assumption of an enhanced between-item integration (cf. Chapter 1 and Zimmer & Engelkamp, 2000). Contrary to these data, the authors reported in their chapter further results that they interpreted in support of their own view that relational information is enhanced by performance. One effect was that, even in SPT, memory was enhanced if subjects were informed about the categories, and another was that in one of their experiments the SPT effect was larger with than without categorical information (Table 4.5 Exp. 2). However, in my opinion, these effects do not really contradict the position that performance does not enhance relational information.

The first effect supports the concept that *explicit knowledge about the categories* included in a list *enhances relational information also in SPT*. This is not a contradiction. We explicitly acknowledged this possibility (e.g., Zimmer & Engelkamp, 1989a, p. 166), although we stated that relational information is not enhanced by performing. Even in the context of actions, using relational information should be possible, because in SPT actions are also conceptually processed. The critical question is whether relational processing is *generally better* in SPT than in VT and whether this enhancement generally causes the better memory performances in SPT free recall. Postulating that performance does not enhance relational encoding does not include the additional assumption that it is impossible to use relational information under performance. Therefore, the result is compatible with both positions. (For a discussion of strategic and deliberate versus obligatory and automatic processes in the context of performance and memory, see Helstrup, 1987, and the reply of Zimmer and Engelkamp, 1989b.)

However, even in their own experiments Kormi-Nouri and Nilsson observed that the effect of explicitly given categorical information was not enhanced by performance, as a look at Experiment 1 of their Table 4.5 reveals. This effect speaks more for the assumption that relational information is not enhanced by performance. In free recall, the SPT effect was of the same size with and without categorical information, and also the effect of categorical information was of the same size in both encoding conditions. (The bad cued recall performances in VT are probably due to the fact that subjects were instructed to remember nouns, so that verbs were ignored. In SPT, this was not possible because the actions had to be performed, and therefore the verbs also had to be processed. Additionally, subjects in the SPT but not in the VT condition got real objects during study.)

Contrary to the results of the first experiment in the second experiment, the SPT effect was larger with than without categorical information. However, this interaction was not caused by a change of the categorical effects in SPT but instead stems from changes in VT recall. Providing explicit categorical information during cued recall *reduced* performances in VT, whereas recall was slightly increased in SPT, an effect that was comparable to Experiment 1. In my view it is therefore the VT result that has to be explained and not the effect of categorical cues in SPT.

Additionally, in the literature (cf. the overview in Zimmer & Engelkamp, 2000) many results are reported that support the conclusion that: (a) the SPT effect is as large in related as in unrelated lists, (b) that the categorical organization in free recall is not enhanced by performing, and (c) that the correlation between the amount of organization and the number of recalled items is even reduced in SPT. From these results I conclude that *performance enhances item-specific information but not relational information*. However, even if I reiterate the observation, this does not mean that it is impossible to use relational information in SPT and that specific conditions may exist in which relational encoding may be enhanced in SPT compared to VT (cf. e.g., Steffens, 1999). Such exceptional effects, however, cannot explain the large enactment effect on free recall in all those cases in which performance did not enhance relational encoding.

Sensory and Motor Components

Interestingly, although the authors presented different explanations for the SPT advantage, all attempts share one feature. All authors assumed that the memory trace of the items was enriched by additional components when the actions were performed. These components are provided by processing the instructions for performance and by carrying out the actions.

Nilsson and Bäckman, for example, explicitly attributed the higher memory performance in SPT to the multiple features that were encoded if the items were performed. "The differences between SPTs and VTs come about because SPTs are multi-modally encoded and comprise a variety of features. . . . The multi-modality of SPTs includes the auditory mode, through the experimenter's reading of the imperative; the visual modality throughout presentation and performance of SPTs; the tactual mode by means of handling the objects involved in the SPTs; even olfactory and gustatory modes might be involved if SPTs like 'smell the flower' and 'eat the raisin' are used. Moreover, there are verbal features, and dependent upon the nature of the SPT used, features of color, shape, weight, texture, and sound" (Nilsson & Bäckman, 1989, p. 180). Similarly, Engelkamp and Zimmer speculated that the memory traces are enriched by motor components that are encoded in addition to verbal, visual, and conceptual components (e.g., Engelkamp & Zimmer, 1985). Foley and Ratner emphasized the consequences of actions, both the changes in the environment and the reactions of the social context to these changes and the goal-related pieces of information. Therefore, in their basic assumptions, the various ways to explain the SPT effect are not that different. *Memory is better because something additional is encoded due to performance, which elaborates the memory trace, and these components enhance remembering.* What distinguishes the models are the types of features that are seen as relevant for this effect.

Bäckman and Nilsson focus on the *input* variables involved in SPT. These are features defined by the verbal commands and by the objects used in actions, but these are also the consequences of the actions. Interestingly, however, the output itself was not seen as relevant. It was not assumed that output parameters are registered in the memory trace. This corresponds with the storehouse metaphor in which memory is a depository for input events. In spite of this, it remains unclear why output events are not remembered. On the contrary, from a functional perspective, it is quite useful to remember how one has reacted to a specific stimulus. In accordance with this perspective, Engelkamp's results (Chapter 3), which demonstrated memory for output effects, are quite reasonable. Specific parameters of the actions are remembered, and if subjects re-performed these actions the match of these parameters either support or impair performances dependent on the concrete testing conditions. Furthermore, if actions were prepared but were interrupted just before they were carried out, which in turn hindered their performance, then memory was reduced relative to those cases in which the actions were actually carried out (Zimmer, 1996a). We should therefore conclude that *in addition to input, output events are also stored in SPT.*

However, not only processes during the execution of actions contribute to memory; the *preparation* of the action influences this as well. Actions that were planned are recalled better than actions that were imitated (Zimmer & Engelkamp, 1996) or prescribed (Oesterreich & Köddig, 1995). Additionally, actions that were only planned but not overtly executed because a no-go signal was given to the subjects showed a repetition effect if the same action needed to be performed a second time. However, this effect was smaller than the one that was observed if the action was actually performed (Zimmer, 1996a), and these actions were recalled worse than those that were performed (Zimmer & Engelkamp, 1984). Obviously, both processes—planning as well as the overt performance—cause some memory effects.

Taken as a whole, these results show that all features, from planning the execution up to carrying out the action and encoding the results, elaborate the representation of the action and thereby contribute to the memory of actions. *Therefore, action memory is multimodal memory of input and output features.* It will be discussed later whether this justifies the conclusion that different systems contribute to memory. At least implicitly, the position that action memory comprises multiple contents is shared by most of the contributors. In spite of this consensus, however, I want to add a few remarks to further clarify some consequences and restrictions of this perspective.

First, the demonstration of conceptual influences on memory in SPT does not deny the contribution of output effects to memory. Kormi-Nouri and Nilsson reported that divided attention also reduced memory in SPT, and they used this as an argument against the motor memory approach. However, if multiple components contribute to memory, such a general interference effect cannot be used as an argument against one specific component. Within the motor approach, it is only assumed that motor components, that is, information about the self performance, contribute to memory, but the effectiveness of other information is not denied. (This latter aspect was often overlooked.) At least for a part of the additional processes, focal attention is necessary, and therefore dividing attention reduces the efficiency of these encoding processes. For example, a part of the conceptual processes are deliberate processes, and dividing attention reduces them in SPT as well. If these components contribute to memory, explicit memory is reduced by dividing attention during encoding. In contrast, the suggested motor program is processed even under divided attention because processing of this information is obligatory when actions are performed. I am not aware of experiments in which the influence of divided attention on the activation of motor information was tested in SPT research.   '

Similarly, movement effects do not extinguish conceptual influences. Some effects, which Engelkamp reported in support of the motor memory explanation, had therefore to be reduced in their significance. Other information, besides the motor one, comes into effect here as well. He reported that motor similarity of distractors influenced memory in SPT more than in VT. The rate of false alarms for conceptually *and* motorically similar items was especially high if the actions were performed. However, the size of this effect represents an overestimation of the contribution of motor components to false recognition. In SPT, more memory entries are accessible than in VT, which is supported by the higher hit rates in SPT than in VT. Therefore, even if the similarity of the targets and distractors are identical in the two encoding conditions, the probability that a partially similar target item falsely hits a token must be higher for SPT than for VT. In other words, the hit rates for identical items give the maximum number of false alarms that are caused by the similarity of study and test item. If we take into account this difference in accessibility, the motor similarity effect does not disappear, but it is clearly reduced. This effect does not contradict the assumption that motor information is part of the memory trace, but it shows that this type of information causes only a part of the effect. As with the other effects, this result also shows that a larger set of components contributes to memory in SPT.

Finally, memory performances are not a positive linear function of the number of features. Foley and Ratner reported that the number of movements performed for each action does not correlate with recall performances. If the number of elements determines the memory performances, one should expect that an increasing number of elements causes an increase in memory performance. This, however, was not the case. Similar results were observed by others (Helstrup, 1987; Nilsson, Nyberg, Kormi-Nouri, & Rönnlund, 1995; Zimmer, 1984). In all of these studies, within domain elaboration, performing more actions than just the core movement did not influence memory, although memory was much better in SPT than in VT. In contrast, it was not sufficient that any unrelated action was carried out. In spite of enactment, unrelated movements did not enhance memory (Schaaf, 1988). These results suggest that, for specific effects, it is important that only the "*basic* movement" of the denoted action was performed, whereas the specific details of the movement are not relevant. Comparable effects were reported for recognition. If distractors were conceptually different, false alarms did not vary with the similarity of the movements of the denoted actions, although a strong SPT effect generally occurred (cf. Chapter 3). If recognition is enhanced by performance because movement information is part of the memory record and this movement component is always addressed during recognition, one should expect at least slight similarity effects.

The fact that the number of features is not relevant indicates that the effectiveness of performance is more similar to that of tagging. It seems that *carrying out the actions* specifically *marks the memory traces as performed*, and this information can be used during remembering (Zimmer, 1996b). Another possibility is that the item carries a pointer to an action register, which can be used without interpreting the content of the entry, to which the pointer is directed. If this is correct, the *presence* of a motor component would be sufficient to set up the memory effect. The more specific information on the concrete content would not be available until the program is opened, which happens when the subject runs through it while performing the action. To my knowledge these possibilities have not yet been more carefully tested.

ACTIONS: AN ANCIENT MEMORY CONTENT WITH SPECIFIC FEATURES

Another aspect that was addressed in various ways in several contributions was the idea that *action memory is an evolutionary old memory performance*. Kormi-Nouri and Nilsson (Chapter 4), for example, explicitly formulated that "enactment is more basic than verbal encoding by being evolutionarily older" and that "enactment, in the form of such a biological preparedness, constitutes the basis for optimal processing." Foley and Ratner emphasized the importance of goal-orientation for remembering actions. Having goals and behaving in order to reach these goals is a basic feature of human existence. The authors speculated that *actions* are the interface between the subject and the environment, and, as such, processing of actions and their memory should be evolutionarily old. Guynn, McDaniel, and Einstein referred to specific brain modules that are involved in prospective memory, and, as brain modules, they should be the outcome of evolution. Finally, even the contribution of a specific motor system to episodic memory, as postulated by Engelkamp, can be interpreted similarly. Therefore, in some way, nearly all authors acknowledged the special role of actions in evolution, and, as a consequence, actions have to be considered as a particular memory content. There is a lot that supports the relevance of this aspect, but there are also other features that make the relevance of this argument doubtful.

Carrying out actions is a fundamental behavior of an organism. In principle, input and output systems only evolve in interaction. The output systems need the information of the input systems, and the relevance of the results of the input systems is defined by the usefulness of this information for actions (cf. Gibson's view). It may therefore *enhance the success of an organism if the actions are remembered* that were performed in reaction to a specific stimulus or to achieve a specific goal. In developing this idea further, one can speculate that memory records of self-performed actions, together with the conditions of their performance, are automatically constructed to be used again in future actions.

From this point of view, a complete sequence from input to output may be seen as the basic unit of encoding, and thus such sequences may constitute the units for remembering as well. A prototype of a "complete" memory record would then be a trace of the entire sequence: (a) the encoding of the input event that defines the starting conditions of the actions (productions), (b) the action that was planned and carried out to it, which provides information that may be reused in a future action, to (c) the results and consequences caused by the actions that reflect their usefulness. Such sequences could be the evolutionary origin of episodes, and as a consequence *forming records of self-performed actions may therefore be a basic memory mechanism.* If such a mechanism exists it would cause a biological preparedness for remembering actions. The good item-specific information would be caused by the fact that actions are the pro-totypical units of episodes.

However, attributing the memory efficiency of performance to such a biolog-ical preparedness causes a problem. Speaking of a basic memory process that is used to acquire knowledge about actions and their conditions of execution reminds us of skill learning and schema acquisition. In contrast, studies on subject-performed tasks investigate episodic memory. It might immediately be plausible that skill learning and schema acquisition are influenced by enactment, but it is not intuitively clear why episodic memory for actions should operate in the same way. One might therefore agree that aspects of performance are automatically remembered in some action modules for future enactment, but one might not accept that this also happens in episodic memory.

A closer look at the necessities of action memory, however, reveals that, for an organism, it is not only useful to abstract generic knowledge about actions, but also to keep specific information on the individual actions and use this to encode actions as episodes, that is, unique events. For actions, it is often nec-essary to know that it was a specific action that was performed in order to avoid an unnecessary repetition, and, therefore, records of individual actions should be kept separate, at least for some time. Furthermore, it is often necessary to know details of the performed action because an action that was useful in its original context may be harmful in a different context. Memory records of self-performed actions should therefore be quite specific. In summary, it seems likely that during evolution the conditions that constrain the success of actions have caused actions to be automatically (involuntarily) encoded as unique events, and this may contribute to some effects of self-performance of actions in episodic memory tasks.

The idea of an automatic encoding of actions, however, also raises questions. What are the aspects of actions that are automatically encoded? Are all aspects encoded or do different sets of features exist, some of which are recorded and some of which are not? From everyday experience, we know that we do not remember all details of actions, and, therefore, different sets of features of these actions exist that have different strengths for remembering. Some clues as to which features of actions should be remembered and which should not may be found in the ideas of Goodale and Humphrey. These authors speculated that in the brain, not only one system exists that is involved in perception (and action), but several. Basically, they distinguish two different groups of modules: input-output systems involved in the (low-level) control of action and input systems involved in the conscious reconstruction of the environment (cf. e.g., Goodale & Humphrey, 1998). Goodale and Humphrey took the position that vision evolved "not to enable one to 'see' the world, but to guide their [animals'] movement through it" (p. 183). These authors reported plenty of evidence for this assumption. Several input-output lines or visuomotor "modules" exist that control motor output. Independently of these modules, a different visual system is used in perception and recognition of objects for the organisms' cognitive life.

From a memory perspective, it is interesting that these two sets of modules have different consequences for remembering. The visuomotor modules guide the *actual* performance of movements, and for this purpose memory is *not* very relevant. Therefore, this system may not keep memory records. In contrast, the perception system is linked with cognitive processes such as long-term memory. Therefore, only the perceptual reconstructive system should contribute to memory, but the visuomotor module should not. This has consequences for the suggestion of an ancient memory process. If most processes during the performance of actions are operating within the "memory free" visuomotor module, the existence of an ancient memory mechanism for encoding of actions is not very likely.

However, for the memory effects, this bold interpretation of Goodale and Humphrey's position of action control is probably not correct. It is more likely that some aspects of actions are only transiently represented, whereas some other aspects of the actions are automatically kept in a memory record. For example, specific parameters of actions specified in a low-level visuomotor control of movements, for example, the concrete trajectory of a movement in space, may not be recorded in memory although this information was processed when the action was carried out. In contrast, other movement information may be automatically remembered. As an example for the not-remembered features, position memory could be mentioned. Spatial information of movement was not enhanced by performance. Relative to a pure perceptual condition, memory for the layout of objects—a task that Goodale and Humphrey attribute to the perception system—was not enhanced by performance, by actively placing the objects in their positions (cf. Chapter 1). In contrast, repetition effects for specific movements were enhanced by carrying out the actions during study, even in comparison to planning (Zimmer, 1996a). These repetition effects occurred without memory intentions, and they can be quite specific, as the effects of re-performance have shown (cf. Chapter 3).

In summary, the idea must be restricted that actions are remembered well because they were encoded by an ancient memory process. Such an old mechanism probably cannot exist for each process involved in the control of action. On the contrary, in action control, several modules are involved, and a subset of them may unintentionally produce memory records, whereas others may not. In order to determine the memory efficiency of the different processes and in order to find out which process belongs to which subset, we have to conduct the task analysis of the execution conditions of actions more carefully, and then we have to design suitable memory experiments. Such studies may enable us to untangle the components involved in the execution and control of actions, and they may help us to decide to what extent these components contribute to memory.

THE PROCESS OF RETRIEVAL IN ACTION MEMORY

Active Memory Search versus Pop-Out into Memory

The final component that has to be dealt with in the context of action memory is retrieval. Most of the effects discussed in the context of action memory were encoding effects. However, in the preceding chapters, there were at least two places where retrieval was also a topic. Guynn, McDaniel, and Einstein investigated whether retrieval of prospective tasks is automatic or search based; and Engelkamp as well as Kormi-Nouri and Nilsson searched for retrieval enactment effects.

Guynn et al. contrasted active search of memory with automatic retrieval. These are two possible retrieval modes, which are not only of importance in the context of prospective memory but also in retrospective memory (e.g., Jacoby, 1991). Guynn et al. suggested that in event based prospective memory tasks, the intended action does not have to be searched for, but instead it is automatically retrieved by a hippocampal component (Moscovitch, 1992), which is activated as soon as a target event is processed. The reported results support their view, and I do not think that further discussion regarding this topic is necessary.

Interestingly, a comparable suggestion was made by Zimmer (1991; Zimmer, Helstrup, and Engelkamp, 2000) for retrospective memory of self-performed actions. These authors suggested that the SPT *free recall advantage is mainly caused by an enhanced automatic retrieval process*, which they called a *pop-out mechanism*. This mechanism is a rather passive process and not an active search using relational information, and usually only a small proportion of items is susceptible to pop-out. Only very recent or outstanding events attract this process. Zimmer et al. assumed that the number of items that are included in this status is enhanced when actions are carried out. These items should pop into conscious memory when participants think back to the recent past without an intentional search for specific items. Actions performed "just a moment ago" provide distinct memory entries that can be easily accessed for a short time. This advantage decays when time is passing or when further items are encoded.

The mechanism is therefore most efficient at the recency part of a study list. Because performance enhances the effectiveness of the pop-out process, the recency effect is more extended in SPT than in VT. Zimmer et al. were able to demonstrate this effect in several experiments with list lengths from 12 to 80 items. In Figure 8.2 this effect is demonstrated for the longest list of 80 items.

In all experiments conducted by Zimmer et al., SPT showed an extended recency effect that always occurred when actions were performed during study, independent of further conceptual encoding processes. The extended recency effect was observed when subjects had a verbal surface encoding instruction for the phrases and additionally performed the actions, and this shallow encoding did not reduce the effect. Neither conceptual processing nor strategies were capable of producing a comparable pop-out, and dividing attention during retrieval did not reduce the efficiency of this process. The recency effect in SPT was extended compared to VT, and this effect was also not reduced when a secondary task was performed during recall. These results support the assumption of an automatic retrieval process.

A similar process was suggested by Moscovitch (e.g., 1992, 1994). This author postulated the existence of a hippocampal component that has features comparable to the one we had suggested for retrieval of enacted events. Moscovitch spoke of the possibility that "memories may pop into mind," and that

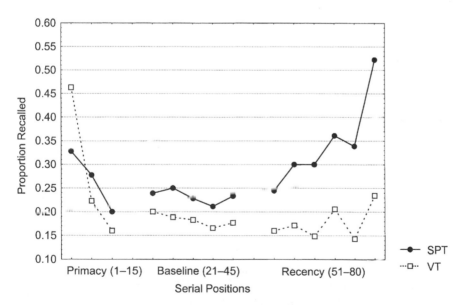

FIGURE 8.2. Free recall performance for an 80 item list. An illustration of the extended recency effect in subject-performed tasks for a study list of 80 items. The relative free recall performances are given dependent on the input positions and the type of encoding (data from Exp. 2 of Zimmer et al., 2000).

this component "responds reflexively . . . and cannot conduct a memory search," and he distinguished this component from an extrahippocampal (frontal) process that uses organization (Moscovitch, 1994, p. 277).

I assume that the hippocampal component can operate on specific mental events similarly to how it operates on external cues. Very distinct and unique events attract the hippocampal component, and due to this resonance they pop into conscious memory. I assume that this pop-out mechanism, based on item-specific information, is enhanced by SPT, and I also believe that this supplementary mechanism substantially enhances free recall of performed actions. Due to a higher proportion of automatically retrieved items, an additional retrieval possibility is created that makes participants less dependent on relational information. Items that pop into mind did not need to be searched for, and therefore memory of these items does not depend on the availability of relational information. The fact that enactment enhances the effectiveness of the pop-out process can explain why relational information is less important in SPT than in VT (cf. Chapter 1). In summary, automatic retrieval should have a greater influence on memory for SPTs than memory for VTs.

However, I ought to mention that the shape of the serial position curve and its dependence on the type of encoding is different in a delayed recall. In a delayed recall, in SPT and in VT, memory performances declined over input positions, and on all positions a SPT advantage was observed that was comparable in size (e.g., Cohen, 1981, 1983). The same result we also observed in delayed recall of longer lists. The retrieval processes are therefore probably different in SPT immediate and delayed recall. This aspect, that retrieval processes involved in SPT may differ from the processes in VT, has not attracted much attention yet in SPT research.

Retrieval Enactment

A further aspect concerning retrieval and SPT is the role of enactment during retrieval. Kormi-Nouri and Nilsson (Chapter 4) summarized a series of experiments demonstrating that *retrieval enactment is not efficient in free recall*, and they took this as an argument against the motor system explanation of SPT. Due to the principle of encoding specificity, they expected that carrying out actions, in SPT, during retrieval should enhance memory compared to a verbal recall. This was clearly not the case. In his comment, Engelkamp already pointed to the fact that, in contrast to free recall, such an effect occurs in recognition. A closer look at the retrieval conditions reveals that differences between these two memory tests are critical for the different results.

Kormi-Nouri and Nilsson's predictions about retrieval enactment were based on the assumption that SPT records are *exclusively* represented within an independent action (motor) memory system and that only this system is used in SPT recall. Based on these assumptions, their conclusion was correct. However, as I, as well as Engelkamp in his comment, had already stated, a different assumption was made by the multimodal memory approach. In this approach, it was only assumed that action records *additionally* contain motor information, from which it follows that their memory records are not encapsulated within a motor memory system. It was furthermore suggested that the relations between actions, inter-item relations, are conceptual in nature, and that even information on the similarity of movements implicitly represented within the motor programs cannot be directly used by the subjects (Zimmer, 1984; Zimmer & Engelkamp, 1989a). The latter assumptions imply that intentional search is based on conceptual information. Finally, in order to carry out a specific action, it must be intended. Based on these assumptions, I want to analyze how enactment during retrieval could enhance memory in free recall.

In the retrieval-enactment experiments subjects were instructed to perform the actions instead of simply remembering them and writing them down. This retrieval-enactment procedure parallels the study-enactment condition. However, although the "enacted recall" is an enactment condition, this task, nevertheless, relies on verbal components. It is very likely that verbal self-instructions mediate the self-performed action during recall. One has to intend to perform a specific action, and this intention is formulated as an ego-oriented, probably verbal command. Therefore, memory in a "performed" recall is similar to memory of the commands.

In order to carry out actions from memory during testing, subjects had to generate the commands in the retrieval-enactment condition as they had to do in verbal recall. The only difference from verbal recall is that subjects had to perform the denoted actions instead of writing them down. Subject-performed recall is therefore not very different from the standard verbal recall. If this task analysis is correct, enactment during recall would enhance memory only if the generation of items (the commands) is enhanced. However, relational information is not positively influenced by performance, and, therefore, re-performing the actions does not substantially influence the generation of items. Retrieval enactment may enhance recall only in those cases, in which performing actions during recall generates new information that is otherwise not available, and if this information can be used as additional cues for retrieval. This possibility was already discussed by Kormi-Nouri and Nilsson.

In summary, due to the conditions of action control and the constraints of the representations, retrieval enactment has no strong influence on recall, independent of the existence of motor information among the memory components. Therefore, retrieval should generally not be influenced by enactment during testing, and, therefore, neither should free recall, although the actions were performed during study. Retrieval is probably influenced only via the pop-out mechanism, and this is enhanced by enactment during *study*.

In recognition, the situation is different. In recognition, all items are presented to the subjects, and, therefore, generation of items does not limit performance. Carrying out an action during recognition that was already studied reactivates movement-specific information, which becomes an element of the memory record during study enactment. This re-performance enhances the contribution of movement information to the subjects' decision. If the actual movement matches the remembered movement pattern of the action, it becomes more likely that the item will be judged as old. In accordance with this, and compatible with the encoding-specificity assumption, it was observed that (re-)performing actions during testing increases the hit rates for old items but also the rates of false alarms for items that are similar in their movement (cf. Chapter 3). Because in recognition subjects are informed which action they should perform, retrieval of the item content is not necessary. The influence of enactment during testing is therefore not an effect on retrieval, that is the generation of items, but on recognition, the match between the actually performed action and the action kept in memory. The fact that performance during testing affects this decision demonstrates that memory for performed actions includes movement specific information.

MEMORY FOR ACTIONS: ONLY DISTINCT OR EVEN SYSTEM-SPECIFIC?

Before closing, I want to make a few remarks in response to the general question as to whether action memory is something specific or if it is even supported by a specific memory system.

First, two different interpretations of "motor memory" exist that have to be distinguished in their specificity.

- The first usage is that some memory effects for actions occur if and only if the actions were processed in order to carry them out and if these actions were actively performed.
- The second usage is that an independent cognitive module, to which specific brain structures probably correspond, contributes to action memory.

SPT Memory: An Effect of Performance

The first interpretation is hardly controversial. In my opinion, the chapters of this book have convincingly demonstrated that instructing subjects to perform actions during study produces very specific encoding effects that cannot be established in the same way by other types of instructions. *Overt enactment must therefore be considered a distinct type of encoding with special memory effects.*

It seems to me that in several circumstances the term "motor encoding," or "motor memory," did not express more than this. It refers to a class of memory effects that are observed if and only if actions are performed during encoding.

As the previous chapters have shown, performance elicits a number of processes that are specific for the enactment situation. Due to the fact that these processes are specific to enactment, each of these processing results in isolation or a combination of them can explain the SPT memory advantage. A portion of these effects is caused by the specific demands of the overt enactment condition. Examples for these are: the focusing of processing onto enactment, planning processes, the activation of movement specific information, implementing motor "programs," the integration of objects into performance, the environmental support created by the carrying out of each action, and so on.

Another portion of effects might usually exist with everyday actions, and in the laboratory the performance of mini-tasks might habitually elicit the same processes. Everyday actions are goal-directed, and these goals cause further processes. Examples of these processes are evaluations of the outcomes and consequences, an increase of ego-involvement, or stronger emotional reactions. If actions carried out in the laboratory are processed in the same way as everyday actions, these goal-directed components may also become relevant in SPT. This is especially true if SPTs were designed in analogy to everyday situations.

If we make the plausible assumption that at least some of these additional processes are memory efficient and that they occur regularly when actions are carried out, memory must be different if actions were performed than if they were verbally encoded.

Due to these effects, I have no doubt that performing actions during study is a distinct encoding condition that must be distinguished from other types of encoding. Performance strongly changes the encoding processes. It is not only an elaboration or an amplifying of semantic processing.

SPT Memory: An Achievement of a Specific Memory System

In contrast to the first usage of the term "motor memory," which does not specify the modules that enable SPT memory, the second view attributes the memory performance in SPT to a specific subsystem. More exactly, it is postulated that a *specific subsystem additionally contributes to memory if actions were performed*. This is Engelkamp's position.

This position was repeatedly misunderstood. The arguments put forward in the chapter by Kormi-Nouri and Nilsson can be taken as an example of this misinterpretation. The (motor) memory system approach was interpreted in the exclusive sense, that postulating the contribution of a different memory system also means postulating that no other memory system is involved in remembering. It was therefore falsely assumed that if a motor system is involved, no other memory component should be used. This position was never stated, and by definition, for SPTs, it cannot be valid because in SPTs subjects have to enact on verbal commands, and they usually have to recall phrases. Therefore, in any case, verbal as well as conceptual processes are relevant in addition to the effects of performance in the narrower sense (cf. Figure 8.1). Engelkamp therefore emphasized that his assumption is that in SPTs modality-specific *and* conceptual information is remembered. As with the first view, he accepts that within the same (memory) system other processes are effective in SPT than in VT, but additionally he assumes that *modality-specific* information contributes to episodic memory as well, and that these modality-specific elements are components of a specific system: the output system.

Modality-specific information is domain-specific knowledge. In SPT, it is information on the movements, and this knowledge is necessary to perform the actions. The units of information were called motor programs because it is assumed that they are used to control muscle movements. Because this information is specific for the enactment of movements, and because it is always activated if actions are performed, Engelkamp spoke of a subsystem. The close relationship of the represented information to the carrying out of actions is the reason he speaks of a motor memory system. Furthermore, Engelkamp assumed that these movement specific contents and processes contribute to the memory trace. The reader might decide for his or her self whether the presented data support this assumption that movement information contributes to memory. It seems obvious to me that, apart from other memory elements, motor information contributes to memory in SPT. However, it is justified to debate whether this *domain specific knowledge* should be called a *subsystem.*

The mentioned features clearly fulfill some of the criteria that were seen as relevant to postulate a specific subsystem (cf. the comment of Nilsson and Kormi-Nouri, Chapter 7). Due to these characteristics, one can justify calling this set of information, with its processes, a subsystem, a specific *module* that is responsible for *controlling actions.* This system may keep memory records of performed actions, and these records may be (re)used in later actions causing (implicit) memory effects. The "motor system" can therefore be called a subsystem for output, similar to other systems suggested for input, for example, the perceptual entry systems (cf. Schacter, 1994).

However, are these arguments sufficient to postulate a specific memory subsystem for actions that also contributes to *episodic* memory? Of course, it is not a completely different episodic task when subjects are required to remember actions. From that perspective SPT is not specific. SPT has only a specific content, but remembering actions also shares many of the processes involved in the remembering of other types of information. This aspect was especially emphasized in the comments of Nilsson and Kormi-Nouri. Additionally, even in the multimodal approach, it is not assumed that remembering actions is solved merely by the use of the motor partsystem. On the contrary, in SPT, encoding and retrieval processes are in contact with all modalities. Furthermore, the same hippocampal component should contribute to all explicit memory tasks. Therefore, memory for subject-performed tasks is not encapsulated within an action memory system. To a considerable extent, in SPT memory, the same processes are active as in a verbal or in a pictorial memory task. This aspect speaks against the claim of a separate action memory system that is independent of other episodic memory systems. What is different, however, is the part system that represents the specific information. Therefore, in my view, it is more correct to describe remembering SPTs as a memory process that uses a specific part system that is unique for performed actions but that nevertheless works in concert with other memory subsystems. I later want to come back to this aspect after I have discussed some neuropsychological arguments that are relevant for this discussion.

Brain Structures Involved in Performing (and Remembering) Actions

In the field of neuropsychology, it is a common view to attribute unique performances to specific brain systems that are relevant for the critical task. In this tradition, specific neural substrates were also postulated for motor movements. If these substrates are damaged, purposeful movements are impaired. The persons suffer from apraxia. Rothi and Heilman (1997) defined apraxia as a neurological disorder of learned purposeful movements that cannot be explained by an impaired executive or sensory system. In other words, although the effectors can be used and the sensory systems function well, the selection and execution of adequate movement, either to commands or to objects, is impaired. This behavioral consequence is caused by an impaired access to motor programs. Similarly, DeRenzi & Faglioni (1999) define "ideomotor apraxia as a disorder that occurs when patients fail to implement the mental representation of a gesture in a motor programme that specifies the correct innervation of the involved muscles" (p. 421).

Both positions share the assumption that humans have a representation of learned movements and that this representation is necessary to react in a purposeful manner to environmental stimuli. This assumption was most explicitly expressed by Rothi, Ochipa, and Heilman (1997), who stated that "to acquire skilled motor behaviour implies that the central nervous system stores information that the individual has previously experienced and that this stored information expedites future behavior. . . . they [motor processes] may be called up from memory and reutilised" (p. 33). In fact, these authors suggested an even more differentiated model in which they distinguished four action components: an "action input lexicon," an "action output lexicon," the "innervatory pattern" to activate muscles, and a representation of "action semantics." For the intentional use of actions the interplay between the action semantics and the action output lexicon is most relevant. An "action is dependent upon the interaction of conceptual knowledge related to tools, objects, and actions (what we [Rothi et al.] call action semantics) and the structural information contained in motor programs" (p. 41). These components can easily be mapped onto the sequence of processes that were discussed in our task analysis of SPT (cf. Figure 8.1).

The impairment of *action semantic knowledge* is very selective and is restricted to actions. Ochipa, Rothi, and Heilman (1989) reported that their conceptually apraxic patient was unable to use tools (e.g., he was brushing his teeth with a spoon), he was unable to mime their use, name the tools when its typical action was presented, or even say what a tool is used for. These problems were not caused by agnosia because the tools themselves were recognized, that is, they were named. This deficit was also not a production deficit because the patient was even unable to match objects with adequate tools without the necessity to overtly enact. It is therefore a specific deficit in action knowledge. DeRenzi and Faglioni (1999) related this disorder to the more general case of impaired object memory in the left hemisphere but with the specific assumption "that these attributes are organised separately in the semantic store and are, therefore, liable to independent disruption" (p. 437). It is interesting to note that opposite cases were also reported. In the literature there are reports of patients who had an impaired action production system and a spared action semantic system (e.g., Rapcsak, Ochipa, Anderson, & Poizner, 1995), and there are patients with an intact action semantic system as well as an intact action production system, but with an impaired object semantic system—these patients cannot name the objects and tools that they adequately use in actions (e.g., Schwartz, Marin, & Saffran, 1979). These data support that object semantic should be distinguished from action semantic, and both differ from action production.

The next component, the *action input lexicon*, has to do with the encoding of a seen action. This component has a direct connection to the action output lexicon and also to the action semantic lexicon. The input lexicon is used when an action is understood (e.g., a seen action has to be categorized) and when a seen action should be imitated. The selective impairment of this component is documented by deficits in imitation or comprehension. Rothi, Mack, & Heilman (1986) reported patients who could imitate specific actions, but who could not comprehend or discriminate these actions. It is likely that in this case the connection between the action input lexicon and the action semantic is damaged. The complementary inpairment was observed by Mehler (1987). He described a patient whose deficit was restricted to meaningless actions which have no semantic representation. In the model, these are actions that can only be performed via a direct route between visual systems and motor systems. Interestingly, also in memory experiments, we found that the routes to actions influence memory. Performing on verbal commands did show memory effects other than imitating seen actions (Zimmer & Engelkamp, 1996).

The final two components are more directly related to the performance of an action. "The *output action lexicon* contains 'time-space' representation for skilled movements or 'movement formulae'. These 'time-space representations' are subsequently transcoded into innervatory patterns and finally these innervatory patterns are played out by the motor systems" (Rothi, Ochipa, & Heilman, 1997, p. 45). If this component is defective, a patient's ability to gesture is impaired and the movement patterns deviate significantly from the standard execution.

Obviously neuropsychological findings suggest the existence of different components of actions which probably have different anatomical correlates: the motor cortex, the supplementary motor area, the lateral premotor area, etc. Activities in the same areas were also found in electrophysiological and neuroimaging studies with healthy subjects when they performed actions or they processed action specific information (Decety, 1994; Deccty, Grezes, Costes, Perani, Jeannerod, Procyk, Grassi, & Fazio, 1997; Gallese, Fadiga, Fogassi, & Rizzolatti, 1996; Grezes, Costes, & Decety, 1998, 1999; Jeannerod, Arbib, Rizzolatti, & Sakata, 1995; Rizzolatti, Fogassi, & Gallese, 1997). Despite all that, the exact anatomical mapping is still under debate. Therefore, and because the details go beyond the intention of this chapter, I will not discuss this topic further here (for more detailed information, especially also on action control, cf. Jeannerod, 1997). In summary, specific brain structures exist that are responsible for the execution of movements, and these structures may always be used when mental operations are performed that make use of movement information.

However, when one is looking at these data, one might raise the question as to what this neuropsychological view on the *ability to perform actions* can add to action *memory*. One might therefore consider these data as irrelevant. From my perspective, however, this is only justified with the initial observation. With a closer look, it seems different. I assume that the same structures that are used in overt actions can be used in other mental tasks and at least partially also in memory. For example, access to action semantic is possible without overt performance if one is looking for that, and it is not clear why this type of processing should not cause memory. Additionally, movement information seems to be activated if humans imagine self-performed actions. Why shouldn't it be possible to activate this information in a memory task as well? In support of this position, I will now mention some results that substantiate the use of the mentioned movement specific structures in tasks without overt movement.

It was, for example, reported that the supplementary motor area showed an increased blood flow if more complex movements of fingers had to be performed. This pattern was also observed if the actions were only imagined (Roland, Larsen, Lassen, & Skinhoj, 1980; Roland, Meyer, Shibasaki, Yamamoto, & Thompson, 1982). Similarly, it was found that brain areas involved in movement perception were active when subjects generated action words to objects or their names (Martin, Haxby, Lalonde, Wiggs, et al., 1995). It was also observed that the premotor area involved in the execution of movements was activated when familiar tools were named (Grafton, Fadiga, Arbib, & Rizzolatti, 1997).

Some recent studies even brought direct evidence for the assumption that brain areas which are involved in the execution of actions also contribute to memory. Heil, Rolke, Engelkamp Rösler, Özcan, & Hennighausen (1999) reported a negative potential shift at the fronto-central electrodes in recognition of performed action phrases which they attributed to the involvement of motor representations in this task. Mecklinger, Gruenewald, Besson, Magnié, Friederici, and von Cramon (2000) observed that the left lateral premotor area was active when subjects held manipulable objects in working memory this effect did not occur with non-manipulable objects. Finally, Nyberg, Nilsson, and Åberg (2000) got evidence for the contribution of specific motor areas to long-term memory in a subject-performed task. In the STP condition enactment-specific areas of the cortex were active during recognition of items. Some brain structures that were only active when the actions were executed during study were active during retrieval of performed items, but not otherwise.

Especially the latter results suggest that enactment-specific brain areas directly contribute to remembering performed actions. This and other results from neuroscience support that those neural structures that execute on-line processing also store information for remembering (McClelland, McNaughton, O'Reilly, 1995). Hence, memory is not a separate storehouse for copies of input events. It is more likely a distributed representation that involves different sets of content-specific components that were active during encoding and were bound by a hippocampal component (Moscovitch, Goshen-Gottstein, & Vriezen, 1994). I assume that in this net not only sub-structures for perceptual processing are included but that also action specific structures participate if they are activated within an SPT task. Because the direct empirical support from neuropsychological studies on SPT memory is small at the moment, this conclusion is still speculative. It is, however, an interesting starting point for future research.

Remembering Self-Performed Actions: An Integrative View

Taking into account all arguments presented in this book, I want to establish three notions about action memory:

1. *Action memory is a specific type of encoding.* Performance of actions activates specific information and it is associated with very specific encoding

processes. These processes and contents cause specific memory effects. Therefore, encoding by enactment should not be dealt with as a modification of other types of encoding processes, such as semantic processing.

2. *Action memory is not produced by a completely independent episodic SPT memory system.* SPT is not the result of an action-specific episodic memory that does not share processes with other episodic memory tasks. Nevertheless, enactment during study results in specific memory traces that include additional information, for example, goal-specific and movement-specific information, and these traces are not generated in the same way by other types of encoding. In my view, the effects that were reported in the preceding chapters strongly support this latter conclusion.

3. *SPT memory is additionally supported by the memory traces of action specific processes that are realized by modules designated for performance.* If we accept that movement-specific information is processed and represented by specific modules, and that these representations keep memory traces, we may also draw this third conclusion. It does not state an independent episodic action memory system. It is only postulated that some modules are additionally active in SPT that are not active otherwise. If we like it, we can call this the contribution of a specific *subsystem to action memory.*

In principle, however, it is not relevant whether we call the latter a contribution of a specific part system or the contribution of a specific informational content to memory that is generated if and only if a specific type of encoding was performed.

Accepting the position that different sets of information contribute to episodic memory and that this information is processed by specific modules, however, has consequences for the conception of episodic memory in general. In closing, I want to say a few words about this effect because Nilsson and Kormi-Nouri (Chapter 7) also discussed epsiodic memory, in general, in their comment. From a multiple component view, episodic memory is no longer a separate and homogeneous memory store, but it is the result of sets of information that probably correspond to specific part systems, and these modulos process information during encoding as well as during remembering (e.g., Fuster, 1995, 1997; Rösler, Heil, & Henninghausen, 1995). There is no additional compartment in which the traces are copied for storage. Episodic memory is distributed over several part systems, and the memory effects are dependent on the type of material involved in the different subsets of these systems.

However, if we do not distinguish memory systems from processing systems, we have to define the feature that makes up the episodic memory task. In my view, the common element of an episodic memory task is the subjects' attempt to intentionally access a specific memory token, which binds together specific sets of features. In an episodic memory task, subjects are explicitly required to remember specific episodes, (unique events in space and time). Usually, an ep-isodic memory task, or a direct memory task, is therefore contrasted with an implicit or indirect memory task in which subjects are not explicitly instructed to make access to a previously experienced episode.

A closer look at this definition reveals that the episodic task can be interpreted from two perspectives. From the *uniqueness of the event* in space and time, and from the *subjects' experience*, which makes this event a part of their own history. Tulving (1984) referred to the latter aspect, the consciousness of remembering, as autonoetic experiences. However, this quality must not necessarily be con-sidered as a precondition of an episodic memory task. On the contrary, might in itself reflect the subjective experience one possible result of an episodic re-trieval. Either it is the contribution of a specific part system to which a retrieved episode is delivered (e.g., Schacter, 1989), or consciousness is a feature of the memory trace that is reactivated as other features, for example, perceptual ones (cf. Moscowitch, Goshen-Gottstein, & Vriezen, 1994). I agree with this as-sumption. If subjects have the feeling of remembering something in an episodic memory task, that is, they recover an event, it is a conscious event. "It is the recovery of a trace imbued with consciousness that makes it feel familiar and immediately recognizable as something that had been previously experienced" (Moscowitch, Goshen-Gottstein, & Vriezen, 1994, p. 644). But, of course, this is not the only mental status that is possible if specific episodes in space and time are retrieved.

For Engelkamp, consciousness was not the relevant aspect of episodic mem-ory. He stated that he is interested in memory for the specific event, and not on the subjects' conscious experience of this event. He wanted to know whether or not a memory trace of a specific item exists, and which information belongs to it, and this could be tested by direct as well as by indirect memory tests. The remembered content could be investigated in the absence of the subjects' con-scious experiences. For example, in experiments conducted in our laboratory, participants perfectly recognized objects as old if they had been re-colored, but they did so more slowly than for items in their original colors; and the latter effect occurred although subjects were not able to consciously decide about the correctness of the colors (Zimmer, 1993). This means that participants recovered the items, (they had a conscious experience of having seen the item before), but they did not consciously recover their color, although some color memory was visible in the recognition times. From this perspective, Engelkamp's position makes sense, in not making the conscious experience of information a precon-dition for episodic memory.

Nevertheless, there is a clear feature of episodic memory that Engelkamp does not refute and that is often used to define it: *the retrieval intention*. Most likely, it is this retrieval intention that makes episodic memory into a unique task. This has consequences for the multiple memory view. If one defines episodic memory by the explicit retrieval attempt, we have only one episodic memory system independent of the modality of the to-be-remembered item (it should be mentioned, however, that this intentional retrieval might also involve specific brain structures [systems].

However, although the retrieval intention is common to all episodic memory tasks, which part system had to be addressed depends on the material. If we make these finer distinctions and look at the part information that is used, we can again distinguish more than one memory system. Dependent on the modality, a different mix of modules is used. I want to call this a *network memory*. From the assumption of a network memory, for SPT, we have to investigate which cognitive modules exist, and whether the same modules are used in the perceiving and the controlling of actions as well as in remembering. Within this attempt, prospective memory for actions is similarly a specific task that partially involves the use of specialized modules, whereas other modules are probably shared by prospective and retrospective tasks. For each module, we must decide when it is used, and then we should be able to list the memory effects that occur if a specific module contributes to remembering.

In my opinion, the same is true for SPT. The reported effects speak for the assumption that remembering self-performed actions is supported by modules that are shared with other episodic memory tasks, for instance, conceptual information, and also by specific modules whose activation is unique to SPT, such as action specific motor information. Therefore, memory for actions is, on a global level, episodic memory, but it is also specific in two respects. First, it is a specific type of encoding that is characterized by the processes necessary to perform the actions, and, secondly, it is a memory performance that is contributed to by specific modules that are involved in the execution of actions.

REFERENCES

Aebli, H. (1980). *Denken: Das Ordnen des Tuns I.* Stuttgart: Klett-Cotta.

Anderson, J. R. (1983). *The architecture of cognition,* Cambridge. Harvard University.

Bäckman, L., & Nilsson, L. G. (1984). Aging effects in free recall: An exception to the rule. *Human Learning, 3,* 53–69.

Brooks, B. M., & Gardiner, J. M. (1994). Age differences in memory for prospective compared with retrospective subject-performed tasks. *Memory and Cognition, 22,* 27–33.

Christianson, S. A. (1992). Emotional stress and eyewitness memory: A critical review. *Psychological Bulletin, 112,* 284–309.

Cohen, R. L. (1981). On the generality of some memory laws. *Scandinavian Journal of Psychology, 22,* 267–281.

Cohen, R. L. (1983). The effect of encoding variables on the free recall of words and action events. *Memory & Cognition, 11,* 575–582.

Craik, F. I. M. (1983). On the transfer of information from temporary to permanent memory. *Philosophical Transactions of the Royal Society of London, B302*, 341–359.

Decety, J. (1994). Brain areas responsible for the generation and control of reaching and grasping. Anatomy with positron emission tomography. In Bennett, K. M. B., Castiello, U., & et al. (Eds.), *Insights into the reach to grasp movement. Advances in psychology, 105* (pp. 109–126). Amsterdam, Netherlands: North-Holland/Elsevier Science Publishers.

Decety, J., Grezes, J., Costes, N., Perani, D., Jeannerod, M., Procyk, E., Grassi, F., & Fazio, F. (1997). Brain activity during observation of actions: Influence of action content and subject's strategy. *Brain, 120*, 1763–1777.

DeRenzi, E., & Faglioni, P. (1999). Apraxia. In G. Denes & L. Pizzamiglio (Eds.), *Handbook of clinical and experimental neuropsychology* (pp. 421–440). Hove: Psychology Press.

Ellis, J. A., & Nimmo-Smith., (1993). Recollecting naturally occurring intentions: A study of cognitive and affective factors. *Memory, 1*, 107–126.

Engelkamp, J. (1997). Memory for to-be-performed tasks versus memory for performed tasks. *Memory & Cognition, 25*, 117–124.

Engelkamp, J. (1998). *Memory for actions*. Hove: Psychology Press.

Engelkamp, J., Mohr, G., & Zimmer, H. D. (1991). Pair-relational encoding of performed nouns and verbs. *Psychological Research, 53*, 232–239.

Engelkamp, J., & Perrig, W. (1986). Differential effects of imaginal and motor encoding on the recall of action phrases. *Archiv für Psychologie, 138*, 261–273.

Engelkamp, J., & Zimmer, H. D. (1983). Der Einfluβ von Wahrnehmen und Tun auf das Behalten von Verb-Objekt-Phrasen. *Sprache & Kognition, 2*, 117–127.

Engelkamp, J., & Zimmer, H. D. (1984). Motor program information as a separable memory unit. *Psychological Research, 46*, 283–299.

Engelkamp, J., & Zimmer, H. D. (1985). Motor programs and their relation to semantic memory. *German Journal of Psychology, 9*, 239–254.

Engelkamp, J., & Zimmer, H. D. (1994). *The human memory: A multimodal approach*. Seattle: Hogrefe.

Engelkamp, J., & Zimmer, H. D. (1996). Organisation and recall in verbal tasks and subject-performed tasks. *European Journal of Cognitive Psychology, 8*, 257–273.

Fuster, J. (1995). *Memory in the cerebral cortex: An empirical approach to neural networks in the human and nonhuman primate*. Cambridge: MIT Press.

Fuster, J. (1997). Network memory. *Trends in Neurosciences, 20*, 451–459.

Gallese, V., Fadiga, L. Fogassi, L., & Rizzolatti, G. (1996). Action recognition in the premotor cortex. *Brain, 119*, 593–609.

Gentner, D. (1981). Verb semantic structures in memory for sentences. Evidence for componential representation. *Cognitive Psychology, 13*, 56–84.

Goodale, M. A., & Humphrey, G. K. (1998). The objects of action and perception. *Cognition, 67*, 181–207.

Goschke, T., & Kuhl, J. (1993). Representation of intentions: Persisting activation in memory. *Journal of Experimental Psychology: Learning, Memory and Cognition, 19*, 1211–1226.

Grafton, S. T., Fadiga, L., Arbib, M. A., & Rizzolatti, G. (1997). Premotor cortex activation during observation and naming of familiar tools. *Neuro Image, 6*, 231–236.

Grezes, J., Costes, N., & Decety, J. (1998). Top-down effect of strategy on the perception of human biological motion: A PET investigation. *Cognitive Neuropsychology, 15*, 553–582.

Grezes, J., Costes, N., & Decety, J. (1999). The effects of learning and intention on the neural network involved in the perception of meaningless actions. *Brain, 122*, 1875–1887.

Heckhausen, H., & Beckman, J. (1990). Intentional action and action slips. *Psychological Review, 97*, 36–48.

Heil, M., Rolke, B., Engelkamp, J., Rösler, F., Özcan, M., & Hennighausen, E. (1999). Event-related brain potentials during recognition of ordinary and bizarre action phrases following verbal and subject-performed encoding conditions. *European Journal of Cognitive Psychology, 11*, 261–280.

Helstrup, T. (1987). One, two, or three memories? A problem-solving approach to memory for performed acts. *Acta Psychologica, 66*, 37–68.

Heuer, H. (1985). Wie wirkt mentale Übung? [How does mental practice operate?]. *Psychologische Rundschau, 36*, 191–200.

Jacoby, L. L. (1991). A process dissociation framework: Separating automatic from intentional uses of memory. *Journal of Memory and Language, 30*, 513–541.

Jeannerod, M. (1997) *The cognitive neuroscience of action.* Oxford: Blackwell.

Jeannerod, M., Arbib, M. A., Rizzolatti, G., & Sakata, H. (1995). Grasping objects: The cortical mechanisms of visuomotor transformation. *Trends in Neurosciences, 18*, 314–320.

Koriat, A., Ben-Zur, H., & Druch, A. (1991). The contextualisation of input and output events in memory. *Psychological Research, 53*, 260–270.

Kormi-Nouri, R. (1994). Memory for action events: An episodic integration view. In *Doctoral Dissertation Department of Psychology.* Umea: Umea University.

Martin, A., Haxby, J. V., Lalonde, F. M., Wiggs, C. L., et al. (1995). Discrete cortical regions associated with knowledge of color and knowledge of action. *Science, 270*, 102–105.

McClelland, J. L., McNaughton, B. L., & O'Reilly, R. C. (1995). Why there are complementary learning systems in the hippocampus and neocortex: Insights from the successes and failures of connectionists models of learning and memory. *Psychological Review, 102*, 419–457.

McDaniel, M. A., Robinson-Riegler, B., & Einstein, G. O. (1998). Prospective remembering: Perceptually driven or conceptually driven processes. *Memory & Cognition, 26*, 121–134.

Mocklinger, A., Gruenewald, C., Besson, M., Magnié, M.-Noelle, Friederici, A. D., & von Cramon, D. Y. (2000). *Separable neuronal circuits for manipulable and non-manipulable objects in working memory.* Submitted paper.

Mehler, M. F. (1987). Visuo-imitative apraxia. *Neurology, 37*, 129.

Moscovitch, M. (1992). Memory and working-with-memory: A component process model based on modules and central system. *Journal of Cognitive Neuroscience, 3*, 257–267.

Moscovitch, M. (1994). Memory and working-with-memory: Evaluation of a component process model and comparison with other models. In D. L. Schacter & E. Tulving (Eds.), *Memory systems* (pp. 269–310). Cambridge: MIT Press.

Moscovitch, M., Goshen-Gottstein, Y., & Vriezen, E. (1994). Memory without conscious recollection: A tutorial review from a neuropsychological perspective. In C. Umilta & M. Moscovitch (Eds.), *Attention and Performance XV (pp. 619–660)*. Cambridge: MIT Press.

Nilsson, L. G., & Bäckman, L. (1989). Implicit memory and the enactment of verbal instructions. In S. Lewandowsky, J. C. Dunn, & K. Kirsner (Eds.), *Implicit memory: Theoretical issues* (pp. 173–183). Hillsdale: Erlbaum.

Nilsson, L. G., & Craik, F. I. M. (1990). Additive and interactive effects in memory for subject-performed tasks. *European Journal of Cognitive Psychology, 2*, 305–324.

Nilsson, L. G., Nyberg, L., Kormi-Nouri, R., & Rönnlund, M. (1995). Dissociative effects of elaboration on memory of enacted and non-enacted events: A case of a negative effect. *Scandinavian Journal of Psychology, 36*, 225–231

Norman, D. A. (1981). Categorization of action slips. *Psychological Review, 88*, 1–15.

Norman, D. A. (1988). *The psychology of everyday things*. New York: Basic Books.

Norman, D. A., & Rumelhart, D. E. (Eds.). (1975). *Exploration in cognition*. San Francisco: Freeman.

Nyberg, L., Nilsson, L. G., °Aberg, C. (2000). On the basis for the enactment effect: Evidence from brain imaging. Paper presented at the 27th International Congress of Psychology in Stockholm, Sweden.

Nyberg, L., Nilsson, L. G., & Bäckmann, L. (1991). A component analysis of action events. *Psychological Research, 53*, 219–225.

Ochipa, C., Rothi, L. J. G., & Heilman, K. M. (1989). Ideational apraxia: A deficit in tool selection and use. *Annals of Neurology, 25*, 190–193.

Oesterreich, R., & Köddig, C. (1995). Das Generieren von Handlungsvorstellungen im Modell "Netz erinnerbaren Handelns" und der Tu-Effekt. *Zeitschrift für Experimentelle und Angewandte Psychologie, 42*, 280–301.

Rapcsak, S. Z., Ochipa, C., Anderson, K. C., & Poizner, H. (1995). Progressive ideomotor apraxia: Evidence for a selective impairment of the action production system. *Brain and Cognition, 27*, 213–236.

Ratner, H. H., & Hill, L. (1991). The development of children's action memory: When do actions speak louder than words? *Psychological Research, 53*, 195–202.

Rizzolatti, G., Fogassi, L., & Gallese, V. (1997). Parietal cortex: From sight to action. *Current Opinion in Neurobiology, 7*, 562–567.

Rösler, F., Heil, M., & Hennighausen, E. (1995). Distinct cortical activation patterns during long-term memory retrieval of verbal, spatial, and color information. *Journal of Cognitive Neuroscience, 7*, 51–65.

Roland, P. E., Larsen, B., Lassen, N. A., & Skinhoj, E. (1980). Supplementary motor area and other cortical areas in organisation of voluntary movements in man. *Journal of Neurophysiology, 43*, 118–136.

Roland, P. E., Meyer, E., Shibasaki, T., Yamamoto, Y. L., & Thompson, C. J. (1982). Regional cerebral blood flow changes in cortex and basal ganglia during voluntary movements in normal human volunteers. *Journal of Neurophysiology, 48*, 467–480.

Rosenbaum, D. A. (1991). *Human motor control*. San Diego: Academic Press.

Rothi, L. J. G., & Heilman, K. M. (1997). Introduction to limb apraxia. In L. J. G. Rothi & K. M. Heilman (Eds.), *Apraxia: The neuropsychology of action* (pp. 1–6). Hove: Psychology Press.

Rothi, L. J. G., Mack, L., & Heilman, K. L. (1986). Pantomime comprehension and ideomotor apraxia. *Journal of Neurology, Neurosurgery, and Psychiatry, 49*, 451–454.

Rothi, L. J. G., Ochipa, C., & Heilman, K. H. (1997). A cognitive neuropsychological model of limb praxis and apraxia. In L. J. G. Rothi & K. H. Heilman (Eds.), *Apraxia: The neuropsychology of action* (pp. 29–49). Hove: Psychology Press.

Schaaf, M. G. (1988). Motorische Aktivität und verbale Lernleistung—Leistungssteigerung durch Simultanität? *Zeitschrift für experimentelle und angewandte Psychologie, 13*, 501–518.

Schacter, D. L. (1989). On the relation between memory and consciousness: Dissociable interactions and conscious experience. In H. L. Roediger & F. I. M. Craik (Eds.), *Varieties of memory and consciousness* (pp. 355–390). Hillsdale: Erlbaum.

Schacter, D. L. (1994). Priming and multiple memory systems: Perceptual mechanisms of implicit memory. In D. L. Schacter & E. Tulving (Eds.), *Memory systems 1994* (pp. 233–268). Cambridge: MIT Press.

Schwartz, M. F., Marin, O. S. M., & Saffran, E. M. (1979). Dissociations of language function in dementia: A case study. *Brain and Language, 7*, 277–306.

Shallice, T., & Burgess, P. W. (1991). Deficits in strategy application following frontal lobe damage in man. *Brain, 114*, 727–741.

Shimamura, A. P., Janowsky, J., & Squire, L. R. (1991). What is the role of frontal lobe damage in memory disorders? In H. S. Levin, H. M. Eisenberg, & A. L. Benton (Eds.), *Frontal lobe function and dysfunction.* New York: Oxford University Press.

Steffens, M. (1999). The role of relational processing in memory for actions: A reversed enactment effect in free recall. *Quarterly Journal of Experimental Psychology: Human Experimental Psychology, 52A*, 877–903.

Tulving, E. (1985). How many memory systems are there? *American Psychologist, 40*, 385–398.

Vallacher, R. R., & Wegner, D. M. (1987). What do people think they're doing? Action identification and human beahavior. *Psychological Review, 94*, 3–15.

West, R. L. (1986). Everyday memory and aging. *Developmental Neuropsychology, 2*, 323–344.

Zimmer, H. D. (1984). *Enkodierung, Rekodierung, Retrieval und die Aktivation motorischer Programme* [Encoding, re-coding, retrieval and the activation of motor programs]. (Arbeiten der Fachrichtung Psychologie, Vol. 91). Saarbrücken: Universität des Saarlandes.

Zimmer, H. D. (1986). The memory trace of semantic or motor processing. In F. Klix & H. Hagendorf (Eds.), *Human memory and cognitive capabilities* (pp. 215–223). Amsterdam: North Holland.

Zimmer, H. D. (1991). Memory after motoric encoding in a generation-recognition model. *Psychological Research, 53*, 226–231.

Zimmer, H. D. (1993). Sensorische Bildmerkmale im expliziten und impliziten Gedächtnis [Sensory features in explicit and implicit memory]. In L. Montada (Ed.), *Bericht über den 38. Kongreβ der Deutschen Gesellschaft für Psychologie in Trier* (Vol. 2, pp. 458–465). Göttingen: Hogrefe.

Zimmer, H. D. (1996a). Performing actions during study enhances retrospective memory and facilitates future actions. Paper presented at the International Conference on Memory, Padova, Italy.

Zimmer, H. D. (1996b). Subject-performed tasks enhance item-specific information but not context integration. Paper presented at the XXVI World Congress of Psychology, Montreal, Canada.

Zimmer, H. D., & Engelkamp, J. (1984). Planungs- und Ausführungsanteile motorischer Gedächtniskomponenten und ihre Wirkung auf das Behalten ihrer verbalen Bezeichnungen [The contribution of planning and execution to the generation of motor memory components and their influence on memory for the verbal commands]. *Zeitschrift für Psychologie, 192,* 379–402.

Zimmer, H. D., & Engelkamp, J. (1989a). Does motor encoding enhance relational information? *Psychological Research, 51,* 158–167.

Zimmer, H. D., & Engelkamp, J. (1989b). One, two or three memories: Some comments and new findings. *Acta Psychologica, 70,* 293–304.

Zimmer, H. D., & Engelkamp, J. (1996). Routes to actions and their efficacy for remembering. *Memory, 4,* 59–78.

Zimmer, H. D., & Engelkamp, J. (2000). What type of information is enhanced in subject-performed tasks?

Zimmer, H. D., Helstrup, T., & Engelkamp, J. (2000). Pop-out into memory: A retrieval mechanism that is enhanced with the recall of subject-performed tasks. *Journal of Experimental Psychology: Human Learning, Memory & Cognition, 26,* 658–670.

Zimmer, H. D., & Engelkamp, J. (1999) Levels-of-processing effects in subject-performed tasks. *Memory & Cognition,* 27, 907–914.

Subject Index

Author Index